Words to Our Now

Imagination and Dissent

Thomas Glave

University of Minnesota Press

MINNEAPOLIS • LONDON

Excerpt from "Children of Our Age," by Wislawa Szymborska,
in *View with a Grain of Sand,* copyright 1993 by Wislawa Szymborska;
English translation by Stanislaw Baranczak and Clare Cavanagh
copyright 1995 by Harcourt, Inc. Reprinted by permission of the publisher.

Excerpts from "Heavy Breathing," "To Some Supposed Brothers,"
and "Does Your Mama Know about Me?" by Essex Hemphill, in
Ceremonies: Prose and Poetry (New York: Plume/Penguin Books, 1992).
Reprinted courtesy of the Estate of Essex Hemphill.

Publication information for previously published essays in this book
is on pages 263–64.

Published by the University of Minnesota Press
111 Third Avenue South, Suite 290
Minneapolis, MN 55401-2520
http://www.upress.umn.edu

ISBN 0-8166-4679-1

A Cataloging-in-Publication record for this book

Printed in the United States of America on acid-free paper

The University of Minnesota is an equal-opportunity educator and employer.

12 11 10 09 08 07 06 05   10 9 8 7 6 5 4 3 2 1

To
Ms. Phyllis Monica Melbourne
—yet another
who (like those of our beloved
Teacher,
and others)
also knows
her true and ancient
properties

Contents

Baychester: A Memory

AS WE STEP FROM THE CAR OUT ONTO THE GROUND THAT is still muddy from last night's gentle rain, feeling its sucking at our feet as we imprint our soles on it, a light breath of spring blows the first scents of wildflowers to us: shovel in hand, I close my eyes and breathe in, deeply. Queen Anne's lace and honeysuckle, I tell my father, above me at my side; already preoccupied with our coming tasks, he smiles at my youthful enthusiasm but does not reply. These thicker morning fragrances, which never find their way as easily into dreams as do those of night, are soon replaced by the briny smell of Eastchester Bay, just off to our right, as we also become aware of the oddly delightful aroma of what we've come for: horse manure, to be dug at the Italian-owned Pelham Bay stables, directly ahead, for my parents' garden. With luck, we'll return home with several large garbage bags full, to empty them out later on the soft, loamy beds my father has spent the week preparing at our home in Baychester, a few miles north of here. There, they'll lay spread upon the ground, drying in the sun that each day now lasts a little longer, until we're ready to plant the seedlings which in adulthood will bear the vegetables my parents love: eggplant, summer and winter squash, onions, red cabbage, romaine and iceberg lettuce, and corn; allowing a little here and there for our still-straggly strawberries, the grapevines already clambering over the white-painted arbor beneath the front-lawn apple tree; some for the mulberry tree (whose berries have no taste) that nods heavy shade over our rabbit hutches; and—how can we forget?—some also for the seven fig trees that each spring emerge naked and groggy from the tar paper, plastic, and cardboard we've wrapped them in for the winter. The flowering cherry trees will get some, as will the apricots, pear, and plums. "You mean you have all this in the *Bronx*? On so little land?"—so a million passersby will ask, have asked, on their way to or from the elevated subway, to or from the nearby apartment towers of Co-op City. (And in a *black* neighborhood, too? their question seems to imply, although almost all of those who will ask are black.) They will ask us this throughout the season, until the arrival of those long, heavy, burning days of summer when the early crops yield. My father—Daddy, as I always call him—will respond with a Jamaican-of-few-words musically accented simple "Yes"—lowering his gaze as if ashamed for the speaker at the obvious silliness of such a question.

We continue on, stepping carefully along the downward path from the car to the stables, aware now of the whinnying of horses—something of a miracle in a place that has already become more well known for nightly siren discordances and gunshots than for the honks of geese, which we also hear. In migration to points farther north, several pairs flutter down this morning to fuss and rest on the bay. Perhaps a few of them will decide to summer here; the marshy ground on this side of the bay and to the north offers plenty of good nesting sites, out of reach of would-be pests and assassins. As we walk on, a screen of fragile spring foliage above our heads shimmers with each breeze off the water: a pale green life network along stems that bend but don't quite break beneath our fingertips' incautious curiosity. The time is sixteen years ago, a Saturday morning pulled from my memory, in this moment beyond fear, before any knowledge I will someday have of death and survival and the usefulness, cultural and otherwise, of masks. I am twelve. Knobby-kneed, ashy-legged, I follow Daddy on the path. Today and every day, for as long as I can remember, he—only he—is master of the world.

This recounting serves by way of explanation in this present as to how I came to be in that other time and place. But in the moment, the actual moment of *being* and *feeling,* none of this explanation—this logic—matters. The backdrop tapestry of the day and its sight-wonders serves merely as an excuse for my coming along on this trip. I'm really here to watch trains, pretending all the while that I'm with Daddy doing something important—something adults will call "useful." The year is 1977, six years after Amtrak's acquiring the rights-of-way and passenger-service rolling stock of the nation's major railroads; we're lucky enough to live in what Amtrak calls the "Northeast Corridor" of the country, near the former New Haven Railroad's trackage to Boston, which runs right past the Pelham Bay stables, out over the low bay truss bridge (over which I've walked many an afternoon and early evening, daring death or simply not understanding its actual possibility), and on, obscured by woods, past the golf course, paralleling the New England Thruway to New Rochelle and Connecticut. As we press our spades into the rich, dark, earthworm-filled manure, I'm uneasy and alert, constantly turning back to face the tracks, afraid I might miss something of vital importance. Daddy begins to whistle, an old Jamaican song from his childhood, words I barely remember but attach to summer nights spent beneath banana trees in my great-grandmother's house as three headless roosters hopped about in dying frenzy outside and sea-wind lilted into the house to leave a trace of Caribbean salt spray on our lips.

Daddy loves this work. You can tell just by watching him. He loves the breeze ruffling his hair, the free feeling of being out in the open near water (one of his unrealized dreams was to own a tall-masted schooner and sail the seas forever with shark-colored dolphins slicing the waters at his heels), away from a city he hates (the people are "unmannerly," the pace too fast); he loves the rich horseshit that he knows will produce the wine-dark eggplants he adores and the fat tomatoes my enterprising mother sells. This year he is sixty-one, one year away from the diabetic onslaught that will sharply diminish his gardening days until it finally kills him ten years later. As I labor beside him, I think of all he doesn't know, or all I think he doesn't know: how I am slowly, painstakingly discovering a world very far from his own, through a medium he revered in his other, younger life as a journalist—books—but in this case none of which he has read. C. A. Tripp's *The Homosexual Matrix,* for one. For me, in my furtive readings of it on the subway each day on my way to school in Manhattan, it has begun to clear a way through a fog that still terrifies even as it exhilarates. By now I've learned well the shrieking violence the "H" word (now the "G" word) produces—not so much from my parents as from the boys my age and older who, at school and in our neighborhood, carry a wicked pugnacity in their necks and fists about the subject. Hatred has come to them early via the killing cruelty of a long line of harsh expletives that only begin with the word "faggot." The feeling of that received hatred—the daily slamming of its fists into my face and the taste of my own blood drawn by the most vicious of these boys—is already steadily steering me away from what I'm learning can be, in this context, the danger of direct, ambiguous eye contact with other young black men, young men outwardly just like me, who hit first and ask questions later, as their parents probably did with them. I still carry this fear, along with the constant rage and shame that I've ever been afraid, am still afraid, have ever *had* to feel afraid, at all; remembering with that fury and shame that to this day I'm still extremely wary and skeptical of those black men who in convenient circumstances glibly call themselves "brothers," as I'm still wary and skeptical of those black women who capriciously call themselves "sisters"—both of whom then in their own peculiar type of fear, loathing, and hypocrisy often inflict violence on black gay men and lesbians whenever we are found either not to be useful or (far worse) too close to home. (The word "faggot" itself is to me as nasty a form of violence as the

perennial spit-nastiness in that classic American word "nigger.")
I've never seen or sensed this type of violence in Daddy—as proud
of his image of his son (something I can't quite yet understand)
as I will someday be of him (something he'll never completely
know). Through texts such as Andrew Holleran's *Dancer from
the Dance* (of which in this time I understand neither its "in"
jokes and encoded language nor the not-so-subtle racism of some
of its characters, and will not until I reread it fifteen years later),
The Church and the Homosexual (I'm still something of a "good"
Catholic, entranced by incense and the mysteries and the beautiful red ceremonial robes of bishops), and *Gay American History*,
I feel myself evolving into something forged in a half darkness
of conscious longing and unselfconscious naïveté, unbeknownst
to Daddy; soon, to my horror and later sadness, to grow away
from him in his coming illness as, fleeing the possibility of his
leaving forever, I take refuge in charting my own self-discovery.
Becoming. To return someday, fully armored, to the depthless
riches of my father's garden.

Today, however, digging, I know nothing of any of this. An
express train bound for Boston, silver-sided, hauling nine cars
that don't yet bear the Amtrak blue-and-red chevron logo, comes
clacking up the tracks toward us. The overhead electrical wires
hiss, as, disturbed, the waterfowl roosting on the bridge rise up
into startled raised-eyebrow patterns. The horses, off feeding in
the distance, barely move. We turn slowly to watch the train.

"Look at the *pan*tograph," I shout, pulling on his arm, "that's
the thing on top of the engine that connects to the overhead wires.
Know what the wires are called? The *cat*enary." This is enough
to make me dance for the rest of the day—both having seen a
train, and such a dramatic one, and having been able to share
this knowledge carefully culled from too many model-railroad
magazines. (Are there trains like this in Jamaica, I wonder? But
no! I remember that time visiting the town in Clarendon parish
where Daddy was born and raised, learning in the midst of all
that headiness and excitement that Jamaica National Railways,

known locally as "the diesel," *does not use* electric trains.) I'm already in Boston with this train as it hurtles northward over the dark, low, rusty bridge, on its way to the affluent Connecticut shore. The catenary is high out of our reach, magical, something that neither the subway nor the Long Island Rail Road, in their adherence to boring regular old third-rail power, uses. Daddy's brief nod, so like my mother's stern glances, signals me to return to work.

What do I know today that he doesn't? Almost everything, I dare to think, eyeing those squiggling earthworms at my shovel's end with distaste; but not much, I finally hope. Except for this: that with the lengthening of these days, men who have already learned the power and seduction of music-in-hips, slinky men who fold shapely muscle and sinew into tight jeans and boots that click out their own city rhythms, have begun to interest me. I've already begun to leave the North Bronx, the trains to Boston, and the loud neighborhood bracelet-jangling teenage girls (who laugh at my abashed fearful silence in the face of their bold how-can-you-resist-us flirts) for the streets of the West Village in lower Manhattan, where I'll watch these men in awed and sometimes skittish fascination: their slinks, their confident sashays past those like me whom they will generally ignore—we're too young still for most of them and can make little sense of their complex ritualistic signals. This summer, I will also learn of a problem that won't make sense to me until years later: that is, that most of these men seem to be white. They, the most visible ones, whose teeth gleam from billboards and magazine covers and—unless the call is for HUGE (and probably "dangerous") penises—from sex ads. Mustached and plaid-shirted in the style of the day, flicking disdain in their wrists and what comes across as a self-protective outer disdain in their shoulders—what I think Eudora Welty signifies in her story "No Place for You, My Love" when she describes "human imperviousness": what many people call, simply, attitude—what so many of us receive so willingly from those who hate us and dole out so brutally to those who don't;

that infuriating thing which hoods eyes and carves haughtiness in chins. Naturally by now I've been warned implicitly and explicitly numerous times by family members, friends, and general experience and observation not to trust white people, ever; not to let them ever get too close; if they do, the warnings tell me, I must keep something, many things, the essential, precious, private part of the spirit-self, the gentleness, the personhood, out of their reach, protected and safe from the reckless and inevitably destroying touch they've perfected—what my entire stateside family learned quickly through their own dehumanizing experiences as black Caribbean immigrants to the United States, and before that in their daily lives under British West Indian colonialism; the general lesson black children and adults in this country learn early on, without too much pain, if we're lucky. What will these new worlds teach me that my parents and grandparents and aunts and uncles, in their love and anxiety, will never be able to protect me from? To my unaccustomed eyes and ears, raised on a street where the comfortable scents of rice and peas and curry goat and bammy breathe from houses along with reggae wails, these new, mostly white people of the Village, who will live through the years before a ravaging epidemic whose horrors will claim many of our lives of every color and sexuality, will be the ones who spend summer weekends on that place called *fireisland,* out of sight and mind; who attend the opera and speak of *Tosca* (who? what? is she? he?); who sit in Village sidewalk cafés holding hands in the new enthrallments of romance and attraction (how I envy them!—their assurance, their ostensible imperturbability), sipping something called cappuccino, as they eye each other in ignorance of the fact that, intuitively, with a deep, creeping disappointment, I'm already anxiously eyeing them for someone who looks like me but whom I almost never find—or, when I do, he almost never sees what looks like *him,* nor apparently does he wish to—he having become an elegant, expensive black drape wrapped about the necks and arms of one of them. Like many white people before them, a number of these gay white men seem to have no problem expressing contempt and derision for what they've been raised to view as contemptible—blackness, and other ethnicities—as at times, between moments of warmth and generosity, some of them will express another sort of contempt for each other, in the coldest of glances. A contempt for the gay brother or sister, a contempt for the self. (As, too often, we as black gay men, lesbians, and others have learned to do to ourselves and other people of difference, having learned well from our former and sometimes contemporary masters.) They will continue to display an awesome capacity for this sort of contempt well into the future, to this very day; with such practiced skill and societal approval, they will surely continue on long afterward. Thus, to me, in their hands, in that way, some of those few now-and-then glimpsed black men willingly evolve into new, bastardized creations formed out of the dregs of an old consciousness—they become the "it" of Gwendolyn Brooks's "Bronzeville Woman in a Red Hat," desired and feared and finally brought to heel, in a way, beneath the possessive-benignant paw of an owner: an it-thing to be fondled, stroked, assessed for the largesse of its thighs and presumed ferocity curled in its crotch. In this time and place, my younger eyes have trouble understanding exactly why he (or it) so frequently doesn't seem to mind his role as such a pet; my adult eyes will feel the fury that will tell me more than I can ever make sense of at twelve—indeed, more than I can stand to know, sometimes, when I begin to make sense out of it as an adult. It is 1977, nine years before Joseph Beam (thank God for him!) will edit and publish *In the Life: A Black Gay Anthology*; four years before Isaac Jackson will found the Blackheart Collective, which will publish the writings of black gay men, and fourteen more years before I will discover it; twelve years before I and others will experience the silencing chill of Essex Hemphill's furious recital of "Now We Think" (". . . as we fuck") in Marlon Riggs's award-winning film *Tongues Untied*, whose title is taken from a British-published minianthology of five black gay poets; fourteen years before Hemphill will also edit and publish *Brother to Brother: New Writings by Black Gay Men*, the Beam-conceived follow-up anthology to *In the Life*; fourteen years before Assotto Saint,[1] another stalwart maverick in a time of great ones, will edit and publish *The Road before Us: 100 Gay Black Poets* (*one hundred* gay black poets? How far we've come! Who would have bought/thought of/dreamed of such a book in 1977? Yet who *was* dreaming of it then, in silence, in tongue-tied abject loneliness?). And how many years before I meet Barbara Smith and cherish her *Home Girls* anthology, discovering there the voices of Audre Lorde, Pat Parker, June Jordan, and so many other powerful black lesbian writers; and how much more time before the founding of Other Countries, the New York–based black gay men's writing collective; and how many years, months, days, before what else? How many?

In the midst of all of this I think: Where are the gay Jamaican voices? Where are the dark men who walk along those roads to Constant Spring market or Saint Catherine market or along the streets of Port Royal at sunset with Irish potatoes and breadfruit in their burlap bags and a pair of heavy dark eyes awaiting them at home? Will this century's history leave us only Claude McKay, one of the foremost voices of the Harlem Renaissance, but who—understandably for his time—was never able to come out as being of Jamaican descent *and* gay?[2] Where are the gay—*openly,* proudly gay—equivalents of John Hearne, A. L. Hendricks, Roy Henry, Mervyn Morris, Roger Mais, Stuart Hall, and John Figueroa?—to name only a few. Where are the Jamaican openly lesbian counterparts to Olive Senior, Lorna Goodison, Louise Bennett, Velma Pollard, Christine Craig, Erna Brodber, and Opal Palmer Adisa—once again, to name only a few?[3]

In this regard, amid the silences and the voices of more than a few contemporary popular Jamaican singers screaming that we should be killed on sight, so far I know of only one challenging voice: that of the highly gifted writer Michelle Cliff. Lyrical, angry, haunting Michelle Cliff. A large personal voice. Prose that is poetry, lifesongs and threnodies. My nationhood-sister, like me an outsider both there and here. Her bravery and willingness to speak out as a lesbian privilege all of us and enable me, in particular, to do the same from the District of Look Behind, where we can't safely live, or up north, where, at least in the larger cities, we would like to think we can, and often don't. But where are the others? In a land where water and trees are never silent and ghosts speak nightly from mountaintops, who has enforced and colluded with this conspiratorial hush?

Still, in 1993 (what we consider "modern times"), what we have available in print by African American lesbians and gay men are Bibles to me. Their works are severe speaking mirrors into which I look, now, and see several hundred lonely, laughing, desperate, silly, enraged, loving versions of myself and the men whom I dream of loving. Nineteen seventy-seven—what feels like a century before these scattered eyes will look out and see signs that tell each other, Yes, we exist. Here. Surviving amid the terrible hushes and the violence that daily threatens our lives. Safe only as long as we stand together—something we *must* do, and learn to do better, no matter how much the roaring mouth of that violence frightens us.

That *we*—the all-important We. Writing these words, I think of them—all of them whom I know now, whom I have known, whom I first met in the harsh enclosed spaces between silences and nervous laughter, behind shuttered eyelids, even as in seeking escape from bullies and bullets I've become something of a wanderer—as have so many of us. As I think of my father's body decaying these years in his grave, yet walking with me, *seeing* with me as surely as in those lonely discovering days I sought so many beyond the infuriating sheen of cold blue eyes that were so sure they had the power to make me disappear they even had me convinced. *Vanish,* that coldness said, "Vanish"—and I did, partly unmindful of injustice; always preferring life among the invisible, particularly if they're my own. I remember: becoming. Making my way from the North Bronx downtown to that unremarkable Harlem street where, in a building across from a littered, tattered excuse for a park, high, *high* above it all yet *in* it, I learned of love between nights of pink Champale and cheap reefer joked out from the singing, beer-chugging (and often loudly antigay) Puerto Rican young men on the corner. The young black men who—restless, dreaming, agonized, wandering—also walked those searing streets of summer: walked, in that time, not yet clad in the 1990s high hood fashion of pants purposely-casually slung low on hips, so that you could still see quite clearly beneath their jeans and shorts the shapes and curves of their firm, high, beautiful behinds; as, inevitably, you recognized the pain and out-rage in their eyes as something also completely yours—another commonality beneath and beyond the skin, another responsibility beyond yet deep within and privy to the fear: the determination to survive the ravages of that outrage and to do everything in your power to ensure that they too survived it if possible; no matter how fiercely it insisted, spurred on by those who had made it and named it, that you die. *For no, we would not die.* And still say No. Surviving the moment, continuing on. Seeing: up high, looking out: the roach-filled kitchen where a Siamese cat with the same smoky eyes as those I came to love drowsed to winter fatness in a corner, uncaring, unseeing, stretching out claws to somnolence as two black men unashamedly, between awkward giggles, kissed. As we knew then and know now that even now those other worlds we know outside our selves and sometimes within our selves will not make easy room for the (to some) threatening sum of this equation. Recalling: that long tree-lined street of brownstones and broad-windowed buildings where long brown eyelashes drooped over checkerboards and feisty old black people mistrustful of our youth turned up their (often light-skinned and proud of it) noses at two young black men who entwined smooth dancer-limbs by day and went apartment hunting by night, swaying that curious swing in the hips the old folks hadn't seen since they'd left behind the pine hills of North Carolina, the red earth of Georgia, the verdant Florida flatlands—and segregation and the fiery cross. Becoming. As my father still walked with me there and I learned the meaning of slow music-in-hips. And nights of barbecued ribs on the fire escape, the thick greasy bodies of scurrying scavenger rats far below, awaiting our bones. . . .

But no—I'm still here, still working beside Daddy on that spring morning of trains and geese and horseshit. Already becoming a wanderer who will eventually return to a past beyond complete recapturing in this North Bronx land that raised me, I'll continue to work beside him, through all the years, slinging horseshit into our plastic garbage bags as we dream, separately, of what we both still have a chance to become amid the encroachments of so many discrete personal confusions. Remembering all, making more sense out of this becoming process as we drive up to Maine (*past* Boston!) to move me into my first year of college there, where I'll study that new austere foreign landscape of cold sea and lobster shacks and pines in order to make it a true part of my memory; celebrating the chance that will later come for winter evening walks over gently arched bridges in what will still be, in 1982, Leningrad (where, in that too-cold air, I'll imagine myself in Paris, wondering if the coldness in white people's and other strangers' eyes, and the occasional unexpected kindness, is any different there or elsewhere from what I see in the cold Russian-Soviet city, or on the North Bronx's largely Italian Allerton Avenue). In this urban mélange of ice and czarist cake-architecture, the train lover's eyes glide toward the blue sky-sparks of electric trolleys on Nevsky Prospekt as they also seek out the dark wooden-seated *electrichka* that speeds with comfortable train noise from Finlandsky Voksal station through snow-covered woods to the *dacha* village of Olgino and farther northern points on the Gulf of Finland; a place where I think of home, reminded of the Throgs Neck Bridge lights we see from Baychester Avenue, as I watch those other city lights across the freezing gulf water green their way into Leningrad evening life.

The process of connection and remembrance continues: as I walk through six sultry Southern Hemisphere summer nights in Buenos Aires, two *porteños,* fascinated by my dreadlocks, will chase me down one of those wide café-lined avenues with their cameras, shouting "Bob *Mar*ley! Bob *Mar*ley!" in not-so-innocent and obnoxiously playful ignorance—what a black traveler in Latin

America, particularly one who looks like me, comes to know as unavoidable. (Later, amid recollections of annoyance at such foolishness, I'll learn easily enough to laugh at this—recognizing that it must be an honor, surely, for anyone, and particularly for a border-crossing Jamaican American in transit between notion-terrains of nationhood and cultural discovery, to be called out as Bob Marley, anywhere.) To my outsider eyes, and to their young ones, perhaps, we are far from *la guerra sucia,* far from *The Official Story,* far from those drowning tragedies the mothers of the Plaza de Mayo, thank God, will still not let us forget. (I remember: Today is Thursday. At three o'clock the mothers march, and I am there, recording.) But there is warmth here, too, often framed by deep sadness: apart from the ubiquitous poverty that rings so many Latin American cities like swollen neck sores—a poverty which in this region of open veins ringworms its way into the scalps of still too many Jamaican and developing-nation children everywhere, as it encrusts their bare feet and dusts over the mottled faces of their dead siblings—I remember the light of longing in a Cuzco *indígena's* face when, admiring her llama, I tell her that I've just traveled by bus from Chile up to this part of Peru, and, yes, I live in the States, and, no, I'm not rich, haven't got a swimming pool, haven't got a house with two cars, haven't got a beautiful blonde *gringa* girlfriend; her light vanishes. There will be the warm coffee-scented *Come, tell us how you live* conversations with northern Argentines in a public park in San Miguel de Tucumán, and the moments of tears shared over cups of *tinto* with a woman in a small house in a city high in the Andes, when we talk about the recent deaths of people close to us: her husband, my sister. We still haven't recovered, and still tell each other so. I take notes: on what I remember, who and what I see, who I aim to be, and who I continue to become. Recalling: in Colombia, walking chilly Bogotá's Carrera Septima beneath those dark-green Andes—what Bogotanos locally call "los cerros," the hills, which flank the city's eastern side from south to north—thinking of García Márquez and his *costeño* world to the north, a world I'll come to know in some small part during Holy Week; yet remembering—how can any of us forget?—the eight-year-old Bogotá prostitute whose clients pay her five hundred pesos more—less than one U.S. dollar at current exchange rates—if she will *not* insist they use a condom; the ragged twelve-year-old boy missing two fingers and an eye, at two o'clock a.m. selling cheap candies to weary unsmiling adults on a city bus; visions of Bogotá's (and Lima's, and Santiago's) well-appointed, wealthy sections, where some residents employ doormen and guards to protect them from possible robberies and kidnappings by guerrilla groups (this protection usually works most forcefully against what occurs most frequently—the arrival of people begging at the door for food. In 1992, during city- and nationwide electricity rationings that cloak Bogotá in dangerous darkness for four or more hours each day and night, the power is turned on here first); but also, in Bogotá and the other cities, visions of poorer living areas, where people live practically *in* the dirt, often without water and electricity and even without walls—what our homeless in the United States share with those we dare to look down upon; and—perhaps most terrifying—the five or so Bogotá drag queens mowed down by (army? police? "cleaning squad" terrorists'?) machine-gun fire early one morning, apparently because they simply existed, dared to exist. Neither *El Tiempo* nor *El Espectador,* Colombia's two major (and conservative) dailies, will carry any reportage on the murders. These nameless victims, along with so many impoverished children and countless others who wind up in mass graveyards of the anonymous unwanted, are called by many simply, coldly, *desechables*—disposables.

Remembering: that as a black male who is also gay, I and my brothers and our black lesbian sisters are considered "disposables" throughout the world, throughout time past and present, in our own black communities and in white ones. This is clearly the case in Jamaica and most other Caribbean nations, and is certainly true in the supposedly more "progressive" United States. What will the force of this virulent hatred mean for our futures, and who will decide once again which of us is disposable?

And: will we stand together when the time comes for *us* to face that machine-gun fire? All of us? Beyond our prejudices?

(Remembering: The August 16, 1993, issue of *Stonewall News*, a New York gay weekly, features an article entitled "Amnesty International Denounces Treatment of Mexican Activists"; the article opens: "Amnesty International has expressed 'deep concern' over the arrest and ill-treatment of two gay activists by Mexican authorities. Other sources report that in 1992 *at least 23 gay men were murdered throughout Mexico by conservative death squads associated with the military or the police*" [my italics]. Such anti-gay/lesbian violence persists as I write, in this moment, throughout most industrialized and developing nations of the world; in many, with the increasingly prideful visibility and organizational effort-struggles of lesbians and gay men, it shows an unconscionably marked increase—so we learn from those lucky enough to survive the tortures to report them, or from those who grieve over lovers, family, and friends lost to disappearances, strategically repressive violence, and summary executions. We know, or ought to know by now, that the real-life dramas haven't changed. Neither have the characters. Will we be so smug, irresponsible, and selfish as to say, "It's their problem"—and leave it at that? What will *this* mean for our futures?)

There will be evenings of racing dolphins (my father's dream) in the frigid South Pacific waters off the island of Chiloe, Chile, bringing to mind the wonderful works of Isabel Allende, whose magical writings, along with those of García Márquez and others, are so related to the magical writings and beliefs of peoples of African descent. The scents of mango and guava rising off the pages of *One Hundred Years of Solitude* or Rosario Ferré's *The Youngest Doll* instantly remind me of another family garden in Norbrook, Jamaica, where not Barrabás but Marcus Garvey's voice comes to us by sea. When I return to Baychester, it will be with another type of knowledge of the richness of those ingrained textures, sounds, and sights. In those musical Jamaican accents and in our harsher Bronx cadences, in the smells of curry goat and sorrel and memories of ashy legs and cold cream and some of the small-town ways in which we live here—far from perfection but with spaces of occasional clarity between the relentless redness and confusion—everything of Toni Morrison's Ohio towns exists; everything even of Faulkner's far-off Yoknapatawpha County, and Flannery O'Connor's stark tree-edged Georgia fields—something of what the Jamaican writer Vic Reid wrote about so powerfully in *The Leopard* and *The Jamaicans*. With these realizations, an immeasurable solitude becomes clearer in you still out there, my exact and imprecise reflection, larger than myself and in your particular solitude owner of a darker knowledge than I acknowledge yet—or in some other life, some other moment of being, both owner and essence of something I've already carried and acknowledged. As Daddy discovered who I was in my new worlds simply by my one day telling him what he'd always known and had never hated, so now have I learned of *place*—that is, that these places are mine to return to and always will be: the North Bronx of my memory or that green, blue-mountained island of my parents; the firm hand of a man in my own joined by the lasting power of my father's living spirit-grasp, guiding. Whichever, or all, if I choose; recognizing these places' pernicious dangers and hatreds of who I am—who *we* are—as I attempt to live as I *have* to live, telling the truth, as my parents raised me to do. In this, I hope that I'll neither fail along the way nor be killed for aiming to live my own truth, *our* truth, as I—we—refuse to be silenced. There will be time for all that and more. And time, too, for me to tell my father how much, how very much, I love him: how much I love the sweat on his neck as he hoists bags of horseshit into the car, the sweat shining on his face as he strains over those tender seedlings that tremble in his hands; how I love and mourn the glance of useless dreams in his beautiful cloudy-clear eyes, the soft gray hair on his head, and his always-formal courtliness—things I won't be able to say to him until shortly before he dies, yet still things that have never left me. Today, sixteen years ago or right now in the present, our *we* still exists in our acknowledged differences and strengths woven into the dream of a shared continuing history, the dream of so many still-silent and silenced voices throughout the world that are part of this We, inseparable from it. We can never let it be erased. *It will never be erased.* Today we carry the horseshit home, as yet another train passes through this memory, as yet another someone of this we—you, or him—walks here. I close my eyes and breathe in, deeply: the new long season breathes out its beginning. Deep in the blood, beating. Discovering. Becoming. Yes.

1994

Toward a Nobility of the Imagination: Jamaica's Shame (An Open Letter to the People of Jamaica)

BECAUSE IN FACT WE ARE NOT NOBLE. WE ARE COWARDS, hypocrites. Hysterical in our hatred and ignorance, seeking to cast aspersions and impose ostracism via state and social persecution—death sentences—upon those whom we consider already damned. Upon lesbians and gay men: those whom we would briskly vilify as "sodomites" or "abominations"—denunciations heard in recent public discussions about homosexuality in Jamaica.[1] But how swift and smug our judgments. How devoid of simple human compassion. How shallow our reasoning.

In truth, we as a society barely know what the word "humanity" means. For in failing to love and support our fellow humans who are gay and lesbian, we are hardly human. This, only one part of our shame.

Have we fallen so far into the abyss of historical amnesia that we have (willfully, purposefully) forgotten? Forgotten that only as recently as the last century our ancestors, who burned and rioted against their masters so that we might bask and shine in freedom's ennobling light, perished beneath the plantation's whip, withered in cane fields beneath vicious suns, opened ravaged thighs to rape, to torture, to unimaginable degradation? To utter inhumanity?

Slavery, it was called. Slavery. Black bodies packed thousand-fold into ships, black hands manacled at the wrist. Flesh ripped, feet broken, brands steamed white-hot into skin. They are not human, they are animals, the masters said. So echoed the innumerable colonizers who followed them—who, late into the twentieth century, believed that we as black people, "out of many, one,"[2] were unfit to govern ourselves; to make laws as human beings for ourselves, and live peacefully, lovingly, nobly, amongst ourselves.

In our present willingness to persecute and destroy our gay and lesbian brothers and sisters—our children, parents, aunts, grandparents, uncles, cousins, and friends—have we proved the masters correct?

With such a brutal history—need we say it?—we should be the noblest people in the world. Self-governing at last, survivors of the most heinous atrocities against humanity the world has ever known, we should long ago have acquired a braver, more generous, more noble imagination: the ability to envision goodness, even greatness, in all things, and most of all in ourselves; the ability to love ourselves—*all* of ourselves, irrespective of color, class, gender, or sexual orientation. But we have not. Our flag flies proudly, yet we are not proud—or we are so falsely, mired in the arrogance that, writ large, adores dishonesty. In our present mean-spiritedness and self-enslaving ignorance, we are quickly on our way to becoming worse off than what many have consistently attempted to make us.

I am gay. Jamaican. And proud to be both. That flag of green, black, and gold is my flag; that national anthem, my anthem; those people in Cross Roads and St. Mary and Clarendon—every parish—mine. All mine. I am them. Of them. My ancestors' blood yet tells me so.

Many of my fellow Jamaicans, however, would not have it be so. "You shoulda dead, bwoy," they would say. "Gwan with that nasty foreign business," they would say. (Indeed, some of them have said.) "We shoulda shot you the first chance we did get," they would say. Shot, stabbed, stoned. Boom bye-bye.[3] It has been said.

Dead? I, and my lesbian sisters and gay brothers, who are sisters and brothers of us all? Cutlassed down in Half-Way-Tree? Shot on Molynes Road? Burned out of house and home (or to ashes) in St. Catherine?

No, no. Absolutely no. It cannot be so. For we are here, we are you, we are part of you. We are Jamaican, human, alive. We are your neighbors and your friends. Your helpers, coworkers, bosses. We serve your food in restaurants, clean your streets, fix your cars, and bury your dead. We nurse you and your loved ones back to health in hospitals and bring forth your children (and our own, for many of us also are parents) into the world. We tidy your homes and live in them.

We process your loans and bank accounts and teach your children. We drive the taxis you hail, arrest the criminals you fear, catch the fish that you fry and steam, repair the roads on which you walk, and even fly the planes and steer the boats that carry you to places beyond your most hopeful dreams. And in this there is a kind of nobility, for—like many other members of this society—we do a great deal without asking much in return, except that we be allowed to live our lives without fear of being harassed or gunned down. We are, indeed, everywhere: like you. But you have not often asked us who we were because you did not want to know, and even when you knew, you denied it. Thus you were able to say, "Mi never know a gay smaddi yet,"[4] or "Battyman, man royal,[5] de whole heap a dem nasty so"—without acknowledging that the woman who sold you yams and bread-fruit this morning or last night might be a lesbian, that the man who drove the bus you rode to work might have gone home later to the kisses and love of another man, that the women who work as security guards, or pharmacy clerks, or as sidewalk vendors on Orange Street and King Street might be dreaming of loving each other—what is normal and is true. That we have always been here has always been true in Jamaica. We are not a new "fashion," not something brought back by an ICI from Curaçao or North America.[6] We are not a disease, nor are we damned.

We are none of the terrible things many would have us be.

But we were not asked compassionately where we were or how we lived, and so—as far as many were concerned—we did not exist. But how ignoble is such imagining; how it reeks of narrowmindedness and spiritual selfishness. If we honestly intend to occupy this earth, and this country, in each other's human service and in peace, these hateful prejudices are far from the best imagining of our lesbian and gay sisters and brothers we as Jamaicans can do. Such mean imagining in actuality pays dim tribute to the formidable legacies handed down by our brilliant national heroes, and to figures such as the late, great Bob Marley and Michael Manley[7]—visionaries who believed, not coincidentally, in the transcendent and enlarging possibilities of freedom.

Regarding deliberations on homosexuality (and on so many other critical matters facing us in this country), I charge my fellow Jamaicans with the necessary human task of becoming more noble. I exhort us to be great, spiritually and in the acts which that spiritual magnitude will motivate. I press us toward compassion. We are not there yet. None of us can live as our greatest, grandest selves while we continue to despise and denigrate so many who are, ultimately, ourselves—our fellow citizens, lesbians and gay men included. The masters' lessons of oppression, like their brands on our ancestors' flesh, still burn into our brains. Our greatest prophet singer admonished us: we must free ourselves from mental slavery—from bigotry, hatred, and selfoppression. He knew that none of us would ever truly be free until all were. As members of the modern world, we must know that freedom cannot be granted selectively: we cannot grant freedom to some as we continue to oppress—"downpress"—others. We must work toward a nobility of the imagination, and spirit, that rejects the shame of our ignorance, as we recognize that all of us, heterosexual and homosexual, deserve equal, loving places in society. Until we do so, we will continue to bear the master's marks, and the weight of our shame—our *dis*-spiriting prejudice and ignorance. Anti–Third Worldists and cultural imperialists need not dominate and manipulate us with spurious promises and seductions of foreign aid if we are so willing to alienate and destroy our own.

And so, in this season of God, nearing the close of one of the most violent centuries humankind has ever known, I pray—words offered up to all who will hear: that I and my lesbian sisters and gay brothers will not, as we come forth in love and honesty, be harassed, or killed, or maimed, in this green, troubled land of our own people and ancestors—this island of so many joys and sorrows. I pray that we all will, in this nation that might still be great, walk peacefully away from shame, toward our potential human nobility. The slaves are dead, the masters decayed in their graves; the future, while never assured, can yet be ours, together. We are poised in the present moment, in which all things may change, all ignorance be transposed to knowledge; from knowledge shall come compassion, and from compassion, nobility.

Our ancestors and national heroes knew this. Dying for us, they spoke it. They speak to us still.

Our beginning, then. A new beginning, in this season of God.

Thus is my faith in my own people, that—standing tall—we may all hear. Hear each other. Attend each other. For once, in unity. Heterosexuals. Homosexuals. All configurations abiding, reconfigurings emergent. Wealthy and poor, female and male. Together. Alive. Here. Now.

Kingston, Jamaica
December 1998–January 1999

(Re-)Recalling Essex Hemphill:
Words to Our Now

AND SO ALWAYS, NOW: RECALLING A LIFE AND THE EVER-renascent power of vision that yet fuels the source and matrix of an essence; invoking the *now* of your undying spirit and refeeling it, reclaiming it, it is to you, of course, whom I write, Essex. In this *now* that is here. And always now. Resolute. Writing to you with the certainty that the abiding force of your passion has not ceased refiguring you and your words ever bolder in our memory. We need only hark to the spirit; it beckons. We need only listen; it speaks:

> I prowl in scant sheaths of latex.
> I harbor no shame.
> I solicit no pity.
> I celebrate my natural tendencies,
> photosynthesis, erotic customs.
> I allow myself to dream of roses
> though I know
> the bloody war continues.[1]

We attend the voice. But of course. Yours. As, yes, the bloody wars continue. As viral nights, official subterfuge, and unofficial antifreedom engenderings continue.[2] So attending, conscious of the viral nights and the engenderings that threaten even as, for some, they beguile, we revisit your voice, within—engaging once more those troubled silences, yearnings, from which you always addressed us: those rooms, cells, corridors of blue tones and shadowed dreams where—so it obtained and obtains still—too many of us languished through those returning *now*s of our most pressing need, evoked in your language's echoes and refrains; as, hearing and reading on the open page those lives both yours and ours so boldly-lovingly revealed, we walked most closely with you when we did not resist your calls, and in the walking drew together ever more aligned in the steadfast power of all our names. "The memory cannot replace the man,"[3] one of our brothers in recent years wrote about you; yet we know that it is memory precisely, exercised in judicious concert with the clarifying, edifying words you gave us that configured anew the previously defined and circumscribed—ourselves and others—that will not only determine our survival but embolden it. Ennoble it. It has been said, and we recall: we were never meant to survive. Not here. No, not then or now. Not in the gorge of a grasping empire poisoned by the recurring venoms of its own antihumanity. Here, now, we can never forget that, as you did not survive, others still are falling. Falling beneath the policeman's baton, or raped by it;[4] expiring in the electric chair, decaying along lonely roads after the body has been chained behind a truck and dragged[5]—the body historically and contemporarily fetishized, sodomized, demonized; now again whipped, sawed, beheaded, carved, and marked with swastikas this week or with whatever the terrorism and terror that prevail and fester in depraved human imaginations will next resurrect and refashion from those dis-eased realms. As you would have asked, we must: who, in this now, will next laugh at the opportunity to view "a nigger's brains,"[6] as, shotgun-armed, on Hitler's birthday, they stand viciously cruel guard over his or her eighteen-year-old form and aim their guns in a high school library where these kinds of things simply *do not happen,* as popular prevarications insist. Such horrors should occur only in the "inner city," someone will say, has said.[7] Not "here." Not in this now.

"But we're in the United States," you doubtless would have said; your seer's most mordant irony confronting misconception, sweeping aside revisionist muddyings of present and past. "In the United States, where these sorts of things always happen. But yes, believe it," you surely would have said, "they always happen here.

"In the United States," you might have said, "where such events are always now. Yes. And always here."

Regarding the caveats illumined in the stanzas you left behind, so we might summon your voice admonishing us in this now, Essex. Knowing as we summon that amid the general incoherence and hysteria of our time still reigns the especial brand of expedient historical revisionism that perennially subverts and travesties integrity. That bastardizes honesty. The same revisionism that, by dint of purposefully *dis*placed memory, ever befriends the spiritual lassitude and anti-intellection that disdain humanity's most hopeful ascensions as much as they imperil its ultimate dignity. Our futures would without question be imperiled, you told us, if, sometime discarding vigilance, we dared curtsey to that enduring U.S. mind-altering favorite, ahistoricism; if we dared ever forget—dismiss—the chains and conflagrant crosses, fire hoses and hemp that preceded, that loom among us still, and which were and are inexorably linked to the seductions and self-deceptions of the unconscionable amnesia that, in all quarters, nurtures bigotry and ignorance alike. Seduction bears its price, you told us. The words of lesser poets who repudiated truth and embraced mediocrity's diminished and diminishing returns have long since been forgotten. But you were not and would not be seduced, not in that way, and—only one of your precious gifts to us—enjoined us not to forget. In the fierceness of this *now,* it is exactly the radical art and life-effort of conscientious remembrance that, against revisionism's erasures and in pursuit of our survival, must better become our duty. Memory in this regard becomes responsibility; as responsibility and memory both become us.

In this now, we celebrate your life and language, Essex. So celebrating, we know that we re-recall you in what is largely, to borrow from another visionary, a "giantless time."[8] The sheer giantry of your breathing presence has passed. Now present and future warriors assume the struggles your language named. Those warriors—ourselves and others—will be compelled to learn, as you did and made manifest, that all hauls toward truth—toward truest freedom—will require intellectual and spiritual vigor, not venality; ardor, not arrogance; forthrightness, not cowardice. You taught us: the habit of "tossing shade" at our sisters and brothers has become more than ever an outmoded and grossly stupid one, ill-afforded, born out of our most pathetic shortsightedness and best laid aside. In this now, we will no longer be able to afford the blood sport that we have so long adored—self-contempt—that should long ago have been fitted with both bridle and brakes. We will have to learn, *finally*, that only the most autodestructive joy will emerge from ripping each other when most afraid to love each other because we remain each's easiest targets. We will have to remember *and believe* what Baby Suggs, hands outstretched, told us: to love our skins, our flesh, and above all the heart—"For this is the prize."[9] Centered in a love generous and secure enough to embrace others, but beginning first and foremost with ourselves, our sisters will no longer be our "bitches," our darkest no longer our shame. No more Mandingoizing of ourselves in search of the biggest, blackest rod that will provide us with the most rageful sundering we believe we so richly deserve; to hell with who's-blacker-than-who snipes, who's-more-educated-than-who foolishness. We will know that the claiming of pride in ourselves will require genuinely loving behavior among ourselves—"the prize"—and not refuge in the easy rhetoric whose glibness loves the fleeting moment but loathes the task. Aspiring toward our greater humanity, we will be compelled to *think,* and think better, in short; jettisoning trendiness and catchwords for rigorous self-analysis that at its best will be both compassionate and wise—the site of true sublimity, where reside all possibilities most supreme. Demanding of us that greatness of spirit which you knew we could ultimately attain, you spoke:

You judge a woman
by what she can do for you alone
but there's no need
for slaves to have slaves.

You judge a woman
by impressions you think you've made.

Ask and she gives,
take without asking,
beat on her and she'll obey,
throw her name up and down the streets
like some loose whistle—
knowing her neighbors will talk.

. . . we so-called men,
we so-called brothers
wonder why it's so hard
to love *our* women
when we're about loving them
the way america
loves us.[10]

So you exhorted and exhort us still to question ourselves, and act bravely, humanely, in the questioning. The exercise of listening in this regard can be only a beginning, for, as we must learn and relearn, it is the synthesis of multilayered understanding with humanitarian action that will propel us closer toward that deeper regard for and commitment to ourselves—knowledge critical to our lives in the star-spangled slaughterhouse at the end of the atrocity-littered twentieth century; knowledge we cannot afford *not* to own. You showed us, and we note: lynchings have not stopped but now proceed smoothly on automatic pilot. Assaults against abortion clinics progress from tightly clutched rifles aimed at doctors and patients to stunningly well-hurled bombs. Black churches are torched to skulking ash; a Guinean immigrant is riddled with bullets by police in a city known to boast of its world-liness and "internationalism";[11] affirmative action shrivels; a gay man in Alabama is beaten to death, his dead body incinerated atop an ignoble pyre of two car tires,[12] as a young gay Wyoming student's skull is literally smashed before his comatose form is tied to a fence;[13] Haitian refugees are scorned in south Florida and remanded to the poverty, violence, and state repression they fled; a white supremacist fires shots into a Jewish community center, wounding several children, as he issues his personal "wake-up call to America to kill all the Jews";[14] AIDS and cancer flare among people of color, women and children vanish from city streets and reappear eviscerated on rural-route shoulders, and right-wing hate mongers smile upon it all. Now, right now, somewhere, black women, black lesbians, are being raped, battered, assaulted; now, right now, black men, black gay men, are running for their lives from baseball bats, knives, ravenous police. A butchered drag queen floats face down in a river as another struts fiercely on in her own image; a black baby shudders for the taste of crack; a black teenager contemplates suicide, or suicide on the installment plan—drugs; two black men on death row yearn to hold each other, two black women seeking heat and shelter for their children dream, somehow, of kissing each other's breasts, and which of us, you asked, will be there to testify? What is our responsibility for their survival, you demanded, and what part do we claim in their silence?

What is our responsibility to *all* of them, we must ask, and which of their faces are in fact our own?

You showed us, Essex: employing the compassionate action that transposes to wisdom and love among ourselves, enhancing ourselves and others, it remains our task as the inheritors of your brother-love and vision to charge, uncertain but unified, in chal-lenge of the lingering repressions born out of hatreds renewed and combined. As people of color in a time both giantless (for the moment) and laced with ignorance and widespread capitu-lation, however and to whomever we define it, the destructive and limiting pastimes of self-aggrandizement and serving in the master's house with the master tools will serve not us but only our enemies.[15] It was your vigilance, Essex, along with that of our passed-on seers Audre Lorde, Joe Beam, Pat Parker, and others, that served and serves still as warning that not only language and its power to silence or muddle must be critiqued, but also every aspect of our waking reality, and the malignancies that corrupt and abrade it. We remember:

> Some of the best minds of my generation would have us believe that AIDS has brought the gay and lesbian community closer and infused it with a more democratic mandate. That is only a partial truth, which further underscores the fact that the gay community still operates from a one-eyed, one gender, one color perception of *community* that is most likely to recognize blond before Black, but seldom the two together. . . . We are communities engaged in a fragile coexistence if we are anything at all. Our most significant coalitions have been created in the realm of sex. What is most clear for Black gay men [and lesbians] is this: we have to do for ourselves *now,* and for one another *now,* what no one has ever done for us. . . . Our only sure guarantee of survival is that which we construct from our own self-determination. White gay men may only be able to understand and respond to oppression as it relates to their ability to obtain orgasm without intrusion from the church and state. White gay men are only "other" in this society when they choose to come out of the closet. But all Black men [and women] are treated as "other" regardless of whether we sleep with men or women—our Black skin automatically marks us as "other."[16]

You invoke the *now*; we traverse it. Traverse it knowing that despite this age-old "otherization" of ourselves, our cultural work continues to blossom. Books are written, poems penned; films are photographed into being, dances envisioned and performed; paintings are colored, plays explode out of shy cauls, and music in all forms lilts forth from gazes steadily widening. We move outward in the wake of your lessons. That we have come this far, this long, in itself testifies to humanity's recurring force and shine as it does you and your words' legacies proud. In the giantless time that changes daily to one of our own giantry, in the here of our now, our status as "other" (and who cares what the naysayers think, anyway?) pales beside our passion and strength, fueled by your gifts of lyric and anger, joy and outrage, that, alongside our own, will long outlive the mean-toned landscape through which we presently walk without your presence beside us in the living flesh. As millions of our own are executed globally—Liberia, Rwanda, Haiti; Sierra Leone, the Sudan, the Congo—we remember; as black men and women and our sisters and brothers of color languish (or die) in the rotting prisons and slums of the slaughter-house and sheets and swastikas are donned beneath conflagrant crosses yet flaring, between homo-haters' brickbats still hurled, we know, holding you within our hands and behind our eyes that this *now*, the risky always-second of the present moment that is the unending and beginning spiral of all consciousness, is ours. Is us. Here. "Well, then *be* it," you would surely say, and mean it. "In america," you wrote, "place your ring / on my cock / where it belongs. / Long may we live / to free this dream."[17] The voice of the seer. Long may we all live, Essex, walking through this anti-freedom land; eyes and hands lifted toward our greatest selves as our spirits soar with yours. The flesh, so propelled onward, cannot be erased. The words become our hearts. *We who are alive. With you. In this now.* Graced by that sheen. By that brother-light.

So we progress. Celebrate. Re-recall. The need guiding our hands. In this now that is you, Essex, and memory, voice. Memory voiced. Your enduring gifts, that are always, now.

2000

Fire and Ink:
Toward a Quest for Language, History, and a Moral Imagination

∾

I MIGHT STAND HERE BEFORE YOU TONIGHT AT THIS HIS-toric conference and invoke, by way of paraphrase, the well-wrought words of our departed sister/mother Audre Lorde: that, like some of you, I am a black gay writer doing my very best to do my work, come to tell you that I know many of you are doing yours—that work, its urgency and necessity, that has at last brought us here, in each other's company, together. I could tell you how, over these long yet short years since Audre's passing (ten years this year), I have longed, viscerally, for the sheer force of her powerful voice speaking out loud, once more, among us; my longing the yearning one feels for a mother who one can scarcely believe is physically gone, a sacred chord inexplicably absent. Longing for that voice that, each day, without fail, fearlessly impelled so many of us toward all the struggles and demands awaiting us, writing and the critical task of bearing conscientious witness among them. That voice, now slightly more distant yet echoing. Echoing without end, and within. I could tell you how I still long for Audre to admonish me again that my silence will never protect me as, in this Cyclops that we call "America," I also dream of finally placing my ring on Essex Hemphill's cock, where it belongs.[1] Let Assotto Saint again regale me with his *Spells of a Voodoo Doll,* as June Jordan electrifies me into unflinching memory with her "Poem about My Rights." Let Marlon Riggs untie my tongue once more and jolt me toward new, discovering language and feeling with his poetry, as Pat Parker demands to know where I will be when they come,[2] as they have come before and, be assured, will again: come with their jingoism and nationalist flags, come with their freshly laundered sheets and smoldering crosses; come with their anti–affirmative action shouts, their forty-one (or fifty, or one hundred) bullets, and their assaults against people perceived to be from "the Middle East"—wherever that is—and against people who closely resemble all of us; who are and always have been, at the day's end and the long night's beginning, us. All of us, in continual quest of language that honors, testifies to, inscribes experiences *dis*honored and distorted, when they are mentioned at all, by official histories; experiences subverted and perverted by media circuses whose pundits, claiming knowledge and ownership of "the truth," tenaciously dissemble as actual thinkers. I could share all these thoughts with you and more, but I already know, having watched your faces closely over these past days and tonight, that you have long pondered them; that, toward the shaping of our narratives, the growing body of which provides new meaning and amplitude to the term "modern art," we have all long considered them. It is that common knowledge, of course, that affords us the grand privilege of easy comfort in each other's company here. For if, as African-descended people and artists, we've achieved anything—and we have, make no mistake, scaled heights beyond reckoning in the 137 years since 1865—we have certainly, as this conference attests, achieved a superlative beginning toward the dream of a common language, to borrow Adrienne Rich's encapsulating title.

It is entirely appropriate that this conference uses in its title the words "fire" and "ink." For in casting even only a glance back at our history—a history which, countenanced or not, accepted within ourselves or not, deeply informs the languages we seek to construct in the narrative architectures we assay today—we remember how, throughout every epoch of that history, both fire and ink were used against us, often with horrifying consequences, but also on our behalf. Fire reduced untold numbers of us to ashes as we dangled from sturdy trees, even as the fire of spirits like Toussaint Louverture and Ida B. Wells, Frederick Douglass and the maroons throughout our entire diaspora labored to deliver us. Ink dried on writs and bills of sale that ensured the cold press of iron about our legs and wrists, about our necks, even as, scrawled by other hands, ink shouted off the pages of *The North Star,* proclaiming to the world and ourselves yet again that, yes, we were and are human beings, possessed of hearts, minds. Dignity. Fire and ink never ceased their fierce alliances in our history, as, at this conference, at the start of a new century (though one still only briefly removed from that past), we begin once more that trenchant work handed down to us by all those hands still reaching; hands that themselves struggled to fashion stories to pass on, so that we, and the stories we craft today, might be, and are.

I spent weeks anticipating this gathering with one supremely pressing question: What, if anything, had I learned from that history, and from the departed elders, among others, whose names I invoked earlier? What new questions that, after all this time, finally might not be all that frustrating or unfathomable, and which, if I could just close my eyes and summon the (surely) just-there-and-waiting revelation's whispered words, would make clear to me so much of what I'd grappled to know all these years? Grappled even while, through those years, I often had no idea of, was unable to recognize, the primordial site of that yearning?

Recurringly, in my questioning what I'd learned from all that had preceded and in pondering all that I still desired so desperately to know, I found myself returning to two words, simple ones, that have everything to do not only with the work we do, but also with the critical importance of our writerly beginnings first as readers, scrupulous readers; as thinkers, scrupulous thinkers. Two simple words: *language,* and *imagination.* For we know that if the elders bequeathed us anything at all—anything in addition to passion, determination, and a capacity to survive—they left us language: a way to shape, make felt. Palpable. Imagination:

a way to see, envision; even—especially—to risk a well-traveled word, to dream. This, our inheritance: prismatic language, assiduously polished out of struggle and rage, yes, frustration and horror, of course, but also out of desire: the desire to conjure oneself as one already was but also as one might be, could be; in the act of conjuring and the emblazoning step toward honing the imagined language of those conjurings into the textual forms of narrative—prose, drama, poetry, or other, newly fused inventions—creating oneself, *the* self, into being: the fragmented self, the lonely, keening self. The vulnerable self, the loving self, the thwarted or ecstatic or trammeled self. The self of all selves beset and sundered by life's imprecations and turbulences, but above all its own precious entity: defiant to would-be silencing by virtue of its very existence, vulnerable to misreadings and dismissals occasioned by its insistence on its own voice, but ever profoundly aware, that new, raw, naked self, of all that magnificent open air previously denied it and all at once right there, all about it, for the taking. The selves of those labored dreams in most cases prevailed, to speak through decades—centuries—of enforced invisibilities, to the selves that we become, have become and will, as, through our stories, we create new selves for each other, and others, and all those who will come after.

But then, if only for a moment, we should look closer at these gauntlets thrown down for us: gauntlets of language, imagination, and the triumphant possibilities of the self and its progeny made manifest, even miraculous, through metaphor and allegory, lyric and stanza. For there they are, and here, those departed voices told us and tell us still: the gifts of language and imagination, sublimely consonant with the self. Language and imagination that must be fed. Nurtured. Fed and nurtured not only (if at all) on ideas and books and writing that maintain our comfort, but also on those which impel us into new, difficult terrains. Language and imagination beyond intellectual smugness; beyond artistic mediocrity; beyond the cheap delights of self-deceiving self-congratulation and the embarrassments of dishonest, fraudulent writing mired in its pretensions to truth and actual substance. Make sure that you do well with the imaginative legacy, whatever you do, the voices urged. Make sure that you *honor* us, they emphasized, as you remember. Understand that you have little time to waste. Do not spend that time dishonoring us by indulgence in "diva" games, in Who's King (or Queen) of the Heap Today games, or in "shade"—a despicable practice—or small-mindedness, an ultimate disgrace. No. Do well instead. But even if you don't do well, whatever that means; even if you commit the enviable error of falling flat on your face because you actually dared to risk everything in the face of mockery, envy, and ever-lurking laughter, they told us, remain undaunted, unhampered by fear; and always, *always* strive to be noble in that act of imagining that is now utterly yours: the supreme gift, and its accountability to your fellow travelers, and to all of us, and to the soul.

Part of this talk's title centers on the idea of what I've come to name, and ardently believe in as, a "moral" imagination. The idea and aims of a so-called moral imagination have always fascinated me; even, I know now, long before I articulated to myself what exactly the parameters of such a state of mind and being, ever-expanding though at its best precisely configured, might be. While, fairly early in my life as a reader, I detected some of this imagination's elements in the writers I most admired and still admire, as I observed its traces in the people of everyday life whom I wished most to emulate, it was only fairly recently—some years before the publication of my short-story collection, and after much additional questioning deepened by the joys and demands of increased reading and countless rewalkings through fire and ink—that I arrived at a more satisfactory, more meaningful, more useful understanding, for the human work I knew I wanted my work to do, of a moral imagination's foundation; its foundational tenets and principles, if you will. I knew that for me, as illustrated in the works of the writers I truly loved, my own moral imagination would perforce need to be intellectually vigilant, never slipshod; politically agile and astute, never complacent; vulnerable and receptive to, aware of, the wider world at large: *that* world, out there and in here, beyond the smallness of my personal geography yet intrinsically part of it, attached to it; and always, without exception, compassionate. While sharpening reflections on these concerns, I soon understood that a moral imagination, by its very nature and mandate, would need also to maintain staunch guard against the slippery slopes of distracting, even destructive languages—the mediums of trivialization, banality, and dehumanization that daily surround us.

The very word "moral," of course, especially when linked with the word "imagination," suggests the presence of the political: in a morally centered universe—one external or internal, focused on the well-being of all humanity and all living creatures with which we share the world—virtually every action that one takes, each decision that one considers, bears political, moral, and often, if not always, ethical import. Yet even (or especially) with an awareness of the political dangling just there in the uneven balance that is both circumstance and the inevitable reality of human error, I sought, while exploring the possibilities of a moral imagination's reach, a particular type of freedom: the largesse to feel and think and write and dream whatever I wanted to feel or write or think about, in the way I wanted to—experimentally, iconoclastically against yet within whichever tradition—without the proscriptions of what I or anyone else deemed I *should,* for whatever reasons, think, or write, or dream, in whichever proscribed or permitted way. This sort of freedom—intoxicating in its most secret moments, when the self most permits itself the simplest, rarest luxury of merely being—is, we know, highly elusive, to say the least, among our kind: that is, among human beings who are also social animals; in our case, animals who are also artists who, whatever else we do, are compelled to live and participate in societies contained and delimited by the mores and rules of social controls. Yet this freedom had to exist, I knew. Other writers and other artists (most notably painters, some dancers, and especially jazz musicians) had achieved it. Slowly, as I became more aware of the artistic explosions taking place in contemporary black queer literature—work produced particularly in the last twenty-five years, including the vanguard work of early black lesbian feminists—I realized. Realized that being a black gay writer meant that I could—of course!—write about anything I chose, in whichever way I liked, no matter what anyone else—friends, other writers, or agenda-driven publishers, agents, and critics—had to say. It meant that we all could. Could write first and foremost about ourselves, whom many had not previously deemed a worthy topic in literature, if they'd considered it at all. We could write about ourselves across gender and class; across history, geography, nationality, and certainly sexuality; all the while taking supreme pleasure in those acrobatic imaginative acts. The great significance—really triumph—of these latter points cannot and should never be overlooked, given the world in which we live: a world that continually seeks to write us *out* of existence, literally or otherwise; one that seeks to truncate us, caricaturize and demonize us, when it isn't ruthlessly busy simply ignoring us. It does try to demolish us, that world, and tries again. Yet how miserably it fails in so many of its attempts, as this conference proves.

And so here, if we choose to accept it, is that freedom that, to me, had long seemed so elusive: the freedom to step fully into an imagination that, at its best, is expansive, completely unafraid; one that does not shy away from but embraces risk; what moves itself, finally, toward a truly moral imagination that by its very nature and outlook is imbued with a profound respect for other people's lives. A developed consciousness outraged by cruelty and ever skeptical of the glib rationale or trite response. Viewed in this light, such an imaginative realm demands that we assume the challenge—and challenge it is—of envisioning, as compassionately and with as much depth and breadth as possible, others beyond ourselves—others who, in our truly seeing and feeling them through a creative act that is itself, in the greatest sense of the word, holy, will no longer be, to us, the "other." A marriage of the moral/ethical and creative will require, in the broad human

drama known more casually as life, that we bear witness to the
great and small joys and sorrows of those many lives and deaths;
lives and deaths which, in the abiding drama, are also and always
will be, make no mistake, our own. This task—the assumption
of high-risk, plain old deep *feeling*—is formidable, of course. But
not impossible. Consider it (to borrow Václav Havel's phrase)
an art of the impossible.[3] An art that, at its most essential core,
insists only that we listen deeply to ourselves; that we attend ourselves first, with such bravery and self-regard (self-regard not to
be mistaken for self-aggrandizement or the unfortunate joys of a
corpulent ego) that we're able, after sustained wrestling with the
art—ourselves—to move with equipoise and gallantry through
the selves of others in these enormous adventures we refer to as
life, literature, invention; spirit, feeling, and vision. And while it
might be true that we occasionally stumble in the act of reaching
to imagine and transform the complexities of our selves and others, we also know—should know by now—that such stumbling
is, yes, permissible—indeed, necessary. For it is only through
stumbling, attuned to our own humanity and its inevitable flaws
from which the generous imagination is never excepted, that we
arrive at the richest possible experience and understanding of
what, for every artist and human being, is the preeminent place
for our continued growth and sojourn toward wisdom: humility,
embodied in the simple grace and courage that allow us to admit
that we have, yes, failed. But then, taking into account these truths
and others, we're also obliged to remember that failure—what we
as artists, scholars, and sometime critics call with trepidation or
self-protecting contempt "failure"—is a luxury we all, taking our
rightful place in the human drama, not only can, but *must* afford.
For it is only through what we mistakenly revile as "failure" that
we learn, graced by the humility that itself is a form of freedom,
that failure is nowhere near the terrifying damnation we've so long
been schooled into believing it to be. In acts of imagining and
daily living, we do often fail, it's true. But in the renewed imaginings and breaths that each next moment brings us, we often

succeed, also true. A moral imagination in search of language
and history knows and understands these truths. The steadfast
gazes of our elders and ancestors long ago made it all clear for us.
Didn't Toni Morrison tell us only nine years ago, in Stockholm,
"We die. That may be the meaning of life. But we *do* language.
That may be the measure of our lives."[4] Didn't James Baldwin
tell us more than three decades ago, at the end of his visionary
fiction "Sonny's Blues," that "the tale of how we suffer, and how
we are delighted, and how we may triumph, is never new, [but]
always must be heard. There isn't any other tale to tell, it's the only
light we've got in all this darkness."[5] Didn't Joseph Beam, fast
on the very heels of his brother-forebear, tell us how he dreamed
of "Black men loving and supporting other Black men, and re-
lieving Black women from the role of primary nurturers in our
community. . . . For too long have we expected from Black women
that which we could only obtain from other men. . . . These days
the nights are cold-blooded and the silence echoes with com-
plicity."[6] And didn't Audre finally leave us with the charge "This
is why the work is so important. Its power . . . [lies] in . . . the
muscle behind the desire that is sparked by the word—hope as
a living state that propels us, open-eyed and fearful, into all the
battles of our lives. And some of those battles we do not win. But
some of them we do."[7]

Yes, they did. And yes, we do.

We do, holding fast to memory, desire, language; history, imagining, and hope. Living and writing in hope and history,[8] the
words of our elders and others beside and within us, as we remember that, since our unexpected arrival in this region of the globe,
we have been (and will be for some time) a people of in-between:
between Africa and the Americas, literally hyphenated, as if one
hyphen between two words could even begin to recall or suggest
four hundred years of violence and the nearly *un*imaginable secrets of an amnesiac ocean; between "queer"-ness and "gay"-ness,
"lesbian"-ness and "bisexual"-ness; between home and nation (but
whose "home," and whose "nation"?); between narrow definitions

of gender and gender roles; between too black to be of any use and not black enough; between tradition and innovation, conformity and rebellion; between North and South, or "here" and "there," diasporically speaking; between languages and restrictions, condemnations, imposed on languages; between colony and empire, illegal alien and postcolonial; between poetry and prose, scholarship and drama; between "the academy" and "community"—and which community, by the way? Black, queer, black queer, women's, black women's, black queer women's, zamis', black gay or lesbian but not queer, or same-gender-loving, thank you, but not gay? A community of the world? A global one encompassing all societies and civilizations? Another art of the (im)possible? Which one? Between, but always, in our most centered moments, at the precise and enduring square root of ourselves.

I believe finally that, as people dedicated to intimate and ongoing involvement with the word, it is also our task—*must* be our task—to exercise severe, exacting scrutiny over the many enforced and enforcing languages that daily and nightly so insidiously seek to permeate and corrupt our very dreams: the prevaricating languages of "official" histories, which never possessed any right to officialness in the first place, nor have in any way ever been sympathetic to the actual truths of most people's lives; the tyrannical languages of state systems and pseudo-democratic regimes, all of which have functioned and continue to serve not as languages of true communication and knowledge but as engines of human misery and degradation—the end results of dire unions between despotism and plutocracy; and the consumerist-driven, mind-deadening splutterings of the media, which, in their wild incoherence, debase as brilliantly as they trivialize, as fiendishly as they instigate. As we shape languages of our own *against,* if not in direct reaction *to,* these continued assaults, we must remain ever aware of actual words themselves—what they mean to us, have meant, and will mean in and to our (literary and other) futures. At the same time, we're compelled to guard against our own vulnerability: our capacity to be lulled by these pretend-languages and the thin prizes their systems and ideologies offer for capitulation, accomodation, utter surrender. We would do well to heed the writer Arundhati Roy, still risking her own life as a dissenting voice in her native India, when she tells us:

> We have free speech. Maybe. But do we have Really Free Speech? If what we have to say doesn't "sell," will we still say it? Can we? Or is everybody looking for Things That Sell to say? Could writers end up playing the role of palace entertainers? Or the subtle twenty-first-century version of court eunuchs attending to the pleasures of our incumbent CEOs? You know—naughty, but nice. Risqué perhaps, but not risky.[9]

Roy cautions us, eloquently, that the risks of seduction in the capricious marketplace of commodification and two-bit attractions are pernicious, ever present. Yet at this conference, if only by virtue of its existence and our presence and participation in it, we are taking risks, hopefully of the most ennobling, emboldening kind. Let us continue, then, and, in closing, at last ask ourselves: where does all this leave us?

It leaves us where we began, of course, which is here. Right here, in this room on a state university's campus in a midwestern city, at the breathing nexus of power and force that is this entire weekend's event—but that is also, more urgently and critically, ourselves. It leaves us where we began, but far beyond that place; assembled here among the sacred blessings of ourselves, but not always blessed, nor guaranteed to be when we depart here. It leaves us basking in the afterglow of this conference's safety and pleasure even as we know that we will almost never be safe, nor always caressed by pleasure. It leaves us in this cataclysm we call "America," with uncertain hands bent toward placing, at last, the ring on Essex's cock, where it belongs. It leaves us *Zami*-fied by Audre and shot through to the marrow by Pat and June—still mourning our loss of their physical selves, but charged to pick up their words and run, "open-eyed and fearful," into whatever new, far-stretching work awaits us. It leaves us, hopefully, with tongues *un*tied, edging toward (even if not yet ready for) paying or resisting the price of the ticket, as we step forth to meet the man, or woman, or corporation, or whatever new chicanery the reigning merchant princes of our time will have dreamed up by the time we've exchanged our good-byes. It leaves us, ultimately, poised at the edge of a precipice both fearsome and arresting; one from which we will not, like so many mindless lemmings, plunge headlong into a killing sea, but rather one from which, as one of our teachers told us, "[our] imaginations gaze."[10] A precipice on which, as that voice intoned, we all are "mining, sifting and polishing languages for illuminations none of us has dreamed of." A promontory from which, so standing, we truly never will "blink or turn away."

It leaves us *there,* which is suddenly, but was always, *here.* Now, yes, and again, as, recalling the history that left us unspeakable thoughts finally speakable, we nudge into life the words that will ensure that we, like those who preceded us and perished between brutal infamies of fire and ink, will become, like our languages and our dreams, stories that *will* be passed on, and passed.

2002

Whose Caribbean?
An Allegory, in Part

AND SO IT CAME TO PASS THAT UPON THAT TIME, NOT SO
long ago, in that part of the world, there lived a child who dreamed.
I am not so sure even now as to the definitive facial features of that
child, but I am fairly certain, having myself wandered through
various dreams that became stories that were told and did not fade
over time, that the child was both female and male—a common
enough occurrence in that place of the child's origin at that time,
as, contrary to numerous prevailing opinions, happens frequently
today. The child—let us know him/her as "S/He"—possessed a
slender penis of startlingly delicate green, the truest color of the
sea that s/he had always loved—that sea which licked and foamed
out and back, out and in again, all about the shores of that place;
as s/he also possessed a pair of luminous blue breasts the tone of
the purest skies that, on the gentlest days, nuzzled their broad,
soft chins against the sea. Nipples did not grow at the end of the
child's breasts, but rather berries the inflamed color of hibiscus
in its most passionate surrender to the sunsets and dawns that
for millennia had washed over that place. The child also possessed a vagina and uterus, which, as was common knowledge
among all who knew him/her, produced at least twice or three
times per year, without assistance from anyone, a race of brazen
dolphins—creatures the fierce color of the sun, silver-speckled and
gray-bottlenosed; creatures which, despite the rude raucousness of

their cries upon emerging from between his/her thighs into the light, leaped without fail with the gravest of countenances into those waiting waves.

The child dreamed; again, nothing unusual in what would come to be known by some as a region of dreamers. S/He dreamed of tamarinds, of course, and of star-apples and green mangoes that, eventually rendered senseless by the days' stunning heat, plunged from their trees to ooze their fragrant juices along the largely still unexplored inner paths of her/his thighs. S/He dreamed of plummeting stars providing a last flash of hope (or, in other instances, a vision of death) to condemned slaves, their wrists bound with heavy chains and thick cords on so many mornings and late afternoons on a public square's auction block; s/he dreamed of tormented hands outstretched, at last vanished forever beneath the night-blackened waves of that eternal sea, as dawn brought her/him dreams of violet hummingbirds intent on sweetness and color, and dreams of shrugging mountains, and cane. Always cane. Field upon field of it, whispering. Muttering. Cane thick with secrets but also with the day's tragedies and joys—the few joys there were, could have been, in those times—and, on nights of the fullest moons, the calls of three-hundred-year dead jumbies, or duppies, or soucouyants rising so slowly from the vast water, green dreadlocked and sober eyed, intent on possessing her/his soul, and yours, and mine.

During my many travels to that place and by way of my own history there—that place which, through the wills and workings of Osun and Oya, stealthy buccaneers or cruise ship companies, slave traders or airline advertisements, or a combination of any and all, became what we call today the Caribbean—I have thought often of that child and her/his dreams. In the dreary halls of immigration, while wondering which passport to use on this trip or that one, Jamaican or U.S.—which citizen will I be this time, (re-)entering "my" country?—I have conjured her/him: the (surely) skinny legs, the (perhaps) slightly mottled skin; the all-too-wide eyes and sun-bleached hair which, even this late in human time, yet bears evidence of ringworm, just there, on the scalp; and the gleaming blue breasts ending in those bright red berry-nipples. I conjure him/her, wondering as I conjure if, during this tourist season or the last one, anyone has propositioned him/her for a quick suck of that lovely green child-cock. A few pennies, little one, to touch . . . or no, to *caress* your body, all its secret parts, and most especially that tender place from which, each spring and autumn, braying dolphins emerge into light amid the noise of their own frenzy. A few pennies, relatively speaking, to trail my fingers along those pathways where star-apples and green mangoes, finally bored with an entire lifetime of murmuring hours passed among the smaller secrets of leaves, consent to drop and ooze their most precious parts over your lap. A few pennies, a dollar here or there, and then I, whoever "I" was or will be this year or last, will return to my distant capital, to my own dreams of vengeance against the swarthy and those who, like you, child, threaten through your wild breeding and proven savagery to overrun my peaceful pastures and geometrically ordained, mercilessly swept cities. I will think no more of you until the next time and the next, even though, in truth, I might live quite nearby you; but you will of course understand that you mean nothing to me, absolutely nothing at all; not even your shimmering blue breasts and magnificently green penis finally mean much to me, except during those passing moments in the darkness of unspoken illicit dreams and echoing silence that we share, have always shared—that darkness that is yours, yes, and mine. Darkness and silence shared for all time. For all time, I say, and I am gone, leaving you touched, possessed, not only by me.

When I conjure this child—when s/he speaks to me on dim nights out of waves and centuries of un-voicedness, complete despair—I imagine that s/he yearns for two things only: to be loved, of course, and to be safe. To be able to walk past the mountains that slouch over her/his town, along the glistening shores that stretch just beyond, secure in the knowledge that s/he has never had, could never have: that no one, not anyone at all, will come crooning at her/him with a few pennies, lately grown to dollars, for a prolonged taste of his/her various parts; that no one will run shouting at him/her, wielding a machete, because s/he possesses not only breasts, but blue ones; not only a penis but a green one. S/He prays, I know, that in his/her town and time, s/he will not be perceived, for whatever reason, as disposable (because s/he is poor, perhaps) and thus worthy of erasure or, worse, annihilation; perceived as "other," perhaps, by those among whom s/he has long dwelt, occasionally in the realm of history-tinged dreams, while received as an exotic morsel by many of those in pursuit of sun, sex, and the two-bit, so-called third world trade long ago made a reality by marauders, and held tightly in place by those of today: the IMF, the World Bank, the transnational corporate behemoths, and, first and foremost as nexus of all three, the United (severely capitalist, fiercely indifferent to human and most life) States. In his/her wandering, s/he continues to dream of a stable economy for her/his region, not disastrous exchange rates; of adequate housing and health care, not shanty slums and intolerable taxes; of the freedom of *not* having to migrate to a so-called first world country in search of work and a life-sustaining wage but where, because of her/his color and/or class, s/he will often be even more despised, or despised in a new and different way. He/She imagines what it would be like to be able to remain in his/her country as a citizen with complete rights and privileges, in a nation in which the idea and practice of actual sovereignty are more than measly yearnings scoffed at by presiding (corrupt) officials. No more for him/her, s/he imagines, the long queues in front of embassies where people wait for visa applications to nations interested only in their cheap labor; no more for her/him the insulting empty promises of parliaments and congresses and long-winded, ineffectual inter-Caribbean councils, but *some*thing, something for once, s/he imagines, akin to a place in the shade: beneath the ample spread of a lignum vitae tree or a guango, maybe; somewhere far from the soul- and body-killing work of hacking cane for next to nothing, of hauling fish out of the sea for scraps, of caring for other people's homes and children for much belligerence and scant gratitude. Somewhere well in the shade for the first time in his/her life, where those hands and they alone can at last, in the peace and solitude that are the nurturing grounds for the soul and its companion the imagination, stroke and take pleasure in those berry-tips at the end of his/her breasts, as the ears of the stroker delight in the bawdy commentary of randy hummingbirds agog at the green fullness of her/his penis finally granted leave to stretch out completely to the shading leaves above, and to the sky.

I am certain that this child's whispers rustled through our individual and collective spirits six years ago when, in Kingston, Jamaica, a small group of us, against all odds and good sense but profoundly possessed of hope and faith, decided to form the Jamaica Forum for Lesbians, All-Sexuals, and Gays, or J-FLAG, as we came to be and still are known.[1] Like that child and others, we had obviously begun to believe, even if we hadn't completely acknowledged, that dreams of one kind or another invariably bespeak both hope and faith—the roots of all political civic action. Hope that we could engender social and political change in a nation that, broadened through our efforts, would ultimately be worthy of all Jamaicans: a nation welcoming to all, irrespective of sexuality and perceived gender transgressions. Faith that our fellow Jamaicans would civilly receive us, extend, and, in so extending, grow. Grow into the nation we had and have yet to achieve: the island of matchless mountains that had produced the likes of Paul Bogle and Marcus Garvey yet continues to wage vicious war on itself through the very violence their visions deplored; grow into the nation that could produce lights like Nanny and Claude McKay, Bob Marley and the Manleys—Edna, Norman, and Michael—and Miss Lou Bennett, and Rex Nettleford (this being, of course, a highly incomplete list), as well as redoubtable, though unfortunately homophobic and sexist, talents like Shabba Ranks and Buju Banton, to name only two. There, in that part of Jamaica, in strictest secrecy and with the widest

How-the-backside-can-we-be-doing-*this* expressions on our faces, we seriously attended the child's echoing whispers—that child who I now believe must have been some sort of god/dess. Because yes, man, all right, now, the whispers said. Time fi stop de foolishness and get past de fear and get on wid making a place fi weself inna dis ya country. A fi we time—this time is ours—and no matter wha de people dem a seh, oonu haffi *work* fi mek de people dem understand dat we nah go tek de burning and de fireburning and de acid dash pon we face and de screams pon de road of "Battybwoy!" and "Battyman fi dead! Battyman fi bu'n!" and "Sodomite bu'n inna holy fire!" Mek *one* a dem touch oonu, the whispers said, and see what rass-backside tings happen nex inna dis ya country—and mek sure to know seh dem might touch oonu and bawl out oonu name pon de road and shout dat oonu is a battybwoy or a sodomite. Dem might go do it, because dis is Jamaica. Still. The Jamaica of boom-bye-bye in a battybwoy head, rudebwoy nah promote de nasty man (or sodomite), dem haffi dead.[2] Mek sure seh oonu tek care wi wha yu a do, but oonu *do* it. Inna Jamaica. Now.

Now, I say, which was then, which remains and always will be now. Now, when, if your breasts end in red berries and your penis is green and attractive to hummingbirds and your uterus delivers raucous dolphins unto the world twice or even three times per year, or even if you merely wish to hold the hand of the person, a person, whom you love or desire and that person is the same gender as oonu, oonu had best watch yu backside inna Jamaica (and other parts of the Caribbean, and, in truth, the world at large), and tek care dat de people dem nah chop yu wid machete. Except that now oonu have a choice: to join the company of dreamers who have survived and, for all I know, just might, beneath their sensible tropical clothes, sport blue breasts and green penises and uteruses filled beyond capacity with cavorting baby dolphins. They survived. We did. Survived years of bellicose, religiously fundamentalist radio announcers who denounced us, froth-mouthed citizens who threatened to murder us if they ever discovered who we actually were as people living among them, and a repressive government that to this very day refuses to take seriously or effectively consider in Jamaica's parliament any initiatives that would begin—merely *begin*—earnest movements toward ensuring the lives, safety, and ultimate human fulfillment of its nonheterosexual citizens. And I say "merely," but that "merely" would in this instance be a hugely significant one, and one not at all lost on a government consistently more interested in maintaining the politically expedient status quo and its legacy of corruption than in developing true democracy—the ideal and aim of all humankind. True democracy itself, however, knows that it cannot flourish—indeed, it can barely breathe—in an environment of sustained and enforced ignorance. True democracy delights in having its belly rubbed by lively congress through which wide room for all voices is made. It can no more thrive beneath Jamaican prime minister P. J. Patterson's savage disregard for the lives of gay, lesbian, bisexual, and transgendered people[3] (as evidenced, in part, by his administration's steadfast refusal to consider doing away with the Offenses against the Person Act and its "buggery law,"[4] both of which criminalize male homosexuality in particular) than it can survive—if it ever existed—beneath the vicious neoimperialistic militarism of "president" George W. Bush, a successful election thief and warmongering, would-be despot. The actions and intentions of both "leaders," and of their kin, will always be enabled by a politically apathetic citizenry—by a populace that is complacent, beguiled and intellectually dulled by the allurements of consumerism, perhaps, but in any event comfortably, if dangerously, mired in ahistoricism and the indifference to, and ignorance of, human suffering that an ahistorical intellect bolsters; such ignorance and indifference numbering among the most tragic, yet avoidable, human states.

It is a known fact, of course, that for any form of *actual,* truly practicable democracy to succeed, its citizens will be required—demanded—to maintain a constant, energetic, interrogating engagement with history. The past—"the good old days" for some, depending on one's point of view—is always now; even the most hell-bent demagogue understands these truths. The demagogue or the truly principled head of state also understands (and risks not understanding at our peril) that true democracy, as fragile as the most endangered of ecosystems, requires respect for and attendance to not only its ideals and aims, but also its scrupulous, honorable practice. Actual, practicable democracy quickly fades in the face of hypocrisy and corruption—political chicanery. The harsh irony is not lost on us, of course, and should never be lost on us or forgotten, that in so many modern Caribbean nations developed out of the atrocities of slavery, genocide, and a racism that continues to snarl and lick its chops, what we are unfortunately charged to term, correctly, "almost-democracy" stumbles along as a bandy-legged spectre, crippled in its posture and regularly short of breath. "Almost-democracy" in that still too many Caribbean citizens in the *twenty-first* century (for all that is worth) do not have access to adequate health care, housing, and education, endure poverty's systematized depredations, and, in the case of those of Jamaica and other locales, if they do not meet the requirements of gender role norms and other demands of expected and imposed heterosexuality, are forced to contend with the continued assaults of heterosexist, homophobic tyranny—literal *assaults,* murder and other violences included, all of which rear vicious heads in the context of global human rights struggles. These problems—those of simple, but fierce, inequalities between human beings—are, of course, by no means unique to the Caribbean. In regarding most, if not all, present-day nations, we can easily enough recall and paraphrase George Orwell's apt words from *Animal Farm* (Orwell's admonishings unfortunately increasingly apropos in the post-September 11 world): that all animals are, sure, fine, equal, but some animals are and always have been—yes, of course!—far more equal than others.[5] As citizens of the so-termed modern world, we understand that, notwithstanding Caribbean and other anticolonial movements for independence and their subsequent postcolonial struggles (resistance to, among other scourges, transnational corporate encroachments,

IMF and World Bank machinations, and latter-day dependencies of developing-world economies bound to tourist dollars and enduring "banana republic" oppressions), "democracy," so loosely imagined, is invariably practiced selectively. Thus, in 1980, Cuba, a revolutionary, presumably anticapitalist and ideally democratic society, may expel from its shores by way of the Mariel boatlift the hundreds, thousands, of its citizens alleged or known to be, à la state rhetoric, degenerates: homosexuals, sex workers, the mentally troubled, drug users, and HIV-positive and AIDS-afflicted people among them. In 2002 (and in all the years before) Jamaica may turn a coldly indifferent cheek to the plight of its poor, to many of its children and women, and to all its (identifiably and not) non-heterosexual people—at least those not among the wealthy—as reports, those which are actually taken seriously and documented by the police and government officials, seep through to anyone who cares about another homosexual murdered in Kingston, another stoned in Spanish Town, another burned to death in St. Elizabeth, or Trelawny, or St. James, or—.[6] It is impossible to know at this time how many more of these people have been driven over the years into the trauma of exile or the even greater trauma of applying, as gay refugees, for political asylum in a foreign country.[7] It is also not lost on us that these realities proceed in a country already beset and factionalized by widespread violence, daily, often grisly, murders, all forms of sexual abuse, extortions, thievery, and—the cake's proverbial icing—untenable inflation and taxation. And so in a similar but distinct context, in the late 1990s the Cayman Islands may refuse entry to its shores of a cruise ship loaded with gay and lesbian tourists, many locals greeting the docking ship with hateful jeers and thrown objects, as, at about the same time and afterward, people in the Bahamas do the same. All animals are equal, our various constitutions have extended so nobly on paper, but please do make trial to excise from that list all faggots and sodomites, most of the poor, a good number of women, and certainly all ambiguously gendered children with blue breasts and green penises.

And make trial to remember what is true: that some—Jamaican elected officials and citizens alike—have already made it clear to you how they would prefer that your son become a thief rather than a faggot. Do not forget how, in so many ways, they let you know that, yes, they most certainly would prefer that your daughter grow up to be a (perhaps casual) whore instead of a sodomite. And while, even after all these centuries, too many in so many cases would still prefer that the majority of their citizens, neighbors, children, and fellows turn out to be light-brown-skinned and at least middle-class, educated, and possessed of sufficient coin to purchase deodorant soap, always remember that, under certain conditions, they will be willing to tolerate even the darkest ones and the poor—the missing-teeth ones, the one-legged ones, the ones who stink (those underarms, the need for deodorant soap) and spit in the street; the ones who carry on in public places like wild dogs. They will tolerate even *them,* provided they are not one of *those* people who are not even really people, are they? The despicable ones. The ones who would, just that quickly, become pedophiles. Those who would, without doubt, perpetrate carnal abuse. Need we say which?

With the education and amplitude that time and experience have permitted us, we have learned at least one thing: that political activism is not, nor should it be, a romantic, or, God forbid, sentimental pursuit. It will always require a nuanced, astute, and sometimes even painful historical and social analysis of the society in which it functions, and, toward the greater truth and clarity that are always attainable, a willingness to investigate, dismantle, and move through the fraudulent, truth-debasing and -obscuring statist languages that affirm and maintain the abuses so beloved by dictators, parliamentary and congressional pretenders, would-be thespian pundits, and plain old charlatans. Among the beleaguered, hostile political climates of today's narrowing world, be they Jamaica or Zimbabwe, the Occupied Territories, the right-wing landscapes of a still-fissured German union or the more than ever police-stated United States, the most generous, sophisticated political activism will increasingly *and justifiably* expect of its practitioners nonreductionist, nonpartisan thinking, a widening of ideological/philosophical boundaries, and a disavowal of the single-issue, myopic political imagination. This last looms as particularly critical, given that *no one* in the world lives or has ever lived a single-issue existence. The (brown, black, yellow, white) woman who cuts cane and is poor and functionally illiterate might very well also have a female lover in similar circumstances, who also has (two, three, four, more) children and has experienced abusive treatment at the hands of a man who owns the house from which he evicted both her and her children. The minimally paid (and uninsured, uneducated) fisherman whose skin spans any range of colors remains, irrespective of his yearnings, a (post-)colonial subject vulnerable to the caprices of the presiding powers' geopolitical chess games—powers both at "home" and abroad—whether he sees himself as such or not, whether he views himself as head of his household or not, whether he finally obtains a visa to the United States/Canada/the United Kingdom or not, and certainly whether he sexually desires and makes love to men or women, or both, or not. Along with the fact that the single-issue life is a simplistic myth—a fallacy of use only to the willfully simpleminded—we know too that what Wislawa Szymborska told us in "Children of Our Age" will always be true:

All day long, all through the night,
all affairs—yours, ours, theirs—
are political affairs.

Whether you like it or not,
your genes have a political past,
your skin, a political cast,
your eyes, a political slant.[8]

Regarding the relevance of dreams, we can allow that activism will occasionally begin in dreams, provided that it moves onward from them into definite action. For dreams, mesmerizing though they might be, are not only a waste of time if indulged in for too long, but also simply too nebulous a sphere to bring about any actual, substantive change—or, in truth, anything. And so the child longs to move unscathed through open public space with his/her red-berried blue breasts but must eventually do battle to be permitted full and unmolested possession of them, at least in this world in which we live—this world which, from its very beginnings, has been a realm both centered on struggles for power and dominion and one which, to the best of its ability, has consistently obliterated all traces of the "other" and "otherness." And so the person focused on erotic/romantic interactions with another person of the same gender fantasizes of being able to meander a country Caribbean road while holding the hand of a partner without fear of a machete's sudden slice across the neck, but must sooner or later be prepared to challenge the constricting, policing forces—local, national, global—that impede his or her ultimately human freedom. The woman who lives in fear for her body, if she is ever to become more than fear's afterwipe, will eventually have to work with other women, and hopefully progressive men, toward securing the unquestioned right to occupy, in absolute safety, her body. And whether one marches in Washington, D.C., against a so-called president's genocidal intentions in the name of making the world "safe" for "democracy," or against military dictatorships in Nicaragua, Panama, El Salvador, Guatemala, or Chile (to name only a few of the nations in which dictatorships were financed and otherwise supported, often covertly, by the United States), or whether one meets with grassroots gay/lesbian/"queer" groups in so many small rooms in Kingston, Havana, Port-au-Prince, or Willemstad, the aims are consistently the same: to secure true freedom for all human beings, toward the realization of a world in which the word "freedom" will come to signify more than a mere two-syllable noun that was once a lovely idea that somehow, somewhere along the way on the path of human progression, failed; more than a pithy word of little use or meaning in these, our increasingly *de*freedomized (if we are not constantly vigilant) twenty-first-century lives; more than a silly little word, sadly obsolete, but still to be found, never fear, in our dust-covered dictionaries, on that page, right there, still somehow arresting our eyes among the many *F*s.

I titled this essay "Whose Caribbean?"—wanting to explore, among other questions, the idea of whose Caribbean for the living? Whose for the being, in an ultimately more dignified, more equitable daily life? Whose for the dreaming and the imagining as well as the fulfilling? For the walking on country roads or city streets while holding, without fear, the hand of a same-gender partner? For the walking, unaccompanied, in a female body? In an ambiguously gendered body? For the lyming and the laughter, and the participating without hesitation or shame in every social ritual, including those of family, to which we have and have always had a right? For even, if we are so fortunate, the baring of our shining blue breasts to the vaulting sky, as our penises scorn, if they choose, the ill-mannered behavior of those dolphins still leaping forth from our uteruses?

Whose Caribbean, and whose freedom? But ours, of course. Our very own. Our own, as we know, or ought to know, that such freedom will rarely, if ever, be achieved easily. Our struggles for true democracy just might end in our lives' termination following the swift hiss of a machete's stroke. It is irrevocably true that, in our lifetimes, we will not see all of our ideals achieved, pulled from dreams into actual life. These incontrovertibles aside, however, *that* Caribbean, the one of today and always, remains ours and is (if we never knew it before) us. Alive to these truths, we must never forget that that Caribbean needs us far more than it needs its disdain for and even occasional hatred of some of us. We must remember that we—*all* of us—are indispensable to its future, even as it growls at the complexities our sexualities and political practice bring to its here-and-there intransigence. In an increasingly desperate, increasingly balkanized post–September 11 world, that Caribbean needs our energies, against corporate and global hegemonies; our talents, against (neo)imperialisms; our wills and intelligent resistance, against the destructions and self-destructiveness of inhumane rhetoric, legislations, and ultimately spurious democracies. Whose Caribbean? I ask once more, awaiting a response.

Yes, a response, as, for this brief while, toward the closing of these reflections that will hopefully open to another kind of beginning, we return to the realm of dreams: to the scents of tamarinds and green mangoes and the redolent nostalgia of freshly sliced star-apples. We return to the sea and the shores and once upon a time, which transposes suddenly to this time, which it always was and which it must, in the so-called natural order of things, steadfastly remain; the present ever inescapably itself, never past or future and invariably the most difficult period of "time" for human beings to live in, simply live in peacefully and without rancor, as suggested by words like *live in the present, live only for today*—desirable, yes, even the ideal, without question, but how many succeed at it, how many of us ever seriously consider it?—the past simultaneously forever embedded in the present, in the pain and inevitable horrors confronted by conscientious unblinking memory, in the tragedies and occasional triumphs of history always raveled by so much needless suffering, by the unbearable human misery and degradation that must not, for our collective sakes and the continued growth of this body we call "humanity," ever be denied. We dream, fully aware that we are and always have been much more than dreamers; we engage with sundry phantasms of the past, astonished at how, in that muting light, their faces and hands bear such unmistakable resemblance to our own. Gradually, over the years that slowly lose measure, we learn that things, all things about us, have begun to change: great lavender-furred lions have begun to crawl up out of the sea in search of the coconuts that alone will slake their yawning thirst, as more than a few mountains simply shrug their shoulders and get up and leave, longing all at once for cooler climates in which

they may copulate for all eternity with the low-lying hills they had
in fact, from their very birth, always wished to be. We dream that,
over the centuries, through the millennia, we have done much
work; that we are tired, well exhausted; that, in spite of that great
fatigue, we have, we know, gradually achieved something of high
value. We are confident in the assurance, even as we feel ourselves
so weary, that much remains for us to do: work having much to
do with the words *necessary, vital,* and even *gallant.* Lying there on
the sand as we now do before the late-in-the-day's bronze receding
waves, we are not at all surprised to note the deepening blue of our
breasts, and the yammering flock of hummingbirds, a good three
hundred of them or more, that, smirking as only they can, come
to light and gossip away the evening on the emerald rod between
our legs, now a deeper green than ever—the most secret tone
of the sky. Should we gasp and rise to attention, then, when all
those children, bearing similar colors to our own over their various parts but brighter, come walking across the waves toward us,
followed by all those women, and men, and the additional million
or so fold in between? We should not, of course, and we do not,
knowing as we do upon those sands, before that sea, that, like
ourselves, they have always been there. "Safety," their faces seem
to say, with a hint of "And now in search of—"; but whether the
words are questions or simply quiet statements we cannot—not
in that moment that is also this one, anyway—yet tell. But then
look at some of them now, we think, as they move back out across
the waves. As they fall into those waters, and rise. Rise and fall, to
gaze back at us now and again, pondering our watching eyes as,
with certainty of the work that we know is and always will be ever
so much more than a dream, we stir, aware of hummingbirds busy
between our thighs; aware of our hands reaching just there, in
that way, as, this time, we sense the deepening red of those lively
berries at the ends of our breasts. It is then we know for sure that,
in this dream that will shortly rapidly transform to waking, we
will at last throw back our faces to the sky and hear, not for the

first time, the word—*that* word which makes possible all things beginning with the deed; that word, passing upward from our recently opened mouths: the finally untethered, always respectful, ever necessary human Yes.

2003–4

These Blocks, Not Square
(Five Movements)

BLOCKS

(Theme and variations)

But then you know and see immediately that they are not square, these Baychester blocks. They go on and on, on and on, forever: ragged-edged, bordered by dirty lawns in some places and unkempt gardens in others. Gardens restrained behind fences or shamelessly flaunting their loud colors where the sidewalk ends and arms slung over gates begin. If you are staunch enough and willing enough to walk these blocks as far as they will take you, a soldierly distance indeed, you will quickly learn that you have a superb chance of ending up someplace that is, like here, nearly nowhere: a distant corner of the Northeast Bronx. An unimportant place to all who journey to New York City in search of importance. This place in particular most decidedly itself because it is *here,* it tells you, and no place else. Still a somewhere of gaping green lots (but quickly disappearing) and thickly shrubbed road-bordering patches that now, in the early twenty-first century, are being developed for the multiunit, faceless, undistinguished brick houses that will attract more young, mostly working-class families in search of some space, a few trees about; in search of the scoldings and scutterings of the jays that have not yet fled before so much new building, and the squirrels that remain all year

high above so many perseveringly unsquare blocks. So I choose to
remember it, and so for me it shall remain. Let me recall now the
dirt roads that once crept all about here; the roads that, not that
long ago, witnessed without a murmur the interment of their own
dusty skins beneath smoother asphalt. Let me recall the thrashing
sounds of stones beneath a car on the dirt road that once was
East 222nd Street: a car in the back of which, as a groggy, half-
dreaming child, I slept as my parents drove onward and farther
past so many endless blocks not square. Let me remember, and
conjure once again as I mourn the neighborhood's changing from
what it once was to me, block upon block of empty weed-choked
lots strewn with the detritus of broken bottles, eviscerated tires,
and upended baby carriages long gone to seed. Let me recollect
and, as I remember, return there—for *there* that is *here* is still
home to me: where I am now, in Baychester on this warm, humid
September night, writing these revisiting words in the dank, dim,
musty, spider- and flea-infested basement of my parents' home.
Here, far beneath slow-soughing trees, on a block not square.

You walk the eternally long blocks, ridiculously long sidewalks
of gray cement and grayer memories, and wonder how much longer they can continue. How much farther will you have to walk,
you wonder, to reach Boston Road? That road known in some
quarters as the famous East Coast–running Route 1: the *road* or
route or whatever-it-is that will take you to either Maine or Florida,
depending on your taste for sun or snow. Boston Road, which
in the southern Westchester town of Pelham Manor, just across
and beyond the Eastchester Bridge half a mile or so from this
Baychester Avenue intersection, changes altogether: no more of
the grimy auto-repair shops and West Indian markets leading up
to the bridge (which is also Boston Road), but more stately houses
backed by quieter streets with increasingly palatial homes, and
lawns that fairly flare healthy green. No raggedness there. Boston
Road, long ago abandoned by the Italian nurserymen—the invariably grizzled, thick-fingered, impatiens-loving gardeners who,
amid their stone statues and fountains and tacky birdbaths, sold

my garden-loving Jamaican parents packets of sunflower seeds; seeds of corn, eggplant, squash; tomatoes, cucumbers, marigolds, and drowsy tulip bulbs. How much farther will you have to walk to reach those English-garbling Italians, now all gone? The stooped men who taught my parents to make chianti? Remembering our next-door neighbor who, before he and his wife departed the area, presented us one Christmas with an impossibly long, maroon-colored bottle filled with wine, the bottle's bulbous base encased in thick straw. Remembering all those hoarse-voiced men and their heavy, black dress–loving women, whose American-born sons and daughters soon enough urged them to flee the neighborhood, for the niggers were moving into it, they said, everywhere: spoiling it, they believed. Destroying it. You won't want to live here too much longer, Mama, Papa, with *these people,* they said. No. *No.* In the years that preceded the later twentieth-century decades when African American and Jamaican families began to move in, those Italians lived all along these long blocks not square; during the early days of our arrival still beside us. Among us. Some of them eventually returned to the Italy they had left, heavy-browed, so many years before. Some moved just a little farther away: up to Pelham Manor, or westward to the other side of Allerton Avenue, or Pelham Parkway, where, many of them to this day hope and believe, they can live unmolested, uninfected by blackness and the filth they insist it brings. Look now at their American flags and the Italian ones here and there along their aluminum awning–shaded front porches. If you walk closer, you might remark on their red and white flowers (geraniums, petunias, impatiens in clay pots and plastic hanging baskets). You might comment on those garden statues of the blessed Virgin in her requisite blue and white, as you note her white alabaster hands perpetually imploring, turned upward to the white-blue-goldwhite of the sky. Look carefully now; cling well to the picture. Later, you will recall with utter certainty that, in just these moments of flags and flag-colored flowers, you were most definitely someplace else, a somewhere much farther away. Not here.

As a child and later a teenager, I walked long blocks not square to my grandmother's and favorite aunt's house. They lived way down (or up) Baychester Avenue, just above it, near the Mount Vernon border, on a raggedy block not square also previously populated by Italians. Names like Ianucci, DeStefano, LaPaglia, and Calcagni once echoed over their street and have been replaced by names like Anderson, Thompson, James, and Melbourne—to a Jamerican like me, recognizably Jamaican surnames. I was walking to my grandmother's Jamaica, not my contemporary one, when I walked those long blocks to their house; as now, as an adult fiercely in love with that island and its maddening, tenacious-unlike-any-other people, I walk once more. Walking to and through Sunday afternoons of tea thickened with condensed milk sold in "tins"—not American "cans"—and English biscuits. Tea served sometime around four o'clock. My grandmother so proudly British colonial, lover of the queen and princesses, and my aunt not far behind her. Then the evenings in that house, in all those houses along those unsquare blocks: evenings of brown-stewed fish, curry goat and rice, and, at Christmas, wine-dark sorrel. Ackee and saltfish with baked bammy for breakfast, and pigtail soup, or pepper pot with gongu peas, for "Saturday soup" and "special" occasions. Calf's-foot jelly, a taste to be reckoned with. . . . Filled fit to bursting with such recollections, that block will never be square. The Jamaicans who now inhabit it will never have it be so. Their accents alone will alter the pavement's course, if their loud swears and country-market laughter don't do it first. My grandmother, aunt, and others just like them and different, filling this place. Commandeering it. Changing it to create blocks not square in a more recent immigrant's image.

Now regard the Latino man on Bartow Avenue, not far from the not long ago built Bay Plaza sprawling mall, on which ground once stretched verdant swamp that attracted hordes of birds, great flocks of night travelers heading steadily south each late summer. On another block not square, he is selling seven-foot lengths of un-stripped sugar cane, and mangoes, and even, in season, Caribbean ginneps. (Depending on where he comes from in the Caribbean, he will or will not call them, in Spanish, *quinepas*.) He is telling you as he stands there waiting for the customers whom he knows will come that, on these unsquare blocks, we are all *here* in the *there* that is both *here* and *there*: Jamaica to Jamerica, once Italian America, sometimes African or Dominican or Puerto Rican America—but always, in this part of the Bronx, way up, *very* far up from the rest of the city. Behind God's back, and glad to be.

WATER

(Scherzo)

There are those who will aver that the Long Island Sound has nothing whatsoever to do with Baychester. They will claim that it is too far away, way over to the east, hidden behind Co-op City and even farther, past Eastchester Bay and the bridge to City Island, but do not believe them. For it is, of course, as you have always known, a presence, waiting just there; caring nothing for those who would deny it. Ceaseless in its lapping refrains.

You would soon enough have anyway noticed how you need never call it. You would have divined that it would come to you, surely, as it had before, as soon as you closed your eyes. You would have felt how, each time, it knew every inch of your wanting it, as, on so many prior occasions, it had thrust itself so quietly against the sky for you that way, stretching. True enough, it no longer is visible from Baychester Avenue, as it was years ago, before the egregiously *un*interesting towers of Co-op City, across the New England Thruway 95, were built. Yet you still sense it; on certain thick nights, such as this one, you smell it; and it will always, of course, fill your dreams.

In those dreams, you will not be drowning, but running along-side it as you have often done, on Shore Road, heading northward toward Pelham Manor, having just left behind the now-and-then wilds of Pelham Bay Park. The Amtrak tracks to Boston will snake

along on your left, to the west, with the pox of Co-op City just behind them. As always, you will love the long curve of the Sound's
back as it comes into view, just around that turn, before you begin
ascending the difficult woods-shrouded hill where, on more than
one afternoon or early evening, you almost stumbled over the
road-slaughtered corpse of an itinerant, though ultimately hap-
less, opossum or skunk. It is entirely possible that—in another
dream, another visitation of the past—you will gaze out at that
water on a sultry summer day clasped well within that earlier
time, holding once more your father's hand in your own. You will
be eight or nine years old in that memory, standing awkwardly
as usual at the fenced edge of the open-air eating area at Johnny's
Reef restaurant, at the very end of City Island. There, you will
note, as you have in recent weeks this past summer, how sulk-
ily the midday haze hangs over the low-slumped Throgs Neck
Bridge off to your far right; how it veils, as if envious of their
smooth shoulders, the low-rolling hills of Great Neck and eastern
Queens, just across the Sound and off to the left. Years later, long
after your father's untimely death and the warm feel of his hand
in your own, you will gaze across at that same view and wonder
what it must have been like for Nick Carraway and Jay Gatsby
to imagine their America from the other side—green light, "the
dark fields of the republic" rolling onward into the night, and
time swept ever backward. You will ponder the wealth of that
writer's imagination whose peculiar visions brought and will yet
bring you much joy, as, at Johnny's, you remember the bewilder-
ing array of items for sale behind the short-order counters (Fried
Shrimp! Steamed Clams! Mussels, Lobster, Oysters!). Yet despite
your innumerable earlier journeys to Johnny's, it is only during
this early-twenty-first-century summer that you recall how, when
you were a child, most of the counter workers were white, as you
notice how now they all are Latino or Chicano—and no blacks
working there at all, anywhere, as far as you can see.
  But the Sound—

The water of all courses that marks things here; sets them off; positions shore where shore ought to be, and invades nostrils with feckless abandon. The water that makes possible the railroad bridge for the Amtrak line over which, back then, with teen friends as foolhardy as yourself, you walked (although you remember that that particular bridge really spans Eastchester Creek, which empties soon enough into the Sound, farther east). In your imagination, this water disdains being called the "East River" beneath the Whitestone Bridge, for *that* is where the Sound, for you, begins!— there, just beneath the bridge over which you traveled on all those trips years ago to Kennedy Airport, to fetch or drop off family friends and relatives, yourself included, arriving from or departing for Jamaica. It is that water, rushing onward to the ocean way out there, that, along with the teal washes of the sun-warm Caribbean, is the oldest water of your dreams.

Much later, you will feel jealous. Jealous over but also enthralled by the fact that the Sound flows all the way up to far eastern Connecticut. Jealous because it is *your* local Northeast Bronx Sound, after all, despite its actual name. But then, you will reflect, why not share it? Why not let those Connecticut people have their Sound too? For they can anyway never have as much as you have, you believe . . . certainly not this stretch of it that is yours, and yours alone. These low waves casing themselves out to the sky—

Yes, and washing over you. Transporting. Washtransporting as you immerse yourself again. As you descend and discover in all that stippled light all the things you have ever feared, and more.

Things you have feared, your deepest voice tells you, *like water. A certain kind of wave or ripple. A peculiar depth beyond all others. But never this water. Not now. Not now as already you have reached beyond Pelham Parkway, beyond—yes, the Shore Road, and—all right, and just a little more along City Island Avenue, then—beyond now the woods where Pelham Manor village meets the shore, and— but you have arrived, are so quickly there, as if you*

Water:

Houses

(Andante)

And so all the new houses. More and more of them now, some twenty or more, all rising into being across the way, on the east side of Baychester Avenue, just north of Givan, itself once a dirt road; just off the Baychester Avenue Thruway exit, not too far from the now Dominican-owned bodega long owned by Puerto Ricans—the bodega-"deli" known locally by many, for years, as "the Spanish store," which years ago began twenty-four-hour operations through a bulletproof revolving window.

Much new housing has risen in the area over the past ten or so years. Much of it looks (unfortunately, unimaginatively) the same. The new houses on the avenue, like their three-story counterparts just behind East 222nd Street (near the old live chicken market), are slapped up in a few months. Their assembling never requires, anywhere, more than a complete year. They appear (and will be) thin walled, thin doored, essentially cheap; fashioned on the outside of pale faux-looking brick that itself yearns for true, centuries-enduring strength. Each house sports a grill-and-glass door over its white front-entry door, and bars over the street-level windows. All are appointed with two to three apartments. (One-family homes, even among the older wood-frame houses, are not necessarily rare, but not all that common, either, in Baychester.) Many younger families—a number of them Puerto Ricans, as suggested by the Puerto Rican flags occasionally hung high from windows, especially around the June time of the Puerto Rican Day parade—have already moved in. You note how the neighborhood's demographics continue to change, this time by way of the wave of primarily domestic, Spanish-speaking migrants.

More recent Jamaican arrivals reside in some of the newer houses west of Boston Road, over by the White Castle and the L & L Farms Produce store in which latter-day Caribbean accents lilt as people shop for the saltfish and snapper, yams, cassava, green bananas, scotch bonnet peppers, and other stuffs that remind them of Home, back there. These Jamaicans, unlike those of my parents' and grandparents' generation, are mostly working-class, in no way British, and not particularly focused on remaining in the United States "until retirement." They move as peripatetically as possible between New York and Home, traveling back for Christmas, when they can afford it, or for brief Easter visits. Their children, growing up in some of the thin-walled houses, will truly be Jam-ericans, the products of two deeply distinct nations and cultures—heirs, as we all are, to four languages: "standard American" English, Jamaican patois, Puerto Rican New York (or "Newyorican") "Spanglish," and African American English; all four spoken at generally top speed, and occasionally mixed, around here.

The houses on that west side of Boston Road also bear the regulated sameness to each other: the same doors and facades, the same squarely or rectangularly cut lawns. The garages which surely must have shared an umbilical cord in the womb, as must have done the second-floor mini-verandas above them. A few of the newly developed blocks, unlike those on the eastern side of Baychester Avenue, are not tree-lined, lending them a summertime noonday harshness: bright sun, white heat, and no escape whatsoever for walkers. Yet, remembering that such treelessness wasn't always so, you only need walk south along Edson Avenue, heading toward the Bay Plaza mall, or along any street that runs through the valley whose western high rim begins at Eastchester Road. In those places you will see, especially on streets filled with older houses, many trees: towering pin oaks, gingkos, and patchy-barked sycamores. So, by way of glancing leaves, is brick-and-cement austerity vanquished.

(But then these words, uncovered in a passing dream: etched, in a ghostly scrawl, to dusk:

Walking these Northeast Bronx streets, I yearn again for the older houses of Mount Vernon. For houses that looked always as if people actually lived in them, died in them, as, over the years, the homes themselves began to sag and settle into the earth. I miss the old frames

*that once crouched upon the blocks about here, and that have now
mostly vanished. Didn't we love life in them? (Yes, we did, another
ghost remembers, as we also fought bitterly in them, and wept.)
Didn't we enjoy the shape and softness of each other's faces? (Yes, and
also hated the boredom and drudgery that daily cursed our hands.)
We owned those tottering frames, you and I. People like us who either
left the earth itself, or sold out to developers. The developers who
came and built over our lives and laughter (and sorrow), and our
deaths. . . . Our houses that were those homes that once—yes, once
upon that time, that time now gone for always, held so much, too
much, to pass on.*

—But I am merely a ghost now who writes these words to you,
that trembling hand scrawls, *trapped in the dream of someone,
many someones, who will never know my name. A sad ghost, myself
haunted by withered trees and their moonlit afterwords. A shade
already fading back into twilight's curl. A caul stretching over my
long-ruined face. A spirit, dream, that utterly refused, even in death,
to creep silently away from so many lingering enthrallments and
refacings of the past.)*

Store

(Intermezzo)

"But then please remember," says this store (L & L Farms Produce,
on Boston Road near Baychester Avenue; Korean owned and
run), "that once, many years ago but not so long ago, things were
different here. Remember that it was not always possible to find
your beloved Pickapeppa sauce up here, or—no!—jerk seasoning,
for which, in those earlier times, when you pined for its bite in
porkskin and chicken backs, you were forced to send word to
someone all the way back in Portland (the only parish in Jamaica
where *true* jerk could be found back then) to put aside a little for
your nostalgia and send it up with the next visiting grandchild
or rum-besotted cousin. Remember," says the store, more sternly,

"how it was when you wished so fervently to bake a cake and could not find *anywhere* about here rose water, or browning, or 'wet' sugar. Or how it felt when you wanted just a little amount of saltfish, merely that much and no more, and no one in this area sold any. Do not *ever* forget," thunders the store, "how, in those earlier times, you were forced to search high and low for ginger, callaloo, white yam and yellow, and cho-cho. How you thought back to evenings spent at Coronation Market in search of those items, invariably found at the feet of a headrag-wrapped, huge-bosomed, boisterous-laughing market woman, spread-legged and ready to curse you for no reason at all through her gold-capped or missing teeth. Here," the store growls, "some parts of your island have come to you—all but the infernal sun, the summer and early autumn rains, and the music everywhere, especially in the language. Remember," the store hisses, more fiercely, "that 'here' has become almost 'there,' and that, living here, picking among the tamarind candy and dasheen, pushing between the Milo and Ovaltine, you will always be between both. Take care that you . . ."—but faded to a whisper. A breath already gone, as all accents mingle and the Korean owners (who employ Mexican men to sort the apples and pears from the Haitian mangoes and scale the bright red, wide-eyed snapper) gaze upon it all—the owners not particularly friendly to anyone, fairly unsmiling with all. The owners who themselves in their most brusque moments are doubtless dreaming of another place: someplace else near water, beneath the long hands of trees. A somewhere impossibly far from here in language and distance, and in time.

PEOPLE

(Allegro vivace)

But now only some, some of them:

The grizzled old man, bent and shirtsleeved, once of North Carolina, slowly sweeping his sidewalk, mourning in a place no one can see his one-year-passed-on wife; the long-legged, smart-mouthed teenager, aware of her relaxed hair blowing in this after-noon's breeze, wondering if *He* (gold teeth, doo rag, a sleek cell phone pressed to his ear, baggy jeans grazing his boxer-shorted buttocks) will be there at the Baychester train station with his fine self, so fine; the tanktop-clad young ruffneck, guzzling Heineken in front of the Spanish store, slouched into his body's pretense of ease, secretly yearning of kissing and being kissed by another man; the elderly orange-haired Jamaican woman, owner of the area's most impressive property (enormous garden, stately fruit trees), shouting from the front veranda at her dreadlocked son to *bring the groceries come, nuh, man*; the quick-heels-clicking morning commuters, crossing from Co-op City on the pedestrian bridge over the Thruway, making steady headway to the train station; Baychester Avenue's last remaining white man, now older than almost everyone else, who for whatever reasons did not flee in panic—now bending carefully over his swept-up autumn leaves; the young yellow-haired Latina girl at the gate of one of the newer houses, shouting into her cell phone *Cause why you laughing for, Manny, that shit ain't funny, coño*; the children shouting in street games along Grace Avenue, along Edson and Wickham; the children whooping in a tag game beneath Haffen Park's ample trees, deep in the valley's belly; all the old people and their ghosts who remember; all the younger people who have already forgotten, or never knew; the raucous, profanely bantering Jamaican taxi men; the grease-coated Italian car mechanics and some of the black men beside whom they work, in the noisy auto shops back by the old-days cookie factory on Givan Avenue; and more, and more, and more and more still. Working and living, all waking and dying in this still-unfashionable corner of the world bisected by elevated subway trestles, the Thruway, and the ever-traffic-clogged Boston Road—up here where all of *what was* shifts and settles as the days cast down their eyes toward the seasons' shrug onward and evenings return, darkening all that breathes and flutters along these streets into the commingled secrets of dusk, night-stillness:

something half-akin to silence that, throughout these parts, does not remain silent, cannot, and never will. Gradually a welcome visitor, like one of us, will come to depend on the mornings, and on them alone, to bring new faces, and familiar ones—each transposed to expectation and something more: the future, perhaps, or merely the dimmest shadings of a life begun in tenderness or ended in rage. All of it and beyond up here, along blocks that remain interminable and ragged, weed choked. Blocks littered by the detritus of years. The years. Blocks that will never—no, not even long after we all are dead and forgotten, utterly nothing—ever be square.

2003

The Death and Light
of Brian Williamson

THIS MUCH IS TRUE: THE BRAVE, LOVING MAN WHO WAS murdered in Kingston last week (on the morning of June 9, exactly) will not be forgotten. His name was Brian Ribton Bernard Williamson. None of us who are gay, lesbian, or bisexual will forget him, and neither will many others.

He was a founding member of the Jamaica Forum for Lesbians, All-Sexuals, and Gays (J-FLAG). I remember him from that time. That was where I first met him—where I first had the privilege of getting to know him. We all were meeting in great trust, hardly sensing at that time, in the latter months of 1998, how daunting and ultimately vital our mission would be. But in 2004, six years later, despite severe challenges to its health, safety, and the morale of its members, J-FLAG still exists—proof of the importance and utter correctness—necessity—of that work. Jamaica's viciousness and hatred, no matter how brutal, could not destroy us then, and will not destroy us now.

I remember Brian as a laughing man: a man with "a head of silver coins," as I sometimes joked with him about his head of curly silver-gray hair. He loved laughing and laughter; though it is often said of the dead even when untrue, he truly *did* love life, and exemplified that love in his formidable bravery where matters of sexuality were concerned. He was not afraid to open and operate, from the late 1990s until only a few years ago, the gay and lesbian

Brian Williamson, September 4, 1945–June 9, 2004

dance club Entourage, right in his home at 3A Haughton Avenue, New Kingston. Entourage, a place where so many of us gays, lesbians, and bisexuals could go to dance, laugh, flirt, party, and share time with friends and loved ones—a place where we could breathe freely and openly, delivered for a few hours from Jamaica's otherwise repressive, hateful antigay environment. At Entourage and in other places, Brian was not afraid to challenge the police, fiercely, when they attempted to harass him. He was not afraid to represent J-FLAG on the radio, using his own name, and to appear on television representing the organization, showing his face. He did it all with great humor and generosity, and lived, until last week, to tell about it. In that regard, he was truly an example to all of us who are gay, lesbian, or bisexual—an example of just what bravery and risk can accomplish.

It remains to be seen whether Brian was murdered specifically because he was gay, although, given the crime's extremely violent nature (numerous stabs with an ice pick to his neck, at least one chop to his forehead with a machete) and his being so widely known as an outspoken gay man—and given Jamaica's unabashed hatred of gay and lesbian people, which hatred gay men and lesbians themselves, not surprisingly, as social creatures and vulnerable human beings, internalize—one would be a bit naive not to wonder. These are hard times for all Jamaicans living on the island, but they're especially hard for men who love and are attracted to other men, for any man who either consciously names himself as "gay" or "bisexual," as well as those who—married, otherwise involved with women, or even confirmed men of the cloth—insist that they are not "that way" or "so," yet seek out other men whenever possible, whenever and wherever imaginable. Many men who desire other men in Jamaica continue to live with an enormous amount of anxiety, shame, and fear. Such is also the case for women who love other women. Those of us who are men, particularly after an incident such as the one that took Brian's life, return to that gnawing fear: will someone strike us down anytime soon because we are "battymen"? How will it happen? With fire? Gasoline tossed over us as we sleep, assisted by a well-tossed lit match? The stench of our burning flesh, and the sound of our screams, bringing sleep-smiles to the sleepers and dreamers who, even at rest, continue to hate us? Will it happen with machetes aimed to rip apart our softest parts? Or with pickaxes, hammers, guns? Knives, or simple strangling? Or will it be "just" a beating? Or a good old-fashioned stoning? Will our father do it to us, or a neighbor? A boyfriend of ours, or a coworker? Will everyone in our community turn on us? Will it happen in the cool, quieter hours of the night, or beneath the sun's blazing afternoon—or just before morning's first shy streaks, on its reliable way in from the East? Will people laugh after our death, as they did after Brian's? Will some cry for us, as many did for Brian? Will people tell each other after our murder that we "deserved" it, or were "asking for" it? Will people in our families be so ashamed of us, and so embarrassed, that they'll refuse to speak about us to anyone, especially when it comes to the men we loved? Will self-hating gay men say vicious things about us—that we were nothing more than a "sketel,"[1] nothing more than a "butu,"[2] so what could anyone expect?

We have all faced discrimination and bigotry from friends, family members, church members, and others; yet many of us somehow manage to survive that bigotry, and even triumph. In that regard, we—male and female homosexuals, bisexuals, "queers"—are truly testaments to survival and the human spirit. Jamaica would be much poorer without our talent, hard work, skills, and intelligence, and Jamaica knows it. Jamaica will be much poorer without the light of Brian Williamson, but the gay/lesbian community, and J-FLAG, will continue, and prevail, as Brian himself would have wanted us to.

Make no mistake: years from now, the world will regard Jamaica in this context the way much of the world regards Nazis today. The future world will rightly view Jamaica's hatred of homosexuals as the equivalent of Nazis' hatred of Jews, as the equal of racist whites' hatred of blacks, as the equal of all hatred everywhere—just as ugly, just as destructive and self-destructive, just as ignorant and narrow. Just as evil. Jamaica's hatred of lesbians and gay men is its own especial Nazism (and most nations have or have always had at least one); Hitler's fury, however, did not obliterate all the Jews, and Jamaica's rage won't kill all of us. It will not even kill those of us who are most vulnerable—those of us who hate ourselves so much precisely because Jamaica has taught us to hate ourselves and other gay people. In our private spaces, we will continue to love and make love to each other. We will continue to tell jokes and drink, play cards and watch TV, nyam our curry goat and brown stew chicken,[3] and drink our rum, Ting[4] and ting.[5] We will live like puss and dog or get on like batty and bench,[6] go on bad[7] or act fenke-fenke[8] and tek bad tings mek laugh.[9] We will still dream of love, like everyone else—and, when necessary, we will take care of each other. If anything, Brian's death should teach us all to do all these things even better.

But it should teach us something else, even more important: that we, and no one else, will have to make the kind of world we want our children to live in. If one of our children turns out to be gay—and I mean the children of any Jamaican, any person, heterosexual or homosexual, since we, too, produce and care for children—are we prepared to send them out into a world that might chop them up, burn them, dash acid on them, or burn down their house? Or stone them? Or cause them to flee Jamaica, terrorized and demoralized, into exile? Or cause them to grow up lying about themselves? Lying to their parents, to spouses, children, friends, family—to everyone? What are we all really doing right now, nearly one week after a brave man's death, to protect our children from that world? From that world which is, still, so unfortunately, this one?

Brian featured on the bottom of his outgoing e-mails a quote often attributed to Gandhi: "We must become the change we wish to see in the world." The idea is useful, but the achievement of its sublime essence requires a tremendous amount of human bravery: brave heart, brave mind and soul, and the courage to expand the mind beyond the prejudices that make us feel happy, comfortable, superior. Are we prepared to try and live this way, if only to keep other people from being killed as Brian was killed, and to save ourselves from such a (literal and spiritual) death as well?

Light a candle, then, for this man who was loved. Light many candles, and remember his name. Hear his laughter—recall it, if you knew him—as you envision his head of silver coins. Remember the shine of his eyeglasses and the shape of his everlastingly, incorrigibly round belly. Remember how much he loved other men, and how very much he wanted them—yearned for them—to love him in return. Remember how much he loved his cat Jonathan and his dog Tessa—poor Tessa, who was there, at home, on the morning of his death. Remember how Brian loved his garden, especially the trailing yellow allamanda flowers on his front lawn's overhead trellis. Say a prayer for him, and say another—yes, somehow—for the terribly lost, terribly maimed person(s) who killed him. Remember how much power, love, and life Brian brought us in Jamaica. Remember how much braver he made so many of us, and how he expanded our entire country. You, dear Brian, whom we will continue to hold right here, deeply in our hearts—closest to our very selves where the earliest breath begins, where memory never ends. Where, amid recurring dreams and sorrow and light, you will always be very, very loved.

2004

Regarding Carolivia Herron's Thereafter Johnnie, So Long Swept Aside: Why?

AND WHY, INDEED? FOR IT IS WITHOUT QUESTION A BRIL-liant work of art. A formidable one. A novel without which, whether we know it or not, we all, every single one of us, would be far poorer. Do not the opening lines of the first chapter, "Vesperus," already provide us some intimation of what we might expect—strangeness, unpredictability, luminousness, and more?

> *Now she is a light flitting through the halls of the Old Carnegie Library. They closed it down, then gave it to the University of the District of Columbia. They stopped having classes there. The black folk left, went up into the Allegheny Mountains when the war started. She gets brighter as evening comes on.*[1]

More, yes, will come; sorrow will come; grief, horror, and great ugliness never far from beauty (the beauty of limpid prose, of allegory, of unsettling myth) will come. Here, quite like a twist-ing road leading into the sea, deeper beneath the sea, all the way around and possibly back to the beginning of the great curved chin of the sea, is the text. Once we have trod upon the road and felt all about us (about our shoulders, about our many parts both smooth and rough, including our smooth-rough hands) that sea, can we imagine the world without it? Imagine night, daylight, consciousness, reflection, thought, imagination, writing, without it? But then perhaps that is precisely the problem—that far too few of us have read it?—have swum the sea? Far too few of us who in fact truly would do much better with it in our minds, but do not yet possess it. So many of us who, not yet having read it, cannot quite envisage just what, precisely, fearless (but then call it merciless) imagination can do. The sort of fearless imagination from which so many of us continue in our daily lives and in our imaginations to shirk, shrink, cower—for we cannot in the light of day or even in the most oblique, shrouding night discuss with ourselves or with others these things, the things that *Thereafter Johnnie* discusses and probes, can we? We cannot discuss incest, much less ambiguously "consenting" incest, in the way the book so lyrically, erotically, unrelentingly does, can we? For certain things, we know, have learned, are simply not permitted. Desire and the need to be daring, to be utterly free, shut down constantly in daily life (consider what is *appropriate*; mind your manners; do not let on that you yearn to be kissed and to kiss, to have someone inside you as you are inside/beside them; restrain your children, like your hands and eyes; banish, after a certain age, all feelings for your mother's breasts)—shut down until some agonizing art opens them up again, if only in secret.

> *A light brightening out of nothing in the Children's Room*
> *of the Old Carnegie Library, out of nothing, because to a*
> *light there is no need for a way of getting there, through the*
> *front door, or through a window, or up from the basement*
> *stairs smelling of urine on days when the mild vagrants sat*
> *in the park.*[2]

But now, here, not quite on my knees, heeding the sound and blessing of nocturnal rain outside and the graceful curl of African violet leaves along a broad white yet still somehow forlorn window-sill, let me be grateful. Let me be grateful to (at least) Brenda O. Daly, Elizabeth Breau, and the late Barbara Christian, who, as feminist scholars, as discerning and brave-hearted scholars, actually assayed, and succeeded in, critical articles about the magnificent, powerfully complex *Johnnie*. (Daly began by calling it an "intriguing" novel, and she was only beginning.)[3] Daly's journey through the novel appeared in an issue of the literary journal *Callaloo* ("Whose Daughter Is Johnnie? Revisionary Myth-Making in Carolivia Herron's *Thereafter Johnnie*," 1995), Breau's in the journal *African American Review* ("Incest and Intertextuality in Carolivia Herron's *Thereafter Johnnie*," 1997), and Christian's in the *Women's Review of Books* ("Epic Achievement," 1991). All three are profoundly insightful, and meticulous. And persuasive. Let me, and other readers and future and potential readers, be grateful that these scholars brought their discriminating gazes to an intricately layered, polyphonic, richly allusive and allegorical novel that is, to be sure, a modern masterpiece within *and beyond* the traditions of African American and African diasporic writing, including the category of women's writing within those traditions; it is a novel that (here a prediction in which I have the utmost confidence) someday, ultimately, will have a powerfully propulsive role in transforming, extending, *reconfiguring* those traditions. Simultaneously, it is a text that surely, for a variety of reasons, frightens—terrifies—some people; and a text that simultaneously is, for me, a daunting text to write about even as I write about it here with all the love and respect and awe I have felt for it ever since first traversing it in the early 1990s, fortuitously recommended to it by a sales clerk at the Schomburg Center for Research in Black Culture in Harlem. Let me be grateful that these critics, these scholars, through their writings and theorizings and conclusions, helped me arrive at a more nuanced, more sophisticated, more alert way of knowing what exactly *Johnnie* had to provide—ever so much more than a story about father-daughter incest. Ever so much more than a novel about the cruel destruction of a middle-class, privileged African American family. *Ever* so much more than the horror of a daughter who is raped by her father (or "seduced" by him, the novel suggests), who also apparently "seduces" him, and who finally drowns herself, leaving behind in grief and unappeasable longing the daughter of their incestuous union—the luckless but enduring ("condemned to immortality") Johnnie. Johnnie, the final survivor, daughter and granddaughter of her "grandfatherfather," John Christopher, and his daughter, Patricia, "patPat."

And more: much more even than the rage and horror of the mother Camille, wife of the incest-inclined father John Christopher. Camille, who after discovering her husband's and daughter's profane relationship and the rape of another daughter, Eva, describes how if, on the drive to the hospital to visit Eva, her daughter Cynthia Jane would just stop the car, she herself could "look down and find out what has happened since the beginning of time, I could see the Trojan War and the theft of Africans, and how they killed the Indians, I could see all the myths when they were born, and I could see all the way down here to the pit of hell, the annihilated, the deceived, the forsaken, the despicable, the wretched, injustice and sorrow and cruelty and despair and torture and lynching and murder and starvation and burning flesh and eyes put out and Eva raped and I would see Eva raped and I would see my husband fucking our daughter, my husband fucking our daughter, my husband fucking our daughter."[4] Camille, who—but how can she survive? How will she manage? Camille, who

Camille
Green eyes, tan orange skin, she lowered her head
    blushing downward whenever he came
Camille
Thin lips, thin waist, thin legs, thin sandy hair curled
    on her shoulder
Camille
She is the one he comes for, she is the one who sows a
    green garden in her mind while seated at the piano
    waiting for him to come. The music.
She is the most beautiful of all.[5]

Let me be grateful that these critics departed from the band-wagonry so common among so many scholars—the let-us-write-ONLY-about-those-authors-who-have-been-written-about-to-death approach to literary criticism and inquiry, as in writing mostly about those enshrined in an evident canon or canon-to-be. Such canons, or hierarchies, without question exist for and among black women writers, promoting excessive visibility for some while relegating others to the margins—to, one might say, at least in the United States, the margins within the margins within the margins. If it is true that, at least in the regard of considering writers for the critical gaze, many literary critics are followers, not leaders—and it does appear to be true, given how many of them so often appear to follow without a blink the leads of other scholars, playing it safe on proven ground as opposed to (though with some exceptions) striking out for unknown critical lands—Christian and Daly, in their serious regard of *Thereafter Johnnie,* took a decidedly unventured path, given how little Herron was known in 1991 as a novelist (though she had achieved some renown in some circles as a scholar).[6] A few other critics in the 1990s also gave Herron's novel the sustained attention it deserved, and to them also I am grateful.[7]

It is surely out of some feelings of rage, and a sense of things simply not being *right,* that I chose to write this essay. Indeed, it was without question due in part to those feelings, and to my excitement about Herron's writing—writing which immediately struck me as both iconoclastic and challenging—that I knew for years that I would someday write these words, and ultimately couldn't imagine not writing them. Some years ago, *Time* maga-zine ran a cover story on Toni Morrison ("The Sound and Fury of Toni Morrison," January 19, 1998), in which, at one point, the article's author asserted that Morrison "single-handedly" pro-vided African American women their voices in literature. It was a nice thought, and a grand one, but egregiously incorrect, and, in its incorrectness, infuriating—as, I suspected, or at least would like to believe, it would have annoyed Morrison, who certainly

knew and has known intimately for decades the difficult landscape African American women writers, and all black women
writers, have had to travel. To state categorically that Morrison
"single-handedly" provided African American women with a
voice instantaneously erased the works of numerous other African
American women writers—among them, I fumed in a letter sent
to *Time* that the magazine shortly thereafter published, Octavia
Butler, Paule Marshall, and Carolivia Herron.[8] (Paule Marshall,
of course, is simultaneously a Caribbean and an African American
writer.) And many more. Morrison herself once stated in an inter-
view that, at least in the United States, there existed only so much
room for so many African American women writers in general,
and far less for those who diverged from the expectations of what
a black woman writer *should* write about and *how* she ought to
write about it—expectations held, to be sure, quite strongly by
many black and other of-color readers, and surely held also in
who can tell how many cases by those black women writers who,
intimidated or successfully conditioned beneath constricting
(sexist, race-ist) ideologies, internalize and genuflect before the
constrictions. In an era of much simplemindedess and stupidity
about what American blackness is "supposed" to be, who and
what American black women are "supposed" to be and what exactly black people are "permitted" to—"supposed" to—engage
about in public discourse (including as such engagement the
practice of literature and other art forms), such rigidities would
assuredly crowd out who knows how many black women writers who might have dreamed of daring to write about the topics
Herron has risked, as well as those who might wish to assay their
own journeys with the sorts of experimentation *Thereafter Johnnie*
contains, and in which it consistently succeeds.

Consider this sampling of some of the proscriptions for black
women writing in the United States:

Do not write about domestic violence. (Alice Walker and
Michelle Wallace, among several others, got pounded for that one.)
Do not write about lesbianism. (Audre Lorde, Anita Cornwell,

Barbara Smith, and Pat Parker, among many others, got severely trounced for that one.) Leave by the side of the road misogyny. Do *not* venture into critiques of black nationalism—the "nation" meaning mostly, of course, ostensibly heterosexual black men. (In such a "nation," homos and women are visa-less hopefuls—but perhaps we, too, someday, if we behave as we ought, might secure full citizenship, or at least functional green cards.) Leave entirely alone discussions of rape and other sexual abuses, including any mention whatsoever of the dreaded "I" word, *I-n-c-e-s-t*. And for God's sake, if you must write about incest (notice the disgust just creeping toward our nostrils), *do not* write about it as a consensual thing—*the* truly unthinkable imagining. If you do so, rest assured, you will bring down the wrath of both women and men on you in such a venture, to say nothing of those among us constantly concerned about what white people will think.

Morrison, Naylor, Hurston, Jones, Bambara, Petry, Marshall, West, Lorde, Walker, Shange, and a score of other black women prose writers made, and in some cases continue to make, their various contributions to the totality of black women's, and all black people's, art and expression, but why, I wondered and wonder still, has Herron's luminous artwork been so generally overlooked even by many black (male and female) writers and critics? Why, aside from its unrelenting gaze at incest and subsequently deeply corrupted family relationships, is *Thereafter Johnnie,* "difficult" reading though it might be (it *is* an intricate, even labyrinthine journey, and it does require scrupulously paid attention—a tough call for readers in an age of, by and large, diminished attention spans and thinned reading skills), such an unknown text? Why is it not a cornerstone in (African) American literature—a text, as Gloria Naylor wrote on the original edition's back cover, "for the ages" in diasporic literature? If Gloria Naylor, with whose salutary words in regard to this novel I agree, feels that "it [is] ironic that critics at large have been bemoaning the fact that American literature has produced no counterpart to James Joyce in vision and structure and that such a person has now appeared within the ranks of Afro-American literature," why do so many readers apparently know nothing of *Thereafter Johnnie*?

Because the book is, as mentioned earlier, "difficult"? But so are many books that are considered so, yet linger on and are even beloved by many (though also hated by many). Books that are consistently read, taught, absorbed, constantly regenerated, re-introduced, resurrected. How quick and simple a read is *Ulysses,* or *Finnegans Wake*? *Absalom! Absalom!* is no party cruise, nor are the *Iliad,* the *Odyssey,* and the *Oresteia.* (I invoke these titles purposely, for, though radically different in numerous ways from *Thereafter Johnnie,* they are epics as it is an epic.) *The Way of All Flesh* endures and is loved. Visible. Also seen about town, at least in readers' circles, are *Heart of Darkness, Vanity Fair, One Hundred Years of Solitude,* and *The Magic Mountain* (incidentally a favorite book of Herron's). *Jude the Obscure* endures, and *Tess of the D'Urbervilles,* and most of Hardy's most famous works; as do *The Portrait of a Lady, The American,* and *The Golden Bowl.* A heap of them. And so—?

I could say, quite correctly if somewhat sweepingly, that if only because most of those aforementioned titles were written by white, heterosexual, Christian men and were long ago inducted into the canon of Western literature, their narratives—at least, one might guess, in the West, and certainly in the racially anxious United States—will be around for a while. The lives of white men—the lives even sometimes of gay white men—*matter,* many people of a wide range of colors believe, and are *interesting,* in contrast to those of black women and black people in general, unless the discussion is centered on sex, sports, or popular music. Race-ist and racial myopia (who cares what blacks write, especially if they try to write "literature"?) are certainly legitimate culprits in the large invisibility, for a more "general" population,[9] of Herron's novel—but what about gender? That is, what about perceptions regarding what is *still* considered appropriate or inappropriate for women to write about—perceptions complicated, when turned toward black women, by the race-ist lens's distortions?

What to say and know about bigotry-informed beliefs that insist, even if occasionally quietly, that black women writers *should only* write a certain way (equal stress on the "should" and "only")—write in *the* tacitly or otherwise prescribed way—about the approved topics? As a lover of the word and a humanist, how to feel about the absolutists who would thunder that no self-respecting black woman writer (equal stress here on "black" and "woman") should have any sort of truck with (as Herron does) the likes of John Milton, Shakespeare, Plato, for example? (Leave the dead white men alone; to engage with them in any way is to make yourself a racial suspect, less "authentically" and "verifiably" black per the blackness quotient. To engage literarily, earnestly, with Milton or Shakespeare will be *almost* as bad as—for a black woman—the utterly unthinkable: *dating* one of *them*.) But then how *not* to admire Herron's marvelous allusiveness and legerdemain, vis-à-vis echoes and inversions, with these and other writers? For she does—her characters do—converse with *Paradise Lost*. With *Macbeth*. With the New Testament. With, according to one critic,[10] the works of Yeats, Wordsworth, and so many more, including—especially in the novel's concluding chapter, "Matin"—non-Western, noncanonical storytelling traditions. Is it possible, however, that *Thereafter Johnnie* is not read as much as it might be partly because many people, once again across color lines, have simply no idea how to read a black woman writer (emphasis here perhaps more forcefully on the "black") whose language achieves the acrobatics that Herron's achieves, whose allusions move as far and as ambitiously as hers do? Whose narrative trajectories move within a twenty-four-chapter epic structure even as the events within those chapters leap about in extremely nonlinear fashion? The disturbing gaze at incest aside (both the characters' gaze at, and their prolonged engagement in, incest, plus the topic itself, are equally unsettling, to say the least), has Herron fashioned something so unimaginably new, so radical and previously unseen, that no ways of *completely* seeing *and comprehending* this novel yet fully exist for many readers who encounter it? Is *Thereafter Johnnie* as strange to the eye and mind as Webern's and Stravinsky's music was to earlier ears accustomed to conventionally structured Western music? If this novelist has, as Gloria Naylor says, emerged as a "counterpart" to James Joyce but is a black female "counterpart," does Herron immediately become not only invisible but also impossible, as in Cannot Possibly Exist? But then how to assess her not in relation to James Joyce, as I would prefer not to do, but on her own, completely unique terms, as *Thereafter Johnnie* does demand one do? What then? Does the task loom as impossible because of one's own bigoted gaze?

I personally have no idea, though I have suspicions. While I love Joyce, and could no more imagine life without his perversity and brilliance than I could without the talents of an uncountable number of other writers whom I adore, Herron fascinates me in part because she is (in this way perhaps quite like Joyce) *completely* herself, unlike in any way whatsoever anyone else. If her work is "like" that of other African American women writers (and it is not, generally speaking) because her characters share with theirs blackness, Americanness, and womanness, the likeness is only as valid as the characters of Synge, Beckett, Sean O'Casey, and Brendan Behan (among many others) having in common with Joyce's their Irishness. In reading and rereading Herron's novel, and even in attempting once, with great difficulty, to teach it, I understand clearly once more that I absolutely have not, in this way, seen language and narrative like this before:

The beauty of torture, the delight of slavery, the joy of being tied up bound down whipped beaten drawn quartered stretched broken into the ground is this—the mind is free. Is this, this, there is no way out, giving up is simplified. With warm flesh in shreds, limbs broken torn, guts lashed slashed hung hooked, body held down trussed up bent over, skin fingernails toenails stripped off, breasts cheeks ears eyes stuck stung pierced, feet palms knees elbows shaved and shaved again to the bone, limbs pinned open spread askew separated

*detached, genitals mauled, split, sliced, eliminated it's easy,
so easy, so finally and absolutely easy. It must be endured.*[11]

What immediately strikes one upon reviewing this passage, and in reading the entire novel, is Herron's willingness to take risks again, and again, and *again,* with language: conventional punctuation in *Thereafter Johnnie* becomes another creation entirely—periods, commas, and semicolons take on new meaning, even as, sometimes alarmingly, they disappear altogether. A woman's nickname becomes "patPat," spelled exactly so; repetition is used to emphasize horror, (erotic) ecstasy, and the sheer poetry possible in prose stretched at times to labyrinthine lengths, at other times as direct as impatient rain. Corrupted, depraved family relationships are represented in striking mergings of words: "mothersister," "grandfatherfather," "auntsister"—the visual equivalents of the facts that Johnnie's father is also her grandfather, her sisters also her aunts, her mother also her sister.

What more to say? For years I have felt deeply sad that people everywhere were not grabbing *Thereafter Johnnie* off bookstore shelves and reading it obsessively, passing it on, demanding it back to share with others. For years, after Random House put the novel out of print, I hunted for copies of it in used book stores and mailed or handed the copies I found to people about whom I cared, often whom I considered friends, and who I thought would, as I had done, delight in—or at least be awed by—the journeys Herron provided. ("I felt that I was being eviscerated while reading that book," one friend, a white woman, said some years ago.) Sharing a book one has admired—sharing any form of art—is certainly one of the most intimate ways of sharing those more tucked-away parts of one not at all easily glimpsed in the everyday: the places where one most profoundly feels and thinks (if one considers oneself someone who does feel and think) and can be thrilled—where one actually can *dare,* dare!—to be excited about the world's now-and-then, often startling beauty, and especially, to use Herron's language at the novel's end, "the joy of beautifully wrought things, words that capture each thing you have loved forever."[12] And so it is now that, loving all those things still and hoping that Herron will someday write another novel—"If only she would write another novel, or several," another friend who also admires Herron's work says wistfully from time to time—and hoping that, through these words throughout these paragraphs, more readers will be moved to seek out and sojourn all of *Thereafter Johnnie*—and disdaining the strictures continually placed on black women writers and on so many writers of color and women writers everywhere, including lesbian writers and gay writers and all those in between—those on the "edges," whose work and lives and very beings are not perceived as being of, at, the "center"—with all that and more in mind, how could I now not end here with Herron's own words from *Johnnie*'s end—words I know I will not, of course not, ever forget; words that continue to pull at me even as they make me deeply sad, lonely for the possibilities of human joy so often mired in pain; Herron's words, which become at this point in the novel Johnnie's but then another voice's entirely, completely unexpected, telling us now that at last "the dream was consumed mysteriously and eliminated by strange fire, as well as all of the dreamers, consumed, not one was left, saving only Johnnie, condemned to immortality, Johnnie, thereafter forever, because as I have told you of this last image of the city, now she is a light

a light
alight"[13]

Between Jamaica(n)
and (North) America(n):
Convergent (Divergent) Territories

∞

RETURN: SLOUCHING TOWARD DISSEMBLING

But first of all, he thinks, the accent. His. He is aware of it on this day, in this moment, which, whether in memory, imagining, actuality, or all three, is Jamaica. Kingston, without doubt; upper St. Andrew, to be sure; the two places in Jamaica that, to him, since childhood, ever since he can remember, have been and continue to be, even more than the northern Clarendon and Manchester centers of his patrilineal ancestors, home. Here, at the Norman Manley airport (which in his childhood was called Palisadoes), long before he arrives at his beloved New Kingston apartment, he suddenly becomes once again aware of his quite noticeable U.S. accent, as, having left the Air Jamaica or American Airlines jet behind, he walks toward immigration: toward that enormous room the fluorescent dreariness of which invariably puts him off even as his face grows warmer with excitement over the role of its "officialness" in permitting him—in some cases welcoming him—into the country. There, in that room, nervously shifting from one leg to the other yet doing his best to affect the bored, occasionally impatient Chuh!-nuttin-nuh-gwan expressions on the faces of so many returning Jamaicans—expressions that more often than not match perfectly those of the white-shirted, uniformed immigration officials and are always accompanied, when the lines are extremely long, by sharply sucked teeth, a here-ism he also affects—he ponders his sharp North American *r*'s, quite unlike those of Barbadians: Yes, si*r*, good mo*r*ning, su*r*e, I'll be he*r*e fo*r* . . . the "here" pronounced in that particularly Northeastern North American way, not like the nasal upper St. Andrew *hair* he remembers. He will try, as usual, to affect with the skeptically expressed immigration officer a casual enough "Yeah, man," or even dare to joke—"But yu no easy!"—if the official grants him a shorter time to stay in Jamaica than he'd hoped for, if he is entering the country on his U.S. passport this time, a prisoner of that hated "Visitors" line which, at all costs, he avoids. Because I'm no damn visitor, his bullish mind will always insist, *I'm a rass-claat Jamaican*—and yes, he will remember that hilarious section from Anthony Winkler's *Going Home to Teach,* from which he lifted the line, but not the sentiment.[1]

The immigration officer will, as usual, be either too bored or too weary (or both) to be impressed by his attempts to dissemble as a fully accented Jamaican. He walks out into the baggage claim area, continuing to dissemble wherever and with whomever he can. *Yes, well, you know I was studying in Canada, so my accent . . .*—will be his glib, sometimes urgently felt reply to those discomfiting, even, yes, painful questions put forth by surprised others upon hearing his accent: But you're not a Jamaican? Oh, you come from "foreign"? You're not from here . . . ? He walks out into the beauty and heat of Jamaica, which again, always, bring him close to tears; walks out to whichever smiling face will greet him this time. He will not dissemble with that person, who will assuredly know and receive him as he sometimes likes to be known—a "Jamerican"—but will pretend with the many others to come: with the roadside vendor just past the Harbour View roundabout ("Yao, gimme two Matterhorn, nuh?"—a cigarette name he has never been able to pronounce properly in a patois-ized accent), with the flirtatious sales clerks in the Matilda's Corner pharmacy (a deep *Um-hmm* might suffice there), and with so many familiar faces at the John R. Wong supermarket, in the Cross

Roads post office, in the Bookland shop where he sometimes buys his *Gleaner* or *Observer* (or *New York Times*), and in the Life of Jamaica or Island Life malls, where, religiously, he daily attends to his e-mail. These are a few of the places within the place he calls "home"—the "home" he continues to love in the passionately yearning way he loves it more than anyplace else, except perhaps the Northeast Bronx, itself one quarter of that boisterous region known in his imagination, and not only there, as "Jamerica." But then, he thinks, how can he, the visitor–not visitor, the outsider-insider, fully be of "home" who does not, for a start, speak like those of here?

(And for just a moment, he reflects: because yes, of course, he thinks: language as culture. As signifier, marker, cornerstone, of culture. As interpreter, bonding agent, but also demarcating line of culture. The word "culture" itself occasionally requiring placement between quotes. And so within and between our "culture(s)," let it be known and understood that you speak this way, I speak so, ergo we know who we are, where we come from, and—most definitely and importantly in a world of reified, still murderously defended borders—who we are not. But then where, he wonders, is the in-between language? The language of hybridity, of convergence, even (especially) in the face of divergence? The syncretic language that—like jazz, perhaps, if not reggae and dancehall—insists on fusion? But he will return to these questions.)

In truth, he would not necessarily mind being perceived as a Caribbean or Latin American foreigner here—especially as a Cuban, loving Cuba as he does and as did his pro-Castro, pro–Michael Manley father before him; loving the Spanish language as he does, the many brilliancies of Cuban art, literature, music, and the nation's resolute defiance before unabated northern tyranny. He feels certain that, as a Cuban—as a direct "neighbor" and not suspect "first worlder," as some Jamaicans have dimly viewed him—his relationship to other Jamaicans would be—is "easier" the word? What would it mean for his own peace of mind, when it comes to this place not quite attained, and to his continu-

ing love of and need for this island if he were to come across to all
its faces as a someone from any other part of the region or nearby
Latin America, or, God knows, the African continent? For it
is, of course, his connection to North America by way of his
U.S. accent—the accent that transposes him in Jamaica to that
most painful and, in reference to him, utterly enraging category,
"foreigner"—that most rankles him. While there are U.S. accents
the music and idiosyncrasies of which he truly enjoys—the *O yeah,
I was like so totally like, O my* God, *like* of southern California, the
extremely stretched-out *a*'s and elided *r*'s of working-class Boston
and *pa'kin' my ca' in Ha'va'd Ya'd befo'e meetin' my fatha,* and the
unmatched *Y'all can go on up the road if y'all want to with Mama
and Daddy* of the Deep South—he simultaneously eschews what,
to him, a U.S. accent, especially in this place but in so many
places, represents: the stupidity and wide-eyed ignorance of questions like *O wow, those dreadlocks are like, so amazing, how do you
wash them, or, like, do you ever wash them?* (This question, with
variations between contempt and genuine curiosity and with a
completely different intonation, is also asked by many Jamaicans
and others, of course.) A U.S. accent, especially but not only if it
puts him in mind of oblivious, benighted white people (and not
only them), recalls what he has often witnessed up close as a globally well-known, globally despised U.S. arrogance, solipsism, and
the crassness of what the United States dares to term, but correctly
does term, its "culture"; and a rampant obsession with conspicu-
ous consumption (the U.S. here having much in common with
other nations, including Jamaica) and the self-deluding rhetoric
of trumpeting national mythologies along the lines of We are
the Best, the Bravest, the Freest, the Smartest, the Most Modern,
the Most Most Most Most Most of Anything and Anyone, and
don't the rest of you little third worlders, including you people
(or whatever you are) from "the islands," ever forget it. A U.S.
accent and its undeniable presence in his own body summons
for him thoughts of ideologies of which, as a self-proclaimed
third worlder and determined would-be Jamaican, he wishes no

part—ideologies such as imperialism that (of course) inflame his moral ire and abrade his humanitarian sensibilities and politics. But then what to do about that pesky, persistent, stuck-in-his-tongue accent that just won't go away, no matter how fiercely he scolds it? But then enough for now, he thinks, stepping into the elevator of his apartment building, almost "home." Enough to continue to play with dissembling, affecting occasionally even what he has fantasized as a northern Irish accent ("*What?* You mean y'haven't heerd anything of the An Clochán Liath community of Irish Jamaican Rastas, lassie?" he teases a pharmacy clerk one evening), or a Ghanain one ("In my village," he gravely tells an openmouthed taxi driver one evening, attempting to present what he imagines as "African dignity" while sharing a proverb once recounted to him by a Ghanaian professor, "we always say that when the elders are sitting on the ground, you don't come as a visitor and ask for a chair"). Endlessly amused and fascinated in part by his own silliness—a silliness backed by his profound desire to be seen as one incontestably connected to this place, or, at least, to its relations, as opposed to a nefarious, warmongering one—and the silliness's peculiar (to say the least) inventiveness, he will continue playing at coming across as almost anything else except one of *them* with their *Yeah, like, whatever* accents and their "president" whose militarism and generally vicious foreign policies, passed on by so many other U.S. presidents, he deplores—policies that continue to impact on his people of this place and all vulnerable peoples of the world. And while it is true that, particularly in a time of unconscionable violence against already-suffering millions, he can hardly bear to glimpse on the front page of the *Gleaner* or the *New York Times* the face of that most recent despoiler, it is also undeniable at the truthful day's end that he knows himself to be one of *them* by virtue of where he was born and the U.S. citizen's privileges he possesses, even while insisting that he is also of here. Aware of the atrocities visited by the northern plunderer on all those places and his link, via history and humanity, to those many, he discerns that such uneasy knowledge incurs its own responsibility: to dissent, resist, and work against a greed that cares little, when money and power are concerned, for the engaging differences between accents, much less those between and within cultures.

FOLLOWING ON DISSEMBLING:
OFFICIAL STORIES AND THE JOY OF GENEALOGY

Outright lies, of course, once formed part of his unsettledness about his accent(s). For how many times, before his first book was published and thus when much knowledge about him became both public and official, had he unabashedly lied in response to that most defining, categorizing of questions: *Where were you born?*

"Oh, well, I, uh," he stammered in those times before a quickened tongue overrode the liar's momentary nonplussedness, "I was born in Aenon Town." (Moment of triumph.) And:

Version for foreigners: "Yes, in Aenon Town. O, yes, a small place, I remember it so well, about two hundred people or less, deep in what we call in Jamaica 'the bush.' *Um*-hmm, in a country parish called Clarendon . . . yeah, man, that's right, lovely name, isn't it, I think so too. . . . O yes, quite rural, and the town, O, you should see it, just like old-time Jamaica . . . well, I mean women washing clothes in the river and a church every five feet—" (he finds this joke particularly clever, always pats himself handsomely on the back for it)—" . . . and yes, those hills, man, so gorgeous, you just can't imagine. . . . And *cold*! Yes, well, Aenon Town can get rather cold at times, just like parts of Manchester, neighboring parish, do you know it? You don't, O, what a pity . . . yes, well, I guess I'm truly a country boy, or 'bwoy' as we'd say in Jamaica, eh, by inclination and upbringing, ancestry . . ."

Version for Jamaicans: "Yeah, man, I'm from Aenon Town. Eh-heh, back in Clarendon. Yeah, man, well, not too far from Spalding and Christiana, you know? Known years ago and in past centuries as 'Barracks,' some people still call it so. *Um*-hmm. Did I—what? Did I grow up there? O, no, man, I left Jamaica for the States when I was about three. Yes, three, that's right. But I was born here, so . . . yes, delivered by a midwife. Can you imagine? Um-hmm, so, yeah, man, a so it go. Mi born right ya so. A Jamaican . . ."

Yes, he lied, although he feels much less now the need to do so. For he does love the Bronx, after all, where he was actually born—the Bronx itself a northern "third world" satellite. While he is often amused, and suspects other Jamaicans would be somewhat amused, by someone going so far as mendacity in order to become, be received as, "authentically" Jamaican (*But can you imagine,* he dream-hears some of them saying, *de bwoy would actually tell* lie *fi become Jamaican. And him already have U.S. passport! But see ya, Massa God, a wha dis now?*), these days he is also able to take great pleasure in the meticulous patrilineal genealogy compiled by a brilliant, dearly beloved relative—a genealogy that traces his ancestors on this island and elsewhere to well before emancipation, and includes (here he positively purrs with smugness, but also with sincere joy) *six* Thomas Glaves—among them, in the more recent past, his father and great-grandfather. He is both humbled by and deeply grateful for the gift: that of being able to place some names, some identities and even actual lives, in a severely truncated diasporic history throughout which neither the intactness of language nor the permutations of precise memory could ever be guaranteed, much less the identities and lives of human beings who, in this hemisphere, served precisely as largely faceless *not*-people, *un*humans: an uncountable sweep of bodies for the building of a wealth even today nowhere near their own. The genealogy permits him the luxury of reveling in names that are his own; names that, in his deepest dreams, provide amplitude for the rollickings of his often-feverish imagination, but—most importantly—names that provide him with an incontrovertible historical connection to the land, this land, that not even the most sneering "O, with your 'Yankee' accent you claim to be from here?" question can undermine; yet the very specificity of those names in his personal history and the fact that he can now actually trace, at least patrilineally, his ancestry back to the mid-eighteenth century, saddens his North American side; for he had, of course, shared with so many black Americans the painful heaviness of not being able to know; of memory, names, places, and persons lost, completely irretrievable. Shared the ponderous weight of that collective sorrow: of never being able to determine exactly where I/we in actuality originated, with the knowledge of who and how we are now, and why, connected to the knowledge of who we actually *were,* as opposed to who we were forced to become—a weight borne also by Jamaicans, of course; the diasporic weight often painfully borne by all peoples of African descent in the West. And so imaginatively enabled by this new knowledge of his family's past (though a past yet incomplete, as so many pasts remain), he cannot quite—not in the ways he did before—participate fully in the not-knowing heaviness; for knowing at least what the genealogy has revealed to him roots him irrevocably in a territory both literal and historical—territory that, for now, perhaps even for this lifetime, can be, with the African continent far more than even an entire ocean's distance away, enough, quite enough; yes, and then some.

ADDENDUM I: A BRIEF JOURNEY THROUGH INTERCULTURAL ANGER, REGRET

Anger? Regret? But yes. And deeply felt in each of his (northern, southern) territories. Anger and regret over the contempt he has heard expressed on this trip, on other trips and in the States, that is the lashing of misunderstanding and resentment between Jamaicans and African Americans, African Americans and Jamaicans. A resentment, mean-spiritedness, which often unfortunately employs the dismissive words "they," "them," or "those," as in "Yes, well, those black Americans are always complaining about something . . . ," as in "Those Jamaicans, well, you know how they are, they think they're better than everybody else, especially us . . . ," as in "But those black Americans, you see? Not *one* of them has any ambition . . . ," as in "And, yeah, you know how those Jamaicans are. They don't even think they're black . . . ," as in "But how can those people live in a big rich country like the United States and still not have made any progress? Pure laziness, man." As in, "Yeah, his sister married a white man. Doesn't that sound typically Jamaican?"

Taking into account nationalisms, petty rivalries, and often deeply felt claims to notions of "sovereignty" or "Afrocentricity" of one kind or another, a pair of (in this case) in-between eyes gradually discerns that simple ahistoricism resides at much of the center of these tensions. Ahistoricism, in truth only another word—a softer, more mellifluous one—for ignorance; for the pitfall of internalized racism, a consciousness successfully colonized. For if I who so look like you despise you, what must I feel about myself? Those many hands and wrists, to say nothing of assorted backs and legs, never free to occupy themselves with the day's random delights throughout those days that stretched into years and then centuries, were always the same, geography notwithstanding, whether busy over sugar or cotton, tobacco or cacao, in Mississippi or Manchioneal. Is it possible that an in-between person, by virtue of his very in-betweenness, so registers this need for historical (and thus present-day) coherent connection? His body straining against the constraints of absolute, absolutist, often tribalist territories? He knows that he resents (and often works to correct) African Americans' frequent assumption that—especially within U.S. contexts—"black people" means *only* African Americans; as, simultaneously, he is deeply and morally offended by many Jamaicans' categorical, glibly insulting statements about African Americans, and by those of African Americans about Jamaicans and Caribbean peoples in general. He fumes over and regrets the self-loathing that each population's disdain for the other suggests, especially, but not only, because the histories of both are housed in his body—in each body of every region, commonalities mutually acknowledged or not, lips curled toward the other in scorn or not. His body, comfortable with the language of both, but on the landscape of intercultural myopia deeply unsettled.

BODY: THE BODY DIVIDED, CONSCIOUSNESS SPLICED

If the Jamaican American's very identity is hyphenated, bifurcated—between, culturally and historically, "here" and "there"—then so too is his experience, between and within North and South, of his own body. He recalls his North American body having come of age with, in its interior life, an abiding fear, horror, of lynchings—lynchings of all sorts, even though the most infamous, grisly ones took place far from the northern U.S. city in which he lived, and certainly for the most part well before he was born. Yet they continue to haunt him: images of black men and women dangling from forlorn trees, above crowds of jeering white faces, with so many fingers pointing up at "the nigger." Songs like Billie Holiday's "Strange Fruit" wrenched at his occasionally naive or complacent edges, as did and does still the lynching-behind-a-truck 1999 murder of James Byrd in Jasper, Texas, the shootings of young black people (often, though not always, males) by wild-eyed white police officers, and recountings in the narratives he learned relatively early on to revere: those of Frederick Douglass, William Wells Brown, and the excruciating historical traumas engaged in novels like Gayl Jones's *Corregidora,* Toni Morrison's *Beloved,* Octavia Butler's *Kindred.* His North American memory recalls how often he prayed, as a teenager, that he be permitted by God or someone to reach the age of twenty-one unscathed by policemen's bullets or by the weaponry of enraged and self-despising young black men, his "fellows" and "brothers," who might, he knew, one day, one night, be able to abide no longer, without the savage blessing of hot steel gripped in their hands, something about him: his accent, maybe, not quite like theirs ("How black art thou? How blackly dost thou speak? Art thou black enough?"—three questions on the African American Authenticity Test, not dissimilar to the Jamaican-Fi-True Exam);

or perhaps their venom would be raised by the peculiar, suspect, now-and-then swing of his hips. His North American body recalls the degradation of *grown* white men's spittle aimed for him, and the insulting reach, in the North Bronx Catholic primary school he attended, of first-generation Italian American children's hands into his hair, to determine if, as so many of them suspected, that hair really did feel "like Brillo," like steel wool: misfortunes—in truth, humiliations—with which his Jamaican immigrant parents could little assist him, uninured as they were, unlike more seasoned African Americans, to the capricious landscape. His North American memory summons once more the contrasts between those outrages—not by far, incidentally, daily or even weekly ones—and the childhood he could not have known at the time was, similarly to but differently than his northern one, so well-protected, in Norbrook,[2] upper St. Andrew: a childhood spent partly beneath the watchful mild impatience of (reliably darker-skinned) helpers,[3] gardeners, part-time laundrywomen, and adults who spoke nasally (he realizes now) and who *never*—at least not ever within his inquisitive overhearing—used any of the "claat" words.[4] Adults who by and large scorned patois, and who, on weekends, yammered incessantly with hosts of friends and other relatives on the then ungrilled-against-gunmen enormous front veranda across which white rum and brown flowed like the ever-invoked Jordan. At the time, to his North American eyes, that world was black, filled with black people everywhere, and not, as he would later learn, both brown *and* black, with preferably more of the former, thank you, whenever possible: so those smiling mouths expressed so faithfully, so often, with and without words. He could not have known then, quite, about all those complicated (post)colonial feelings regarding blackness and brownness and, Lord knows, about *hair* (what will they make of his nappy dreadlocks fifteen years later? But no, do not ask); feelings that had, in spite of his naïveté, swirled about, thickening the very air with their ambivalence and anxiety about the dreaded possibilities of blackness's constant encroachments. Blackness in the Manor Park shopping center, which was no "stush" big deal then the way it is now;[5] and blackness in the then more active Constant Spring market. Blackness on JOS,[6] on all the roads, and on television (in those years the lone JBC channel, not the broad cable wealth of today). Blackness in spite of preferences for brownness, not to be denied. A surfeit of wonder and reflectiveness, the self and selves of history reflected. Yet—

Yes, his North American body remembers, as his Jamaican body, in its mid-teenage years, began to resist. Resist in spite of blackness and brownness everywhere and the fact that few (if any) fingers checked for Brillo feel in the hair (t)here, at least not Italian American ones. Resist because, well, as he approached fourteen, as he turned fifteen, he began to learn that he dared not ever yearn for it, conjure it: yearn for the most secret union he desired, which would have been blackness and brownness in a male face and body beside his own, beneath his own, inside his own, as the requirements of compulsory heterosexuality proceeded, implacably, to level themselves on his panicked head and he wondered, did he not?—how he would survive those daily and nightly crushings unto obliteration of his most insubordinate passions, of his self. Would he survive, not attempt to kill himself? (He had not yet reached sixteen.) Survive the unmistakably communicated loathing for that which—at least at that time—would have had to remain unspoken, so execrable was it. Another thing, and certainly one of the worst, aside from pedophilia, which they in polite upper St. Andrew would and could never possibly countenance, associated as it was, *that behavior,* with nastiness, filth, degeneracy: not countenance it, no, of course not during one of their sparkling weekend gatherings and *certainly not* in the presence of children. They developed tasteful enough codes: Yes, my dear, I did hear he was, you know, *so inclined* . . . or yes, that young man is (preceded by an edgy clearing of the throat) Paul's, or Andrew's, or Neville's *friend. Um*-hmm. The longing gazes he exchanged occasionally with boys his age, their eyes and mouths so arresting, he learned soon enough to avert. Do not look at them, do not permit the eyes to graze their various and secret meadows or linger over the moistness of their lips, and above all *for God's sake* do not ever dream of kissing them, of making love to them, of permitting your face even the slightest motion toward the belt buckle and the zipper's teeth ripped apart in your deepest dreams to expose the curled, drowsing animal and its companions awaiting your so longed-for (but ever stealthy) ministrations. He would have to understand—understand *fast*—that there, in the midst of all that blackness and brownness, the gradual demolition of his emerging self (and how many others' selves?) would commence. He would carry that knowledge with him in both his North American and Jamaican memories as, years later, on the sweltering streets of a New York City Gay Pride celebration or along the flat, wide-open streets of Oakland, California, that would remind him so much of the Mona area (those low houses, and the royal palms lining some of the streets on the way up to Berkeley), he pressed his face to another man's, to the faces of men of varying colors, savoring the way their lips and mouths became part of his own, as his hands, as if luxuriating in the ripeness of a Julie mango or jackfruit, gently massaged the promising plenitude of their accomodating buttocks. His North American mouth recalls those kisses, his hands those fondlings, as his northern eyes remember, in New York City's Greenwich Village, the delights of men's hips in tight blue jeans or beneath short, *short* Scottish tartan miniskirts— the high fashion that summer—swinging along Seventh Avenue South, amid so many pointed nipples pressing beneath white cotton T-shirts just beginning to register the alluring aroma of male sweat. Yet his Jamaican eyes—those of the more confident, more determined adult—recall male kisses exchanged at a party, one of many, held way up in Cooper's Hill or Stony Hill for people like him. Those eyes remember smiles exchanged, arching bodies enthralled by music, outrageous flirtations carried on in the most unlikely public Jamaican quarters, and, of course, the romantic interludes that began with glances and ended with—among other things—ellipses. Yet, notwithstanding those husbanded

delights, in themselves acts of resistance, his Jamaican body remains wary. It recalls shouts hurled in recent times, in this fiercely
gender-conscious place, toward him and two other males walking
casually enough one early evening along Trafalgar Road, laughing, sharing jokes: "Why yu a walk so?" the shouter had hurled,
"like yu is man and woman together? A whe yu woman deh,
battybwoy?"[7]—a fleeting interrogation by the JGHP, the Jamaica
Gender and (Hetero)sexuality Police—an interrogaion which,
had it attracted a crowd, might have become both gory and fatal.[8]
He reconjures how once, in a small house tucked among the hills
high above Kingston, he had lain with another man, exposed
to sunlight and dust motes, rigid with pleasure yet tense: tense
that someone, in the heat of that day, might pass too close to the
house and overhear their perforce quieted sighs; tense that, as he
knew then and still knows, they both could have been murdered
by a rabid crowd for that tenuous intimacy, or simply by one furious face mindful in that moment of the usefulness of machetes;
tense because, while necks had indeed stretched in southern and
northern trees "up there" and in so many ways still did, his kind of
people "down here" routinely skirted the risks of being chopped,
burned, beaten, and otherwise annihilated—as they did, though
somewhat differently, "up there" also, of course. His kind of people
even as so much blackness and brownness abounded and all had
supposedly been formed "out of many, one."[9] And so what will
the connections finally be, he wonders, between a noose dangling
its grotesque fruit and a crowd screaming that *Chi chi man haffi
dead*?[10] What are the connections between his fear and the fear
of all men "so inclined" to share, in this country, intimacy with
another man behind scrims of enforced shame and never-far-off
dread, always somewhere just there, outside the window, beneath
sighs? And so where, he wonders, between and within both his
bodies, is the region, a region, of peace? Of final safety? The place
between North and South where he and others like him can at
last integrate their straining parts as their bodies strain against
those of other men? A place where, even in this place where who

he is and how he loves and desires are still not considered topics for polite conversation, he can formulate a language, *the* language, that at last, for once, will neither proscribe nor obscure—no, nor encode—but provide full voice for who he is and how he loves, how he lives? A language that will provide voice effortlessly, to be as warmly received as the casual words of others regarding their engagements, weddings, and admiring gazes at, comments about, those of the opposite gender, which attractions are not only permitted daily room but in fact championed out loud in public, we're-all-presumed-to-be-heterosexual (or had better be so) dominated space: what *they* with their sanctioned, wildly cele-brated marriages and engagements have always taken so much for granted, but in which neither of his bodies nor minds has ever been able to participate comfortably without much dissembling and a slow, agonizing evisceration of the soul; the soul a property few on this island have ever, outside the expediently excoriating rhetoric of religion, granted him and his kind.

ADDENDUM II: UNIVERSITY

But then, on the heels of "him and his kind," what about this university? The very university to which he was so graciously invited to share these thoughts today? What should his North American–Jamaican mind make of this exalted institution's ap-parently steadfast refusal to engage academically and rigorously with the burgeoning, cutting-edge field of (as it is known abroad, and as it has become more known of late in not far-off Latin America) queer studies? Queer studies being, of course, not only the discipline of reading texts by gay or lesbian authors or texts with homoerotic themes, but also the application of a so-termed "queer" reading to any text, or scholarly practice (deconstruction-ism, poststructuralism, postcolonial investigation, and certainly gender studies), or historical terrain: a frank, critical inquiry into the homoerotic public and private spaces of slavery, for example, or a focus on the black male body in Jamaican history as object of (white and black) male desire; an earnest turn toward the still largely unexamined area of same-gender desire and sexual and romantic bonding between slave women. Today, on this university's campus, several years into the twenty-first century, a Jamaican American imagines, and imagines that others are surely imagining, the possibility of intellectual thrill in discovering and forthrightly examining homoerotic images and themes in Derek Walcott's poetry, or flashes of same-gender desire in the fiction of Olive Senior. He wonders what it would be like to *de*-heterosexualize assumptions about presiding masculinity in Kamau Brathwaite's poetry, as deeper insight is gained into how Velma Pollard's poetry and fiction speak perhaps lesbo-erotically to the lesbo-erotic tenderness shared by so many coming-of-age girls in the works of Jamaica Kincaid. But then is it possible that even now, in 2003, there still exist reactionary agents on this university's campus? Agents who find the idea of such scholarly endeavor literally unthinkable, its practice impracticable? Agents who fear that students' parents would revolt (to say the least) over such "controversial" academic inquiry? (Yes, the same parents who would doubtless permit their children to imbibe without care inflammatory, profane, often sexist and homophobic dancehall lyrics.) And, well, those parents might scream, as perhaps well they should. For then, surely, a dialogue   dialogue, not shouting match—might truly begin, with the eminent University of the West Indies at its helm; the university insisting in that dialogue, as the appropriate (inter)national institution and icon that it is, that in a rapidly transforming, allegedly "modern" world, knowledge and scholarship of *any* kind cannot afford to drag their feet. They cannot proceed apace outside Jamaica, per the example of queer (or lesbian-gay) studies, as if Jamaica were not in fact a member of the larger world and the university itself not a critical and much-needed engine in a global and globalizing intellectual community. Conservatism and its many runny-nosed cousins should by now, especially in the vital arena of education in this, our "developing" world, be deceased—the vestigial unspeakables and unmentionables of tight-lipped British colonial reticence jettisoned. Queer studies, nonheterosexual people, and their literature and theoretical practice are, yes, it cannot be denied, here to stay forever, even in God-deliver-us-from-*those*-people Jamaica. It is, but must not be for too much longer, an unflattering reality that the esteemed University of the West Indies has not greatly contributed to—significantly partaken of—the expanding discourses that already, in so many other parts of the world, have begun to widen both the practice and interpretation of literature and scholarship in this new century and also challenged Western attitudes about normative constructions of gender and inflexible gender roles. What responsibilities is UWI not fulfilling to its nonheterosexual students, and to everyone, by refusing to engage more daringly—consistently, openly—with sexuality questions? (To date, UWI has not especially encouraged gay and lesbian social/political student organizations on any of its campuses, either—another glaring fact, unfortunately relevant to this discussion.) The Jamaican American who expects more from the university he reveres thus snarls at its—in this regard—intransigence; he stamps his feet, yanks in fury at his dreadlocks, and generally puts up a fuss, wondering in frustration and impatience when the institution he so admires will venture, ennobled, into the exciting tides out there, ever rising. He wonders the same about the institution's many redoubtable intellects who have, by way of their varied work, taught him so very much over these many years. Simultaneously, he remains aware that the warm invitation extended to him to share his work today reflects great generosity of spirit and progressive thinking, especially given the fact that those who invited him had surely already known of him as a consummate example of the love that once dared not speak its name so rapidly having become the love that absolutely will not, for God's sake, ever shut up. He smiles now at their watching faces gathered for this presentation, and trusts that, despite their possible astonishment at his brazenness ("Leave it to a (J)American," some of them will doubtless later reflect, wryly shaking their heads), they will begin to attend his complaints which are not only personal, not only pedagogical, but also political, and ultimately humanly correct.

Following on the Body Divided: Hair

But then how this particular agent of masking aids him in the dissembling necessary for survival here. How it hides him and one of his most essential truths, obscures one part of who he truly is, as, by way of that cloaking, it protects him. Protects him, he knows, from the assaults that, on this island—at least in Kingston—surely would, he fears, come: assaults hurled toward his face, more soft looking, feminine looking (assisted in no small way by what he knows to be his large, vulnerably expressive eyes), were his face not shielded—masculinized—by the slender goatee and mustache that frame his lips and cover his chin; assaults that would surely come, he fears, were his scalp not topped by its mass of unruly, thick, orthodox-Rastaman-appearing dreadlocks, which even (or especially) during the days' sweltering heat he keeps constantly pinned up and secured beneath a dark green dread "tam," lending him an even more orthodox "natty dread" appearance.

He fears the shouts that he is certain would come: snarls of *Battybwoy, Chi chi man.* He knows that, even at his age, his face possesses a boyish, but slightly girlish, smoothness to which many men, in varying instances, react—perhaps especially men in Jamaica, where sexuality in general is so often privately fluid but publicly vilified for being so; where the too-obvious sway of male hips, by and large, can lead to public taunts and threats of (if not actual) violence, depending on one's particular connections to power and status in a given community—a (patriarchal) reality in no way unique to Jamaica. But how pleasant, he thinks, to be hailed so warmly by all his Rasta brothers (but if only they knew! he often thinks, nursing an inward smile): hailed on the roads, in shops, on drives into the countryside, in the affectionate, caring, though generally masculine way Rastafarian men acknowledge each other:

"Yes, natty!" they hail.
"Yes, Lion!" they shout.
"Bless-ed!" they greet.
"Yes, Bingy!" they call.
"Far-I!" they shout.
"Yes, dread!" they hail.
"Yes, Fada!" they greet.
"Rastaman!" they call.

Utter joy for him? Delight? But of course—and more, tinged only occasionally by anxiety. And so he revels in it. Revels in the recognition by other Rastamen—lions black, brown, and every tone in between—of his (though faux, by orthodox definitions) Rasta self in relation to their own, and by extension his black male self. He loves their acknowledgment of blackness and brownness—of kinship and communion, with Rastas of any color. *Out of many, one,* at least in this regard, in the realm of fleeting perceptions. He especially loves their recognition and appreciation of (some) black body aesthetics: of this hair, not colonized. This hair for itself. And so he would, of course, like to get to know some of them in a more sustained way; to move closer to some of them, and even press himself against them eventually for the feel of their warm flesh next to his, the glory of their smiles up close (yes, recalling those who sport pleasant smiles, but also those whose smiles and general health were long ago encroached on by poverty), and their scents of sun and sweat, of skin and hair that are also his own. He would like to get to know so many of them, these Rastamen who greet him as a brother (but if only they knew), but—the several sexist, misogynistic practices and beliefs of orthodox Rastafari aside, all of which give him severe pause—how to get to know more truthfully those who utterly despise his way of loving and desiring, his way of being and the so profound pleasure taken in that way? How to tell them that, in this place of much palpable human rage and despair, he sometimes fears them? Fears that even (especially) were he to come to know some of them in the more intimate way a few of his friends have done, an unpredictable fury might sometime rise out of their eyes, as clearly it did toward more than a few unfortunate men eventually uncovered in varying states of decomposition, cases quickly tossed aside by the police. Here—anywhere?—there is no way to be sure that, in the intimate embrace of one of his dreaded brethren or someone else, an ice pick might not be plunged into his throat, and plunged again and again, after the most prolonged traversing of terrains and deepest desires. Pointed steel to slice away all memory of hidden pleasures taken: lips locked, secrets swallowed, and the reliable aftermaths of guilt and self-disgust.

Much better, he knows, to return to hair. To hair that, in some parts of the United States, renders one most visible in an "exotic" way to uncomprehending eyes; to eyes that crave some union of their own flesh with the fetishized, perceived-to-be-virile-and-untamed—a visibility attainable in those eyes even as, before their steady gaze, the regarded subject-as-object is rendered most *in*visible, unknown. The same invisible-rendering eyes that, vacationing on this island's north coast (yes: bodies lounging about in all those resorts he hates to visit, loathing as he does the sight of so many Jamaicans simpering before so many salmon-skinned culturally clueless foreigners; bodies lounging about in complete ignorance of—for a start—how those who wait on them are treated by the hotel owners), seek out the faux-Rastaman "beach boys"—the men who provide, at cost, sex for tourists, the majority of the clientele white women from Europe and North America. The men known as "Rent-a-Dreads," "Rastitutes," "Rasta sketels," or "Rasta rascals."[11] Men of whom he himself is wary, who themselves have made dissembling an unparalleled art.

(And then he also remembers that, his nappy locks notwithstanding, some of the Rasta brethren whom he greets will—after a quick scan of his "uptown"-looking clothes and shoes and even the light brown of his skin, somewhat unlike theirs, though light brown dreads exist—dismiss him as a "boasy dread," as a "Hollywood dread," as an "uptown dread," as a "Manor Park dread," as an "upper St. Andrew dread": as an apparent member of the privileged classes who decided to dread perhaps to shame and outrage his parents in Jack's Hill or Russell Heights; a someone who chose to rebel against Mummy and Daddy and Grandmother back in Cherry Gardens [and to whom, they know, he will always be able to return] by determined and perverse slumming as a locksman. Family outrage assuredly ensued on the heels of his hair growth, and scandal, remonstrances, between many loudly sucked teeth and hands thrown up in the air to Jesus, but they still paid for him, didn't they, to attend university at UWI or, better yet, abroad. ["What? You mean you didn't send him to UWI?" "UWI, what? No, my dear. Princeton."] Still bought him a car, furnished him with the sundry delights required for living—and yes, continued to warn him about *those people downtown,* among them several dreads.)

Hair: the sort that, among the upper St. Andrewers he knows and occasionally scorns and yet to whom he regularly feels so connected, causes eyebrows to rise, lips to (but slightly) curl. Hair that, in so-impressed-by-itself, perm-loving, brown-worshiping upper St. Andrew, draws questions both voiced and unvoiced: *But why do you wear your hair that way?* (Or, more frequently, out of his earshot, to others: *But really, why does he . . . ? 'sus Christ, and such a nice young man . . .) What do your parents think? But you'll eventually cut it off, won't you?* (Eliding, at that last question's end, the "please.")

Hair that, once upon a time in Jamaica, could have led to him and others like him being arrested, hauled and cuffed about in public—fiercely beaten—by the police. Hair that the police might have cut off right there on the road if they chose, *very* ungently, before a largely approving public's eyes. It will always be important, he knows, to remember that time in the country's only too recent colonized past. Important to recall today, in an era of continued police viciousness leveled primarily against the poor, the time when Rastafarians, men and women alike, were far from beloved by "the authorities." Important to remember when Rastafarians, famous musicians included, were persona non grata, as, in a different but similar way now, they still are perceived to be by the country's middle and upper-middle class, and by so many good Christian ladies and gentlemen . . .

Hair that transforms him into a walking, living oxymoron: a Rasta battyman. What none of his Rasta brethren, with luck, will ever know about him. Hair that, on his head, in his (historical-ancestral) memory and imagination and those most private inner-most spaces in which all things are ineffable and where language can never serve as fruitfully or immediately as metaphor, so much of what Jamaica most means to him resides. There, on his head, beneath his dark green, sun-bleached tam: locks protected, that protect. Above his eyes, but part of them. Above his mind, but invincibly of it.

WHILE DREAMING: LIMINALITY, LITERATURE

And so now regard the wayfarer who dreams. Who yearns for two cultures/languages (or more) fully consonant with one another within the same body, his own, as, deep in the dream, he remains fascinated by the divergences: of language, history, historical imagination, and the specifics of locale and time. He dreams, fascinated but daunted too by how much *literature he has yet, for his especial purposes (and partly toward greater integration of all his parts) to absorb. For no, he has not yet read that novel by Erna Brodber, nor that one by John Hearne, but then what about that novel by the African American writer Ntozake Shange, and the luminous book of essays by her fellow Amiri Baraka? What about the works of Latin American writers, without whose work he knows, no matter how insistently teal-toned the dream, he could not live? Without which he would, he knows, more poorly imagine, and which, by way of the fictions of Gabriel García Márquez (for one), first introduced him to the literature of the Caribbean?—for it was in the pages of* One Hundred Years of Solitude, *wasn't it, that he first saw the words "mango" and "guava" in text and truly* felt *the Caribbean all about him? (But yes, of course: as he dreamed. Dreamed and, with wild thirst, drank in those words and similar ones in the works by other Caribbean writers he would later read. A world of star-apple kingdoms edged by snapper-rich seas that all became his very own.)*

Dreaming: long paths toward the works of homo North American writers like Andrew Holleran and John Rechy, which, along with the works of Audre Lorde, another here-there person like him and also a Caribbean one, provided him with an entirely new, what he likes to conjure as "intersectional," way of imagining. He walks in dreams alongside the works of Caribbean-originated homo writers: Dionne Brand, Nigel Thomas, and the Jamaicans Michelle Cliff and Makeda Silvera. And then not least the literature of the rest of the Caribbean and, ultimately, the world. . . . But no, one evening breeze whispers (or really hisses), do not even begin to dream about jazz or dancehall, hip-hop or reggae, r & b or salsa and ska . . . no, nor about merengue or rock or soca—or, goodness knows, the romanticists, classicists, and those deeply cherished ones of the baroque. Dream on, the teal washes of imagining all about you, but over the years he has (you have) yes, absolutely, grown exhausted before the ever-growing piles of literature and here-there information, history and language—in actuality languages and processes of envisioning by way of culturally bequeathed divergences—to be absorbed. Dream-wondering once more, this time as he labors (you labor) to craft narrative language, what would be a language of in-betweenness? Could it ever exist? A liminal language of (yes!) hybridity? One well beyond, not encumbered by, the absolute presiding language(s) of one place or the other? A means of voicing not weighted by the presiding dictates and rules? Rules of How One Ought to Be in one place or the other? A means of voicing not saddled by presiding—dominating, delimiting—imaginings of "blackness," of The Only Ways to Be Black—Jamaican, African American?

But in this dream, he will not fret. No, nor rant. For he does still believe in and hope for the possibilities and surprises of language that, like desire, desire both vilified and celebrated, becomes fluid, protean, and capable of constant reinvention.

He dream-recalls: "I want you in the liminal stage," that pair of hands wrote, connected to a face known to him, "In the in between place . . . In the most vulnerable, in the most tentative. In the place where one thing is about to change into another," those hands wrote, years before the face with its odd mouth would share warm words with him, "In the hanging, gorgeous strange place between poetry and prose. . . . In the space between fiction and essay,"[12] *those hands wrote. He dreams, in spite of his questions regarding convergence still looming largely unanswered. He proceeds, both of his bodies within and about him. Restless. He moves forward more skeptical than ever regarding the ultimate usefulness of "territories." Of territorialism.*

RETURN

And so at last the time looms for his return. For departure. But a return *to,* departure *from,* where? For he realizes now that all of his regions are (and in one way or another of course always were) both convergent and divergent; more than ever before, he holds them all within his bodies and minds in such a way that, over the years, they have begun, slowly enough but with frequently discernible speed, to integrate. Yet such integration could not ever be and still isn't easy; one reason of several why he has often felt "here" when "there," of "here" when "there," and vice versa—which returns him to his question of a departure from where, internally speaking, to where? For by now he also knows that, long ago, in keeping with his overall bifurcated yet merged cultural-historical inheritance, he internalized the languages, cultures, and histories of both places, even as, in varying moments, he resisted one or the other, hid behind or within one or the other, and struggled through it all to discover, invent, and reconfigure an ultimately more useful, more adaptable means of knowing. It has become at least somewhat more clear to him now that, while his Jamaican body may still fear for the swing of its hips or the ambiguous glance in another man's eyes along certain roads even as his Jamaican mouth recollects the sweetness of June plums savored on the tongue before the swallow, and while his North

American body may still, in this year or the next, fear for its neck eventually ending up in a noose or some more subtle, ingenious form of horror directed toward his brown-black or homo body (or the two combined) even as he revisits sea-edged Cape Cod twilights and the warm grasp of a particular hand he clasped right there on the beach, in public, before largely unimpressed eyes, his bodies are at last—at least through these words' closing pages and the time spent in sojourning them—fairly converged. On a morning not too far off, he will find himself on a plane nosing its way above clouds that, to his relief, in spite of war and much global mayhem, will have remained serenely themselves, quietly indifferent to the truculence of human beings and the passing of years; the sea, so far below, will, also to his relief, continue its slow-backed crawls toward the shore. The plane will land, the passengers will debark, and he, joining them, will feel once again the particular air of that place against his face—the coolness or harsh coldness of the North, the warmth or punishing heat of the South, or—entirely likely—something, like him, manifestly in between. He will walk through the familiar airport, tasting again, as he senses the country's rhythms about him, that rage at a bellicose "president"; or the thin disgust, that commences in the nostrils, for a corrupt, prevaricating prime minister—feelings that will end hopefully not only in sucked teeth but also in vigorous dissent.

And then suddenly, before he knows it, he arrives at immigration. The same dull, glaring fluorescent lights overhead; the same sadness within him, coupled with mute anticipation, at a journey ended, another beginning; the same bored, workday faces everywhere, all of them imparting to him some fresh intelligence about this part of the world, and without doubt about himself, about one of his several selves. He slowly puts a hand in his carry-on bag, in preparation for what he knows the immigration officer will soon request. Which passport will it be this time? he wonders. The large blue one, or the smaller?[13] He feels them both, fingers them both, in the carry-on's protected pocket.

His turn at last in the line. He steps forward.

"Your travel documents, sir," the immigration officer says.

He extends the appropriate passport, knowing which one it is not by looking but by its size and thickness against his palm.

The immigration officer receives it, looks carefully at him, compares the passport photo with his face, briskly stamps the documents, and hands everything back, to his surprised pleasure, with a smile. He believes he heard the words "Welcome home," or "Welcome back," but already, walking once more between remerging worlds, he has begun to make his way to the baggage claim area, after which, as always, customs will follow.

He claims his bag, grateful that all the gifts he brought for friends and family were not damaged. He walks toward customs, which this time, he knows, will be a breeze: a cursory enough search in the "Nothing to Declare" line, and he is free. He walks toward the area exit, wondering how that face, the smiling one that he knows will be waiting out there to greet him, will appear this time. He quickens his steps, remarking the cadences of a familiar language around and within him.

"Home," he thinks. The (t)hereness of (t)here.

And last of all, he thinks: the accent.

2003–4

On the Difficulty of Confiding, with Complete Love and Trust, in Some Heterosexual "Friends"

BUT THEN BY NOW YOU HAVE LEARNED THAT WHEN REFERRING *to them—indeed, even when thinking about them, as you often do—you must suspend the word "friends" between quotes. You have learned by this time (or ought to have learned by now, given all that they have already shown you, that you have plainly seen) that, when using the word to refer to them—to those particular heterosexual people who claim to be your "friends"—you must distrust the word; regard it and them askance and with all suspicion. For when, given what they have revealed to you over the years of your "friend"-ship, were you ever completely certain that they truly were friends? That they really considered you and others like you an actual person, not an aberration? Not something experimental and "interesting," or one of "those people" who can be* so funny, so acerbic and outrageous and—*when?*

And so it has been true that from time to time—often—you have wanted to confide in them. Very much. Of course. You have wanted to tell them how things were and might have been for you that week, that month; on those two clear days between ponderous rain during which you waited for and spent time with *him*—the man you loved at that time, hoped to love; were working so hard at loving. That man whom you desired, about whom you thought and dreamed and—yes, whose most intimate smells you summoned beneath you and beside you as, alone, on so many nights and tepid afternoons, you rubbed yourself back and forth on those spreading sheets and imagined being with him, within him, beside him, for what would have been still more secret and unknowable time. Between rain showers and clear days, nightfalls and loping dawns, you wanted so much to tell them how those hours passed for you in so many ways, and how they passed—the minutes, interludes, silent stretches—for him. But those confidences would not have been all. Surely you would have wanted them to know how the hours had passed for another friend severely in love (but will he never stop yearning? some of his friends had wondered); for a friend caring for a sick lover (but when will he himself take time out to rest?). You would have wanted to tell them about that ex-lover recovering from a gay-bashing, about that other friend distraught over his mother's illness, and—of course!—about the new acquaintance hell bent on enjoying the hell out of this club, or no, *this* club, he had laughed, let's hit *all* of these clubs, let's dance until—! (And how that laughing man had held on to you and pulled you in his direction with the zest of someone utterly free, you remember . . . how you and all the others in that evening's company had laughed in return, not entirely easily, and accompanied him, twirling, for a night of sheer abandon and joy.) You have wanted to tell all of these things and more to the married couple whose photograph you once lovingly nestled on your dresser between cherished leavings of the dead and souvenirs of the sea; as you have wanted to do with the engaged couple who departed last week for Martinique, or with your dear woman friend and her man "partner"—all of whom have claimed to be "friends," and all of whom have been kind to you on several occasions, it is true, and clearly care about you in some way.

And so why wouldn't you tell them? Why would you choose not to confide in them about the first time you noticed the soft creases in a youngish man's face, that testified to how he would appear to the world when he reached sixty years old, if he lived that long? The creases that appeared somehow only when he spoke, wistfully, about adopting children with a man for whom he cared but whose continued presence, for so many reasons, could no longer be guaranteed? That wistful yearner shared with you exactly the sorts of things you have so longed to tell them: how, for instance, you have loved one man in particular so much, for the longest time, even as—not surprisingly—you have dreaded loving him so much. You have loved him, you have wanted to tell them, as assiduously and imperfectly as they have cared for each other—the wife her husband, the husband his wife, the woman and man each other. Their flaws in loving are yours, too, and his, and everyone's. Regarding them, you wonder: did they, so community-supported ("But they really do have a *per*fect marriage, such lovely children," etc.), ever fear making a life together in the way that you, today, fear making a life with him? (Yes, for you cannot forget how, only two weeks ago, he gazed so serenely at you and asked if you would be with him—"Will you be with me?" he asked.) Did they ever cower before the expectation of two lives lived lovingly, intimately, steadfastly together? What would their fear have felt like—smelled like? How would it have (or would it have) trembled and itched at the tips of their fingers? Would they, feeling the dampness of a humid rain-soaked afternoon or the aggregate salt of years, eventually have regarded each other in the way you trust you never will regard him, and wondered if, after all these years, they had done "the right thing"? Wondered if they had each finally received what they had always hoped for and wanted, in the ways they had hoped for and wanted it? Would they have said, as you might hope to say, *But all right, then. Because this* is—*yes, no mistake*—*what we always wanted. What we have. Each other, and more.* And how, *how* you would like to ask them all these things, and share that untold number of your own, but you cannot. Not with this woman or this man, because—

Well, but there they are again, as they have always been, responding to your imminent disclosures with the same reactions. The same slightly clenched fists (*Why* must he speak about these things and those people? the fists say. Isn't it enough that we care about him? Why does he have to bring all of *them* into it? their furrowed brows tell you once more). The same glazed-over eyes—No, we don't want to have to imagine, when he speaks about *desire,* how *those people* have sex with each other—please, no! Then that familiar hooding of their eyes; their voices sand-thickened; that awful twitching somewhere south of the nose, and the chin, at the sullen edge of its own precipice, half-mastedly holding its own against outrightly communicated disgust. Now your hands and throat itch toward providing some sign that you wish to speak about him; about what it has been like and will be to be with him. As you privately exult in the sway-swing of his hips when he walks toward you or away from you, you note how they, halfway attendant, clear, once more, their throats; you see how their eyes roll (to where, or whom?) and how, just so skittishly, they hem and haw about how the dishes simply *must* be cleared from the table right now (the end of a dinner party to which they invited you, at which few other nonheterosexual people were present). They mutter, not entirely disingenuously, about how the children must now be put to bed, because well, yes, they would sleep down here in the living room if we let them, can you imagine?—and then we'd never be able to talk amongst ourselves, would we? And, of course, what they imagine you have to say in all its filth and perversity (words they would never use in front of you) isn't fit for children's ears—it never is, they have made tacitly clear time and time again. And so as you stutter toward some form of speaking, you learn that they must make some urgent phone call—yes, to Kuala Lumpur, Port Said, Dar es Salaam, Dallas! Or no, they must tune in to some critical TV show—an epic series on the melting polar ice caps, or the latest word on the continuing chemical ruination of inland seas. They must wash their hands, vacuum crumbs off the tablecloth—crucial tasks, hell to pay if they aren't done—or they must run out quickly, *very* quickly, for something earlier forgotten. It will be a loaf of bread this time, although you are certain that you saw—didn't you?—two full, fresh loaves in the kitchen, atop the gleaming white refrigerator, as usual right next to the tongue-clucking Swiss-fashioned clock . . .

Is it painful? Their avoidance, awkwardness, and downright rejection of you and those for whom you care? Well yes, of course. Of course it hurts, deeply. Severely. As always, you would rather not witness their mouths drawn down along the edges, their eyebrows raised not in anticipation but in the dread of *Please don't talk about this now,* their faces say, *we just can't handle it.* You would rather deny that their faces are plainly stating that they positively *do not want* to know that part of you that has everything to do with deep feelings for other men; with the essential human need to love, to desire, to be loved. But we don't want to (and so will not) imagine it, their eyebrows say. We're better off not knowing, and we wish that you would have enough decorum not to *force it down our throats.* And what an image, you think. As if you, non-soldier and complete pacifist, never a torturer for even one day in your life, could ever, outside of intimate and consensual engagement, successfully force anything down anyone's throat.

And here you recognize imposed on you, by way of their stiffened backs and taut brows, a form of exile; ostracism; a delivery of *almost* diplomatically wrought shaming and exclusion that, through a nearly invincible intransigence, banishes you to that most pernicious place: to an outer region of silence where shame, caressed and fortified by prejudice, may triumph. Suddenly, aware once again that you are not welcome to speak intimately with these people about your most pressing vulnerabilities, you feel keenly outside that warm locale where human beings frequently exist most vibrantly, in the realm of animated and intimate, vulnerable conversation; the place where imagination is engendered, amplified, and reconfigured; the place where we all imagine and re-imagine loves, losses, hopes and hopefuls, the chances we took and didn't take, and every regret and joy clutched fast between them. It is there, outside the warm place of deep imagination even as you feel yourself still strangely in their presence (for you are still present; you did not stalk away, nor—for whatever reason—

viciously curse them), that you now watch them. Watch them as they kiss and cuddle—the woman her man, the husband his wife, the fiancée her affianced. You watch them as they kiss publicly: in a mall, in a movie theatre, out in the open on people-thick streets. You marvel at their complete lack of self-consciousness as they neck in all those places, completely oblivious to the possibility of the danger that rarely (unless, in the United States and some other countries, they are a black-white interracial couple) threatens them. They appear so free, so unencumbered by doubt, concern; unfazed by the who-might-be-wielding-a-baseball-bat-just-around-the-corner type of worry that, not without great reason, has stalked so many times before you and other women and men queers you know. You marvel at how they, as the world's personified definition of what love *should* be, take the display of their affection and its pride of place so much for granted. You know, as they cannot, that (unless they are an interracial couple) they will never know the quick release of a publicly held hand as a group of hostile-looking young men approach. They will never know the fury of angry voices shouting at them that their love is not "real," or that it is "filth," "an abomination," "a sickness." To them, all those billboards and TV commercials and films and popular songs extolling "love," illustrating the "correct" kind of intimacy—same-race, same-class, opposite gender couples, and invariably (although not always) young faces—will be above question; for that, you know, is what the world, the world that they know and you know, the same one that formed us all and continues to preside absolutely over too many of our imaginations, *wishes to see.* And then you marvel once more at the fact that, for every particle of ire you have choked within yourself over their smooth disregard for the unparalleled human rights they enjoy—human rights they rarely, if ever, view in such a context—you have never, until now, confronted them with your feelings. You have never told them how it makes you feel when, thinking nothing of it, she refers to him as "Honey," he to her as "Sweetie," but both of them swiftly close their faces and cringe when you do the same, in their presence, with him. You have not yet told them how stallions' hooves have viciously kicked at your temples every time you heard the spittle in a passing woman's comment: "Oh, is he into men? What a waste"; every time you heard another woman's angry lament that "all 'our' black men are either in jail, dead, on drugs, or gay" (and hopefully this last time you heard the word "gay," not "faggots"). You have never discussed the disgust and contempt you felt when—in a locker room, in some other unrelievedly macho space—you were privy, *again*, to a round of boors braying about how *hot* she was last night, fucking Christ, did you see her tits in that blouse, Jesus, and what a pair of legs on her, and that ass, man, did you *see*? Even as you were repulsed by their heavy-testosterone straightstudman talk (which bore an alarming resemblance to some forms of gaystudman talk), you couldn't help but grimace at what you knew would be their absolute repugnance were you even to mention in their presence how lovely his bikini-shorted buttocks had appeared to you the week before, how his hands had moved over you through the dappling of that afternoon and *well now but then how utterly wild you became, a fully-grown man, when the bending evidence of his desire all at once about-faced and saluted his bellybutton that way merely because you had, once again you had* . . . of course. You see once more their eyes closing down as, your face already returned to the thick-misted forests of that private time, you ascend off the ground in a memory of what exactly he whispered into your neck last night as you held him and he told you (of course). You envision their arms tightly folded across their chests, fit to demolish their hearts, as you speak of feeling married to this particular man. You remember the feeling, and yearn so much to share more with them, but will they welcome it? Will they beckon you with a "Please do" and a Come, tell us how you live?

Some will, of course, and some won't. Most so far haven't. Most—even those who have fancied themselves "liberal," "modern," and "broad-minded"—have, until now, tossed you and other queers off with a simple "Umff" of disinterest, or the lackluster

"Oh, really? Huh" wholly devoid of ingenuous, generous engagement. They might have been sophisticated enough not to pitch the old "But why must you talk about it—" (And what exactly is the "it"?) "—and be so blatant?"—but, well, small cheers for that underwhelming achievement. How could you explain to them, in a way they would finally understand, that—as only one example of a prevailing "master" hetero societal script—a woman's pregnancy is and always will be, irrespective of her actual sexual and romantic interests, a public and widely accepted confirmation that sex, actual *sex,* occurred between a man and a woman? How could you make clear to them that even if a woman prefers the companionship of other women, her visible pregnancy will automatically "heterosexualize" her to those who know nothing, or wish to dissemble that they know nothing, of her personal life? How could you make definitively evident to them that, along the way, such a woman will without doubt encounter all too many people only too willing to "forget," in the face of the pregnancy that has "heterosexualized" her, that she is in fact a woman who prefers her own form of same-gender intimacy? How could you make them understand all these points and more, even as you labored to make them apprehend that the sort of sex they take so much for granted—"normative," opposite-gender sex—is precisely the sort of which society in large part (at least in the public legislating sphere) approves, albeit much more so within the confines of heterosexual, preferably monogamous, marriage? As citizens of the world of generally sanctioned, even championed, sex, they would care to hear little or nothing of your transgressive wish—a wish you have heard other men express when speaking about the men they cared for—that he could get you pregnant, or you him. For what would it be like, you have often wondered, to carry his child? To have received him in that way; to have felt, after the shudder and the gasp and the melding of his various parts with yours, his body-hot fluids racing through your insides and on to the places where a child-creature would be formed, held, fed, and protected; the places your man's body did not possess, would never possess. What would it be like to feel his child-thing growing within you, as you watched yours grow in him? To see and touch and kiss his belly ballooning over the months? To gaze, close up, at his nipples swelling, increasingly sensitive, as nausea and the violent need to retch roused him from bed early each morning? To feel the intensifying kicks of that sightless foal that, at the nine-month road's end and another road's beginning, would charge whinnying into the world, causing you, as the first sign of that small head emerged from you, to throw back your head and part your legs, as women have done for millennia, with a scream. . . . But no, you certainly cannot confide such a pondering to them—not to those heterosexual friends, no matter how friendly, to your face, they appear. They would laugh you out of court, and maybe even (but you should be so lucky!) revile you as a pornographer. But then you know also that few homo men would care to hear such a wondering either, ashamed as so many have been and continue to be of their own private parts, and most especially of their private parts that, so effectively, receive, and grip, and hold.

Amazingly, in spite of everything, you will care for these people nonetheless—these couples of the no-problem public kissings and embracings; these people of the proud pregnancies and the wildly celebrated, rice-strewn marriages. Caring for them will always be far better than hating them. You could never truly hate them anyway, having spent as much close time as you have together—and there has been close time. Resentment is easier. It will permit you, in your meaner, smaller moments from time to time, the self-indulgence of cathartic vindictiveness, even self-righteousness. (You hope that none of the foregoing will lead to permanent bitterness.) Resentment of their myopia and smugness; resentment that they would never consider probing more deeply into what it was like for so many who, through tears, stenches and vomitings, ruined bladders and wastings, nursed those who finally didn't survive the epidemic that still rages. The people of the proud pregnancies and approved public kissings will never, for the most part, have any idea what all that was like and still is like. They will find the idea of so many funerals horrifying; unimaginable. With their best goodwill summoned for you, if not for other queers, they will hope that someone finds a cure for this awful disease soon (they will actually term it an "awful" disease), for what a monstrousness that it has taken the lives of so many young people, they will murmur . . . so many women, they will reflect, and so many innocent children. (And no, you will not—not yet, not today—challenge them on their use of the word "innocent," with its implication that some who were afflicted and died were "guilty," and thus deserving of death.)

Years later, you will remember their children: the ones who grew out of tadpole stages while you watched; who laughed, irritated, gurgled, wet, sulked, waddled, snuffled, and did all the other innumerable things, amusing and exasperating, that children do. You will recall how more than a few of the parents—the ones who, finally, couldn't have cared for you that much—never trusted you or anyone closely associated with you to dandle the young one on your lap; to rub away, with oil, an invasion of diaper rash, rock away a threatening storm of tears, or read a bedtime story, in near darkness, about a family of seven ice-skating bears—how clumsy they all were, the story would have read, and how the mama bear's belly jiggled when she fell on the ice! They certainly never trusted you to babysit. *Because, well, you never know,* they might have whispered in darkened bedrooms but would never have said to you, *Why take the chance? Because really, we do love him, we love all of them, but, well.* And yes, well . . . although such conversations might not ever have taken place. They would not have needed to. For such prejudice is deep-rooted and ancient enough to be instantly understood—communicated keenly enough by way of the simplest of glances, the merest shadow-look that supersedes and presciently, effectively supplants the dehumanizing word. And so it would remain for years between you, perhaps: unspoken but understood regarding which of their friends were called on to care for the little ones when they were away, and which were not.

But then who are these people, finally? Who have they been all along? But they are anyone, of course: those whom, in a few cases, you have most loved and adored; those whose counsel and wisdom pulled you back often and gently enough from savage mistakes and stupidity. Your teachers, mentors, advisers; the warm-eyed man with the big laugh whose ear you long bent to discuss professional matters, but little else (and who, you noticed, every now and then exercised his penchant for homophobic jokes); the crinkly fingered woman who laughed at your off-color sallies; your parents; your other relatives; your parents' friends, all of whom had always appeared to like you in spite of *that* (and who felt relieved, and demonstrated the relief, when you didn't talk about *it*); colleagues past and present; and, of course, those whom you cannot describe too precisely in this essay, for they would wonder, Has he always felt this way? But why didn't he ever tell us? Did we really behave that way toward him? Toward *them*? Were we—? They would stumble through those uneasy woods and nick their exposed fingers on the many briars. But you are not yet ready, for too many labyrinthine reasons of your own, to reveal yourself so fearlessly—unabashedly—to them. You are not yet ready to risk so much, and watch them stumble as you learn, finally, what standing taller than ever, well beyond them, feels like. All of them and more. . . . For even now your most painful dreams re-etch their faces clearly for you; their faces and, in other dreams, their voices, muffled beneath the most unyielding water, along with all the things neither you nor they have ever said, nor dared to say.

By and by the months pass, curl into years, and yawn into the enormities of whole decades; entire lives. Moons wax and fade, seas roil, and gazelles graze and vault over their shrinking terrain, as determined vermin and autocrats alike stalk and plunder the continents. Forests continue their primordial complaints throughout every cycle of the earth's growing older to warmer, larger to woefully small, as more weddings and pregnancies loom, hair thins from scalp to scalp, and waists thicken everywhere. By now it is possible that you and he, or another he, have held each other across the yawning years. Perhaps, by now, your life has filled up with so much, in so many ways, that they, with their not-wanting-to-know eyebrows, no longer matter to you. The rage that you nursed against them might, by now, have cooled into something else—something neither altogether friendly nor necessarily to be feared. Still, when you run across them—and you do, the years have not effaced that probability—it is entirely likely that you eschew openness with them. This withholding might have become a habit induced in part by their rejections; or it may linger as some vestige of your own difficult shame, or something else entirely, still unnamed. The years taught you well how to absent from their lives (and not only from their lives) those most You parts of yourself. You became, with them (but hopefully not with others) one of those players supremely adept at compartmentalizing his A (what must never be welcomed) from his B and C (what fights to prevail). And so with some sadness, a little time-tempered anger, you realize that you, too, share some of the weight for this distance . . . for truths never entirely disclosed.

It is still possible that it all will end differently. Possible that trust and love between you, in spite of everything, will somehow emerge. How, you are not entirely sure; nor are you completely certain, in this moment, that you care. For the while, you are content to revel in a morning of sun and dust motes. In a bedroom, on the uppermost floor of a house somewhere, far from any town or city; many living things outside and all around flexing and shouting out their names in deep green, as the air fairly groans beneath its weight of summer, redolent heat, and the lively snaps and whistles of the reawakened natural world. You remark how the motes flaunt their freedom in the rays that slant without fail each early morning through the nearer bedroom window, as you push yourself more immediately into him—whichever him he will by this time have become—and smell, squeeze, nuzzle. Your belly presses into his back; he sleep-smiles upon feeling your knuckles' hitchhike across his broad plains. You both are happy enough holding and being held in this way for all these minutes that will stretch into an hour, or two, or four. You are pleased when you remember the orange juice that awaits you in the refrigerator downstairs, and the coffee, and the delicate, smoothly folded rolls. When a photograph comes into your mind—one once kept on your dresser, lovingly nestled between cherished leavings of the dead and souvenirs of the sea—it is enough for you to murmur, No. Not now. Perhaps not ever. Enough for you to disremember the young, happy, smiling couple in the picture, and their laughter as, beneath tossed flowers, you also laughed and begged them to hold still, please! while you focused the lens and they kissed, through which act (although they might not have known so at the time) they became more of themselves, and more still. For now, holding him and drinking in the sun's outrageous flirting with the day, it is gratifying indeed to dismiss them and a few others like them from memory: she grown more dusty now, ample about the hips, and he slumped everyplace except in his body. Over the years, they have become more part of that other world—that world of which, at least as part of their company, you have become less and less a part, as you have insisted on talking more about him and yourself; on showing and sharing him and yourself; on taking pleasure in the company of others who have had similar tales to relate about past disharmonies, and who too have moved on. Whatever else might happen, you know that for just these hours that will shortly transpose themselves to something else yet again, this quiet joy that you feel—over the day, the tawny flirtatious sun, the feeling of your knuckles across his plains, and his breath, now and then, just beneath your neck—can be enough. Enough to vanquish memories of censorious eyelids, apoplectic ahems, twitching *Please don't bring* it *up* brows and fearful hands safeguarding children. Enough to carry you back to the hours of yesterday and last week that will shortly become the minutes of this unfolding time, when you will once more look at him as you did before . . . as you always have before. When he will return your gaze. When neither of you will need to ask the question to which you both know and have long known the answer, the answer you have already told each other so many times without needing to say it, that, once more, moves right there, without words. And moves again. And settles. And yes.

2003

Panic, Despair:
When the Words Do Not Come
(But Then an Unexpected Journey)

AND WHEN THEY DO NOT COME, AN AWFUL OCCURRENCE that has happened before and will—yes, rest assured—happen again, you do panic, of course. You freeze; slump; retreat into the secrecy and banality of masks, "ordinary" greetings, and pleasantries not at all pleasant, strangely illumined by that smile produced so automatically if not quite easily—that smile, acid-tinged just beneath the surface, which leads, with others, to the dissembling banalities of "How are you?" and "Sure, I'm fine, how are you?" and "How's the writing going?"—the worst possible question in those times when the words will not come—and the forced untruth (yes, forced, for one must always save face, mustn't one?—save face especially with those whom one dislikes, who make one nervous; save face with those who, lantern-jawed, lizard-eyed, and sometimes even somewhat reptilian in the face, are positively predatory in their wanting to know *But what are you writing* now? *What are you thinking about* now?): *Oh, it's going . . . wonderfully, thanks! Got to run! Take care!*

But then stop. Stop right here, now, in the most silent minutes of the silent passing hours, and admit it. Admit that, on the without-words mornings that invariably come, you wish *not at all* to raise your head from the pillow; not ever to take your face out of that blessed, caressing cotton, nor to remove it in any way from beneath the blanket's protective layer. *A kind of womb,* you think, loving it—and no, it isn't hyperbole; for here is the womb once more, after a fashion—a desperate one; here is, somewhat, the nearly next best retreat, withdrawal. Here, your face urgently pressing down into the pillow, is oblivion, forgetfulness. Here is ignorance, utter solitude. *So that I might remain here all day,* you think, *and perhaps even all night*—so you hope, as if reaching to strike a bargain with the god in which you were, O yes, without question, raised so unrelentingly to believe. *And then,* the ghost-fugitive you are slowly on your way to becoming thinks, *let me stay here the day after that and for all the days after that, on and on, on and (yes, of course) never ending . . . just that,* you beg, as only the most desperate can beg. *For now* (and here, more completely, is the voice of the ghost you are now more rapidly on your way to becoming), *now I cannot rise. And so, unrising, I possess absolutely no wish whatsoever to view the outer world. No, nor anyone, any thing, any person, nor any bird, tree, flower, living creature, or rock; for here, stupid though it may seem, self-indulgent and craven and jejune though it may seem, I am, I am . . . I am in this moment utterly incapacitated, joyless and inert. Robbed completely of vigor. And so here I will remain, yes, for as long as the words do not, will not, come: the words I so adore (yes! I* love *them; the words without which life itself is—well, what?* What?*); the words which are the complete joy of books yet to be written, ensconced more reliably in dreams, and the joys and sorrows of those books here still among us; the words of this mind or another, of many minds; the words of so many hearts scattered and sundered throughout the ages (yes, reenvisioning the many who died for love, for example, and the (but who can count how many?) who killed for it; the uncountable number who died worshiping beauty, for instance, and all those who died cursing it); the words of courage and fortitude (of heroes and saints, martyrs and idiots), and the words of love—something in which I do still believe, yes, I will never deny it—and, as always, the words of hope, of poetry, of Give us this day, dear Lord, and Yes, I do love you. I always will—*

I always will. As so happen again the times, as will always reoccur the times, when words, pure language, become love itself.

Love, that always strange yet always completely familiar thing of which we in this world seem, despite our protestations and pretending at indifference, beyond it-ness, above-it-all-ness, to need so much. Words, imagined in the realm of greatest yearning, as a means of finding love, defining it; as a means of shaping it (This is how it feels, this is where it hurts) and sharing with others its permutations, astonishments, exaltations, and erosions. In that regard and others, an act of faith, then, to write; to employ words in pursuit of the belief that one does indeed actually *believe* in something—in love, in the frequent surprising possibilities of other people—as one moves toward the redemptive power inherent in the communal act of revelation: toward the daring, vulnerability, of I have written this, will you read it? I have risked my soul in this, might you caress it? I have felt this, might you too feel it? I have seen this, or thought I saw it—felt it, smelled it, dreamed it—and so would you too care to see it, to smell it, to dream? To dream with me, alongside me, within me? But then perhaps you have already seen it, and it was through your telling me what it looked like and how you saw it that I, somehow, imagined it for myself. Imagined the beauty you tasted, the sadness you swallowed, and the lonesomeness nudging there, just right there, beneath the flesh. I imagined, we did, and it did not quite matter then who we were, did it? In the imagining we might have been any color, any persuasion or inclination. You might have been as fond of swimming nude with orange jellyfish at noon as I was of dolphins' prods, then their pushes and pokes, beneath my bare hidden parts, beneath every wave that licked and buoyed us, buoyed us! An act of faith, of joy and life itself—and so how dim, how very gray and thin the wordlover becomes when the words simply do not come.

Thin, yes; for imagine yourself now sloshing through a world in which beauty and death and glory and suffering and all manner of utterly unpredictable, wonderful things are there, *there*—yet you cannot describe them, for the words are not. Now, sloshing in wordlessness up to your hips (it will soon engulf you completely), how will you record, with truest faith, the expression on the face of that girl, that one, who has just witnessed her father's incineration? (*Yes, we are sorry to inform you,* some voices say, *his car was bombed today.*) How to describe, when the words hold back so doggedly, the plight of those refugees forced to flee their upland homes yet again after still another invasion? The surviving women are old, the surviving children are exhausted, and the men, as always, will either be murdered or pitched into killing cells . . . today it will be Cypriots overtaken by Turks, but tomorrow. . . . How will you say, precisely, "These particular people"—whoever they are—"are arrogant, ignorant"—perhaps referring to those of your own country, or to those of another now joyfully making war—and then show, through metaphor, allegory, through meticulously constructed illustration, how those in question have for the longest time behaved exactly that way, just that insufferably, wrongheadedly, as warmongers, triumphalists—how will you make us know and understand the precise thing when the words, the vital words, have for all these parched weeks languished so far out of sight over *there,* way across the water, in a reserve camp, in the most unknowable place of untelling?

For certain, life does become hollow without them. Hollower. For it is always possible, though never terribly easy, to live without the more conventional forms of love; without kisses, embraces, caresses, intonings, and the *Yes, of course I do*s of intimacy. One can live (though more thinly) without all *that.* It is actually possible to manage—somehow—without arms entwined about the back (your back, mine) and the certain feeling that one really is cared for, deeply. Loneliness is never easy but is fairly inevitable—for, as you learned long ago and will continue to learn as the years pass, "everyone" does not finally find "someone." Solitude often is simply the way things *are,* not necessarily as one would wish them to be. Yet it is far more difficult to live without the words, and perhaps especially without those one has always wished one had written: words like *Innisfree,* like *Wessex*; like *Many years later, as he faced the firing squad,* like *124 was spiteful*; like *So this is where people* *come to live; I would have thought it is a city to die in,* and *Barrabás came to us by sea,* the child Clara wrote in her delicate calligraphy, and *We are talking now of summer evenings in Knoxville, Tennessee during that time I lived there so successfully disguised to myself as a child.* Words like *For I can sooner get used to never hearing from him—the perfect reader—than to not being able to write for him at all.* These words, these and more, harvested from that last invincible province, the imagination, as, with beauty, nuance, poetry, they reinvent—reconfigure—the world that is, finally, this one; this world which will not—no, not ever—cease changing.

Life on this particular evening (late winter; the sky outside in this northern place, far from the beloved Caribbean, dull, gray, and already steel-sheeted, closed for the day, at ten minutes to five; the hours here, devoid of companionship, wretchedly lonely, though warmed somewhat by lamps whose golden glows, like those of a few candles, soften the room, this room, this office in which work with words often, with luck and sheer abandon, leads to dreams) is nearly completely bleak, but cannot—will not—remain so forever. Not when, well beyond the lamp-warmed windows of this room, out there, across the water, over there, in that ancient city, so many people are being killed; decimated. They did not ask for that. They did not ask to be plundered, nor, certainly, did they demand rescue. They did not ask to be firebombed. Now, today or just yesterday, more news comes of still more suicide bombers there; news of their own young men and women, though mostly men, so enraged because the occupiers continue, brazenly, to despoil, will not leave. News arrives of those body parts that continue to litter the ancient city's narrow streets, and of those suspected of whatever today's charge will be rounded up for the nearest internment camp: the ire of the entire world feeding on itself, devouring itself yet again. To see it all clearly, even (especially) from a room made safer by candles and lamps, one must begin with the less (literally) explosive things, such as the woman all at once visible (though she was always there, she has long been there)—that woman, sitting again in that half-darkened room;

sitting, perhaps sewing this time, or mending a basket, or stitching up a piece of frayed clothing (fabric is more expensive than ever these days, in times of embargo or war or dictatorship or all three). Or wait—she is applying her steady fingers to piecing back together a recently shattered ceramic dish—a dish for reasons known only to her most important to her, one she absolutely must save. Regarding her face—those lines, and even the small intersecting scars, about five or six of them, beneath her left eye, curving down to her mouth—it is easy to see that she knows without question the great pain, the actual sundering pain, of giving birth to children without benefit of anesthesia. She has in truth produced many children—at least seven, maybe as many even as ten. She might or might not consider herself "blessed" in any number of ways various religions interpret the word; today, on what has already become another shimmering afternoon, busy at her work, she knows, in this violent time, that she is glad to be alive. No longer young, yet not elderly either, and utterly contemptuous of sentimentality, she will be happy, or at least pleased, each day that she continues to find herself alive. A few of her children—those who have either decided to remain in the war-stressed nation or stayed because they had no choice—ensure to the best of their ability that she always has just enough food; that she is never anywhere close to starving. She has anyway never been what some would term a "large" eater—a good thing, surely, in a land long familiar with famines and outstretched hands.

Yet what will happen to the quick quietness of her fingers, that nimbleness, and the shape of her lowered head against the darkened wall behind her, when she discovers later today that her eldest son, barely twenty-two, died this afternoon—indeed, will die only an hour or so from now when his suicide bomb detonates in the city bus he will purposefully hail and enter, taking seventeen other people with him? What colors will her eyes make, exactly, and how will her eyelids, suddenly shuttered, make sense out of it all? Will they make sense of it? Make sense of her rapidly increased heartbeat and shortened breath? Make sense when she tries to imagine/refuses to imagine which of his splattered parts she would quietly have picked up first, had she been there, and placed *very* carefully—yes, like that—into the straw shopping bag she always carries when she walks into the city. Would it have been, at first, what had remained of his right hand? (But to find the stomach to gather together all his fingers . . . the same stomach that would have hurled toward her parched throat the force of all that vomit.) Or that—that *thing* that was so clearly what had been left behind of his left shoulder? That bit of skin from just above one of his knees—the flesh that had bubbled and discolored years ago, preceded by his toddler's screams, when the raging man who had passed closely enough for his father, now long gone, had hurled boiling water on him.

Would she have looked for the hair that had always insisted more thickly on the right side of his scalp? Would she have gazed absently toward where his big toe—left foot, right?—should have been? The one he had broken twice in some school game so many years ago? But it is still early afternoon, and the bomb he carries strapped so securely beneath his innocuous-looking outer clothes has not yet exploded. Indeed, right now she is almost not even thinking of him as he actually is right at this minute, standing as he does right now quite far from her and that neighborhood where, with great difficulty, she raised all her children. He is standing out in the sunshine in a public square in the western corner of the city, chatting casually enough, if soberly, with an acquaintance who, in a country of remorselessly politicized people and families, towns, neighborhoods, and districts, is unusually not in any way (or so he says publicly) political. The acquaintance, a student of architectural technology at the local secular university, briefly notices the creeping lines of weariness and—tension, is it, or . . . ?—in the young man's otherwise handsome face; a face more handsome than ever today, the acquaintance notices, in the sun's just-after-midday glow. Later, after the tragedy and its stench of human flesh permeates the city's shocked air, he will not tell the news reporters who serendipitously intercept him that anything had seemed "out of the ordinary" that afternoon in the young man's manner. Although he will not know it when the reporters fire their questions at him, it will be his own skin's cold pricklings that will produce in him before their cameras and microphones an invincible amnesia regarding all those details about the young man's actual demeanor, appearance: *Did you notice what he was wearing? Could you discern any type of explosive device attached to his person? Had he ever confided in you about affiliation with any special group? Yes, exactly, as in a fanatical organization? Did he speak to or acknowledge anyone else during the time you claim you spoke with him?* That same amnesia, the literal freezing of his mind (awful, when the words do not come), will not save him from the more forceful questioning of "special investigators" who will "escort" him to that secret place about which he had never had any idea (in that country, their country!—but, as he had always said publicly, he had never been political). In the secret place, where he will spend days and nights, his amnesia will in fact quicken their snarls and punches, and even their kicks, and when they break his jaw and then one, two, then three of his ribs—*These cocksuckers are all terrorists, of course he knows something*—he will scream, cry, and think of his mother and family and the beautiful university campus where he had studied architectural technology and where he had never, he had always insisted, been political. And whether or not he makes it out of the secret place, away from them and their punches and kicks (and later, even their electric shocks, and at night, the threat of being raped by two of them: stiffened flesh used by one, blunt instruments by the other), well, no one can know—who can possibly say? Who can say, if he survives their questioning, whether or not he will ultimately have to flee the country, branded as he will be from the moment of their taking him away as a possible terrorist, collaborator, fearsome renegade? In some places amnesty is hard to come by, exoneration rare. The process he will have endured and possibly survived, or not, will be the one known as "rigorous" questioning. In so many secret places like that one, places of truncheons and thick fists in gloves, the words had *better* come before the broken jaw and ruptured spleen. Before breaking open the cocksucker's face if he doesn't talk.

The woman in the darkened room (dark in the heat of the day, cool in the waning heat of the later day) is not, just now, as she works so quietly, so steadily, thinking of her son, who will soon be so explosively dead. She will not think later—no, and not for days to come—of the mostly completely scorched, nearly unidentifiable parts of the seventeen others he will soon take with him. (Included among them, two very young children, one of whom would have been forced into prostitution had she reached, in three years, the age of ten; a pregnant woman who, had she not boarded that bus, would have lived to miscarry painfully in her fourth month; and a toothless old man, regularly besmirched by incontinence, who fifty-two years earlier had fled a neighboring nation's cataclysmic ethnic wars, his already wavering wife beside him.) Nor does she think of the acquaintance to whom her son now distractedly, even restively, is speaking. As her hands move so rapidly (a glint of sun in the room reveals that she has moved on to sewing), she thinks now absently, now with a burst of longing which surprises and almost embarrasses her in its unchecked and, to her, rather unseemly passion, of the turquoise and red colors of a fish washed up on the beach last week—that same beach where, though old land mines from the last civil war still skulked beneath the sand only a few miles down the shore, she had walked that week-ago morning in search of the looming day's sea mist and the pleasure of its gentle sting in her nostrils; the morning she had waved while walking to a few of the wizened-faced fishing men and women whose faces she had recognized—waved to this one, that one, *Good morning.*

(And yes, she had thought that day, there were so many more new people, more refugees, in the area now; more people flee-ing disastrous [to say the least] conditions in the neighboring countries now. But then flight and the viciousness that caused it had been going on for more than a thousand years, two thousand years; what sort of improved conditions the fugitives believed they would find in this country remained a mystery to her. One thing they most definitely did know was that without too much argument from the presiding local fishing elders, they could do peacefully here what they had done in their homeland—fish—before tyranny's artillery had struck and choked their once primordially clean waters with corpses.)

The fish upon which she had so suddenly come—the turquoise and red one—had moved her to a point she would never have considered it possible, had she ever seriously reflected on it, to be moved, reached by something so—was *earthy* the word? Something so regular, so everyday, even ridiculous, as a fish. (Ridiculous, yes—well, because fish were slightly ridiculous, weren't they? Ridiculous, with those constantly staring, bug-eyed expressions? With those downturned mouths as if all in their world were somehow beyond redemption? Ridiculous in those wobbly, side-to-side movements they made—why move through the world that way, why not find some other way to move, like jellyfish, pulsating, or marlins, arcing and leaping? Why not move like the gorgeous winged rays so fond of the sand-thick water farther up the shore—the rays, so powerful, so sleek, fins undulating?) The fish, clearly having washed up on the shore only moments before and still panting, sides heaving in the last throes of panting distress, had moved her in its complete, pathetic helplessness, haplessness, and in its iridescent beauty gleaming, in the steadily advancing light, off all those scales. Its helplessness and forlornness had chilled her: nothing, she had thought with a brisk shudder, should ever be that helpless; not a child, nor a man either—and certainly not, God help her, any woman. The fish's helplessness had appeared to her a state, she knew now, that could induce in one cruelty, outrage, or (and it was this last that had in fact embarrassed her and embarrassed her now, but only because she had feared and feared still others discovering it in her) deepest compassion—fellow feeling with another creature, even with one not remotely near one's own species, that could sting one to tears of both sorrow and helplessness: there had been nothing for her hands to do to help the creature, what could she possibly have done? In those moments, gazing down in utter silence and absorption at the twitching, gasping form, she had understood that she could indeed do nothing at all: no salvation, intervention, heroism or cure, *for death, here is death,* the fish might have whispered to her and her alone, *death turquoise colored and red and quite literally before you, staring up at you: death, and all that you can do, all that you can dream, is to let me wither before you in the greatest pain imaginable, which from my dying moment onward will also become yours—yes, will forever live within you and haunt you long after I am no more.* Though no fisherwoman ever in her life—O no, far from it—she had ascertained intuitively on first glance at the creature that it was not one for eating; the brightness of the markings, perhaps, had told her so, if not the strangeness of its appearance. She was quite sure now and had been certain then, hadn't she, that she had never before seen such a fish, never before imagined one of its kind. "Sadness" was not enough of a word to describe how she had felt, standing there slightly hunched over in the gathering light, watching the thing slowly expire, gasping so uselessly for breath. It had lain not at all far from the waves, its small gleaming sides slightly heaving, and the gills maybe fluttering or whatever it was that fish did when gasping for air and all at once aware that they, even they, such lowly beings, were rapidly, inexorably unbecoming as, helplessly, before the advance of hours, they reached—generally far beyond the sight of humans—for their dying breaths. *And it is looking,* she had thought. Yes, she had thought that, hadn't she? *The fish. As it dies. Dies in front of me. It is looking at me.* She might have been half-tempted just then to kick it back into the sea; a few sure kicks would surely have landed it back among the churlish waves. But as touching it in any way, putting her hand on it, feeling its moist, clammy, living, respiring, panting *gleaming* solidness beneath her fingers would have been, to her, undeniably out of the question—she, war-, invasion-, and hunger-toughened village woman as she was and had been most of her life would have screamed, she thought, had she dared to touch the thing, those eyes still regarding her so gravely, not at all stoically—she had also feared that she might damage it if she attempted to move it. (A kick, of course, would certainly damage it.) And then also wouldn't the fishing people, the men especially, passing by there and here and armed with nets, hooks, with lines and all the complicated, invariably rusted, briny things common to their trade, laughing and stamping barefooted on the tide-compacted sand and growling as they spat into the sea or spat orders at their sons, baring their enormous hairy bellies with absolutely no shame, no self-consciousness, nothing, just in the way that men like that, men in general (except, she hoped, she thought, her sons, all her gorgeous sons, and especially the eldest), went all about the world as if the world were entirely theirs and theirs alone—men who belched loudly in public and broke wind whenever and wherever they wished with no care at all, who even laughed out loud about such things with their friends—wouldn't they, those men, laugh at her? Laugh at her who, though like them a war-, invasion-, and hunger-toughened village denizen, was still a woman who was not and never had been one of their raucous, hard-bitten kind?—a fisherwoman? Wouldn't they laugh at her on that early morning, out for an uncharacteristic walk among them? (Although none of them could know quite how uncharacteristic it was, not quite knowing her and minding their "own business" as they always seemed to do—though who truly did that in villages such as the one in which she lived, especially one so often so vulnerable to the cruelties of the latest enemy?—and "uncharacteristic," well, yes, it was, that early morning venture, but in truth, in one of her most secret places, she had always loved the sea, adored it—yes, she always had!) Wouldn't they, big-bellied, grizzled, enamored of spitting, enamored of the rude outbursts of their own public flatulence, laugh at her? Laugh at her, a woman of her age, no longer nearly attractive, slightly bent-backed, given to varicose veins and plainly sagging breasts, concentrating her pity and compassion on a—on a *fish?* The gales of it, the laughter, as she was certain it would come, rocketed in her ears, rocketed and ricocheted, reminding her of something else . . . what, exactly? Of the man she had not been able to marry? Or, more precisely, truthfully, the man who had not in any way wished to marry her: that man who, while every now and then dealing her brutal blows across the face, had years ago, his heavy body twisting above her silent one, ground into her what had eventually become all those children. All those children, before, in one of his rages, taking his screams and fists with him, he had finally disappeared one morning. One morning, she thought, and then gone forever . . . picking up speed in her walk and leaving behind, perhaps for all time, that still-breathing fish which she had been so certain, in those moments of her curiosity and compassion, had been watching her. *Looking* at her, she thought, walking faster, *as if to*

Life is not quite so hollow now—not right now. In truth, of course, it never was, quite. It was partially unseen. As she walks ever faster, it is possible, and even easier now, to see—imagine— her face in the darkness of that room to which she will soon return, and where, on another day—the one that has become this one, right now—she will sit and (but for the near future hours of her son's funeral) sit for some time. It is easier now, after having watched her on the beach, to imagine her hands busy at work; to hear her mind occasionally moving with the longing only she can know and the wonder she still feels (though carefully, gingerly) over the sad beauty, and so much more, of a destroyed fish. Seeing her this way is easier to take—for who will she become, later, in only a few hours, when she learns of her son's death and the deaths of the seventeen he will have taken with him?

(The bus in which his bomb will explode—in which his fingers, swiftly, will reach down for that part of the device, and press, or pull—though blasted into shrapnel with most of its windows blown out, will, by early next year, after extensive and meticulous repairs, find itself, to its own tottering surprise, back on the roads—on those same dusty, narrow roads thickened each morning and each night with beggars, cripples, one-legged whores, and mine-disfigured children. And, well, some voices will say, resources are scarce, and bombs . . . if we let ourselves go under for every bomb that exploded here every year—every month—we'd never leave our homes again, would we?—so one public transport official will later be unofficially quoted. The driver actually in charge of the targeted bus that afternoon—the driver who, miraculously, along with six others, will survive—will, two weeks after the disaster, permanently retire at the age of fifty-seven years, and die, four months later, of an aortic aneurysm brought on, several close to him will bitterly attest, by extreme untreated trauma and stress.)

But she is there still. In the quickening dark which, here, always follows the blazing afternoons. Quiet now, as she usually is. Quiet as she will be when (although three of her children will be standing in the room with her) the grave, stiff-backed policemen arrive in her doorway this evening—one of them so young still, she will think with deep sorrow for him as she wonderingly meets his edgy gaze: *so smooth his skin still,* she will think, *but what must it be like for his parents, having their son work in such a dangerous occupation?* She will have some idea, gazing down at his hands, that he and his older colleague have brought her some terrible news. She will immediately know, one of her younger children pressing into her side, that it will be best not to look at either of them. She will look at both of them—look steadily, having no idea even then how much both of the officers will be inwardly quailing before what they are certain will be the unbearable outburst of her grief: that grief, the same one they have seen too many times before: the falling-down, screaming, shoulder-grabbing kind. The one that so swiftly transforms hands to claws and rolls the eyes back in the head. The one that falls down prostrate on the sacred steps of temples, begging (but screaming) for light, air. Mercy. Begging whichever deity to Make It Not True, to Reverse the Past Two Minutes, to Let Me Incinerate Myself in the Bomb instead of Him. Let me submit to rape in the torture cells instead of

my daughter, allow me to feel the lighted cigarettes pushed into
my testicles instead of my father, let me beg for amnesty even if
they all laugh and force me right there in their headquarters to
take it up the ass without any preparation, let me become the
one who dies again and again in fire, in ice, beneath the shining
naked light bulb, instead of, instead of. Please. As sons and lovers
themselves, they know, these two officers, this country's women
and mothers, men and fathers, sisters, brothers, grandparents:
those who, in varying shadowed hours, are the people of the dusty
body bags and the ruins still walking, held together somehow at
the spine, returned from rigorous questioning.

Soon, the officers standing before her, not quite looking at her
and certainly not daring to look at her as she cannot yet dare to
look at her other children (who, after hearing the news about their
brother, will neither want nor be able to meet her eyes yet—no,
not just yet), the younger officer for whose still-smooth face she
feels such compassion will tell her that she will now have to ac-
company them. Yes, right now, please. No, you alone, please, none
of the young ones. He will recall later that immediately after
his words there had arisen some sort of noise, a brief outcry from
one of the younger sons—but that officer, like his colleague, will
mostly remember her silence. How she walked between them, he
will prefer not to recall. His older colleague will remember (but
against his will) how still she was, as if already resigned to her own
death, even though her son who had destroyed others and himslf
with his bomb was not her only child. The officers and the others
who encounter her later that evening beneath the stark light of a
dangling electric bulb will remember her: those small, odd scars
just beneath her left eye, and the peculiar movement, near her
knees and on her lap, of her hands. Will any of them know how
very hard she had tried, if only for a moment, to rush herself back
to a recent early morning and the bright turquoise and red colors
of a strange fish on a beach beneath the sands of which, only a few
miles away, active land mines had continued to doze? Will any of
them, even the younger officer whose eyes she simply cannot catch

now—*Do* not *look at him,* she thinks, hardly imagining that he is thinking to the point of prayer the same thing about her—will any of them guess that in fact she now really has no choice but to think, though impossibly, of him? To recall how, even from infancy, his hair had always insisted more thickly on the right side of his scalp? How, even from an early age, he had loved to kiss his younger siblings and hold their hands, even as he had taken such delight later in ordering them about? The officers will remember her, and she, to her astonishment, will all at once awaken, as if wrested out of the weirdest sort of dream, to find herself among them, a company of strangers, in that place, seated solidly beneath the dangling electric bulb—seated and somehow *not* stroking his hair (yes, for wouldn't he have liked that? Wouldn't my son just have loved that?) or holding his face against the pain he surely would have felt upon the bomb's first searing of his flesh . . . not in her dark house and not near the sea. Just there. Among them, those many faces watching hers, and waiting. Silent, for a time.

Life, not now nearly hollow. Her life. And the words to describe, imagine, feel and then remember, not quite coming, but coming. Coming even as all those present feel all sorts of things; too many things. Too many things like *But now I have no feelings at all,* she thinks, *and no words. No words to say anything.*

Words—

And the world—*that* world, announces this day or night—is still out there. Yes, and in here.

It is difficult to feel her hands, she thinks. Difficult to believe that her hands will not touch . . . no, nor hold him again—

Now, more words—

Summoning—

Yes, and trying to tell—telling—

2004

Regarding a Black Male
Monica Lewinsky, Anal Penetration,
and Bill Clinton's Sacred White Anus

∞

BUT THEN WHY ALL THE SHOCK—MORTIFICATION—
registered so clearly on all those gaping faces? Why that deeply
stunned silence, as if all present had been completely undone by
the question I'd just asked? For in truth, I hadn't meant to shock
anyone, not even myself. I'd wanted only to posit what had struck
me on reflection as a fascinating idea—one that had electrified my
own caught-off-guard imagination. For the question, as it came
to me, had startled me, to be sure; but I'd never thought, given
the general level of evident boredom with everyday life and cynicism evinced by so many students, that they would actually have
reacted they way they did, or even necessarily reacted at all.

And so what was this great question, which, immediately after
I uttered it, seemed to stop time itself? It was simply this, posed to
the undergraduate class I was teaching that afternoon in the fall
of 2001: would the late-1990s U.S. public (and, eventually, anyone
who had access to particular media and information sources) have
witnessed such determinedly intimate reporting of White House
intern Monica Lewinsky's and then-president Bill Clinton's sexual
relationship, especially as produced so unflaggingly in *The Starr
Report*—indeed, would *The Starr Report* itself (published in 1998)
and the furor it generated even have been possible—if Lewinsky
had been not a white female, but a black male?

The accentuation in my question as I'd heard it in my own

head had fallen evenly on the words "black" and "male." A black male. Three evenly stressed syllables. Yet as I looked around the room at the students' stone-still faces, I realized that they were grappling, as I began to grapple, with the implications of different accents placed on different words:

A *black* male? A black *gay* male? A black gay *male*?

A *man*? A *black man*?

Would the United States (and the world) have witnessed such a *Starr Report* passage as the following, had Lewinsky been a black male?

> Ms. Lewinsky testified that her physical relationship with the President included oral sex but not sexual intercourse. According to Ms. Lewinsky, she performed oral sex on the President; he never performed oral sex on her. Initially, according to Ms. Lewinsky, the President would not let her perform oral sex to completion. In Ms. Lewinsky's understanding, his refusal was related to "trust and not knowing me well enough." During their last two sexual encounters, both in 1997, he did ejaculate.[1]

Below, I reproduce that passage with the female pronouns changed to male ones, and "Ms. Lewinksy" replaced with (for example) "Mr. Jacobs," to be imagined as a black male. Let us envision him as a handsome man about the same age as Lewinsky, of fine figure, in his early twenties:

> Mr. Jacobs testified that his physical relationship with the President included oral sex but not sexual intercourse. According to Mr. Jacobs, he performed oral sex on the President; the President never performed oral sex on him. Initially, according to Mr. Jacobs, the President would not let him perform oral sex to completion. In Mr. Jacobs's understanding, the President's refusal was related

to "trust and not knowing me well enough." During their last two sexual encounters, both in 1997, the President did ejaculate.

I replace "Ms. Lewinsky" with "Mr. Jacobs" in another passage of Lewinsky's testimony, from page 57 of the *Report*:

Afterward, he [Jacobs] and the President moved to the Oval Office and talked. According to Mr. Jacobs: "[The President] was chewing on a cigar. And then he had the cigar in his hand and he was kind of looking at the cigar in . . . sort of a naughty way. And so . . . I looked at the cigar and I looked at him and I said, we can do that, too, some time."

And last, a passage from page 79 of the *Report,* with Lewinsky speaking here in the first person. Imagine again here the black Mr. Jacobs:

And then I think I was touching him in his genital area through his pants, and I think I unbuttoned his shirt and was kissing his chest. And then . . . I wanted to perform oral sex on him . . . and so I did. And then . . . I think he heard something, or he heard someone in his office. So, we moved into the bathroom.

And I continued to perform oral sex and then he pushed me away, kind of as he always did before he came, and then I stood up and I said . . . I care about you so much . . . I don't understand why you won't let me . . . make you come; it's important to me.[2]

Note that, in these passages, the imagined Mr. Jacobs, positioned in place of Lewinsky, performs in a sequence of subservient roles: sexually, as the provider of oral sex (the oral sex "bottom" to the oral "top" recipient, in contemporary queer parlance); as a

White House intern, like Lewinsky, subordinate to the president in the official hierarchy; and as a black male *racially* "beneath" a white male—black maleness perceived and defined as the *racial* and *social* inferior to white maleness. Gender-wise, the male Jacobs could equal the president as a male (albeit in this instance a sexually subservient one), were Jacobs not a *black,* and hence "inferior," male. It's significant that the black male Jacobs operates somewhat differently than, but also similarly to, the white female (and demonstratedly heterosexual) Lewinsky. Taking into account pervasive, culturally ingrained images and representations of the missionary position as the "normative" heterosexual sex position, societal stereotypes about which gender supposedly "dominates" (and penetrates) which during heterosexual sex, and the centrality (or at least symbolic significance) of the penis in heterosexual and male homosexual sex, Lewinsky as a woman is a *presumably* sexually subordinate participant with the male Clinton merely by virtue of being a woman. Like Mr. Jacobs, she is subordinate in the official hierarchy as a White House intern interacting with her superior, the U.S. president; also like Jacobs, she is subordinate as the oral sex "bottom" whose penis-penetrated mouth provides the dominant "top" president with pre-ejaculatory pleasure; yet, as a white person, she is what Mr. Jacobs, or any black person, male or female, cannot be: the *racial* equal of the white president. These specifics are extremely important, for presumptions about sexual dominance power—about who exactly might penetrate whom, or about who "should" penetrate whom—become very slippery when we regard an imagined homosexual encounter between the male president and his partner, given that either man can easily penetrate the other, orally or anally. The scenario becomes even more complicated with the entry of racial issues.

To be sure, many, if not most, of the students in the class had not at that time read any or all of *The Starr Report.* Neither had I. Like many other people, I felt as if I had read it simply by having heard so much so often about its outrageous catalog of details. Nonetheless, the students, like me, knew enough about what it contained—"naughty" details about the president's dalliance with Lewinsky—to gaze at me, after my question, with jaws actually dropped and unbelieving You-*couldn't*-have-just-asked-the-question-you-just-asked stares. Gradually becoming more aware of their facial expressions but fascinated by the question's apparently limitless discussion possibilities, I thought: But, well, this question *is* reasonable, isn't it? Reasonable even if the scenes excerpted above from the *Report* with "Mr. Jacobs" in Lewinsky's place appeared "unthinkable," as one (African American, male, heterosexual) friend later chidingly put it to me, and as another (African American, female, heterosexual) expressed it, "inconceivable"? A difficult task, perhaps (but why?) to imagine the white President Clinton and the black Mr. Jacobs placing their hands and mouths all over each other's private parts, but still worthy of sustained consideration, and—as I was beginning to learn—risky, given prevailing race-, gender-, and sexuality-focused bigotries in the United States, including the "illicit"-ness and outlawry invariably placed on—associated with—the bodies of black people in general and black males in particular, heterosexual, homosexual, or otherwise. And so imagining one Mr. Jacobs and William Jefferson Clinton engaged in oral sex did indeed begin to reveal itself as extremely important—iconoclastic—given, in our time, U.S. society's increasingly *un*avoidable intersections of sexuality and racial contexts, paradigms, codes, and metaphors. Clearly, frank consideration of the scenario would make possible compelling insights into gender, gender roles, and the interplay between those roles, ideologies, and the (sometimes) fluid hierarchies of power directly connected to U.S. popular perceptions about race, class, sex, gender, and sexuality. If, as all those dropped student jaws suggested, the idea of a black male interacting sexually, and perhaps emotionally, with the white, heterosexually married president of the United States had clearly theretofore been utterly *un*thinkable—even beyond the outlandish and ludicrous, flung farther into the realm of the fantastic—it could (and should) no longer be, as we began (even if *extremely* unwillingly on the part of some—but again, why?) to consider it.

The Starr Report itself was, and remains, a highly peculiar document, in many ways reflective of the wider U.S. public: simultaneously prurient and policing, puritanical and salacious, censorious and voyeuristic. In addition to the depositions and grand jury testimonies provided by Lewinsky and Clinton, words by supporting cast members Betty Currie (Clinton's personal secretary), Linda Tripp (an infamous friend, or ultimately "friend," of Lewinsky's), and Vernon Jordan (a friend of Clinton's), and the input of several others, including journalists, the *Report* also featured Kenneth Starr's controversial "Grounds for Impeachment" document.

The *Report*'s arresting contents considered, I returned to the idea of a black (gay, or at least same-gender sexually inclined) man in place of the white heterosexual female body of Monica Lewinsky, sexualized by Bill Clinton. A black male sexually interacting with the president's white publicly heterosexual body, perhaps penetrating the anally (and/or orally) receptive white presidential body, and receiving penetration in return. As mentioned earlier, I surprised myself with the consideration partly because, upon voicing it, I felt with great certainty that someone surely must have asked it before, directly or indirectly, in one way or another. Someone, I believed, surely must have reflected on what I would soon discover were the question's deeper resonances and provocations vis-à-vis distinct, yet potentially intersecting, quadrants of power: the "official" power granted to, and legislated by, a nation's elected and supreme governing personage, shaped by historical constructions of the U.S. president—a personage thus far white, male, Christian, and presumably incorruptibly (in Clinton's case perhaps also incorrigibly) heterosexual; the president as perceived and imagined (inter)national iconic godhead—the embodiment of an entity approaching at least kingliness, if not quite total godliness; and the more fluid, less easily discernible power dynamics present in sexual (in this case "taboo") relations between two males in a heteronormative, heterosexist society—a society still wracked by profound anxieties about interracial (sexual and other) intimacy, and assuredly anxious about, if not outrightly repelled by, male-male (sexual) intimacy. Who earlier, I wondered, had asked this Lewinsky–black man–sex with the president question and unearthed in their own excavations the many additional questions that, for me and for those students, would shortly surface?

I quickly discerned that apparently no one, even in lesbian and gay political and academic networks, had. Such silence clearly existed for reasons about which I could only guess. Faced with that silence and what I surmised to be its close cousin—the students' confounded speechlessness—I began to ponder the force and staying power of historically crafted, societally sanctioned "scripts," such as the overarching narrative of presumed (and, more often than not, required) heterosexuality for all citizens (particularly male heterosexuality, and particularly *black* and *white* male heterosexualities), and its enduring normative currency. Simultaneously I reflected on lingering U.S. anxieties over interracial desire and sex. In the United States' racially stratified society, such socially and politically transgressive desire and sex have always been—and remain— both aberrant and dangerous to the established social order; the anti-interracial order involving, and always dependent on, both tacit and de facto racial segregation. Interracial (especially black-white) desire and sex threaten at least one hierarchy of racialized power—that of whites on the social and economic "top," blacks on the social and economic "bottom." The order is easily upset—and feared by many to be so easily upset—by the possibility of black sexual "topping" or "domination"/penetration of a white body, and especially black male topping/penetration of a white male body, with even more disastrous consequences for the black male–topped theretofore *heterosexual* white male body. Suddenly, on the heels of these deliberations on the United States' anxiety-ridden popular imagination regarding matters of sexuality, gender, class, and especially race, the combination of interracial sexual desire with same-gender *male* sexual pleasure and intimacy made even more risky by the (ostensibly) unprecedented addition of the presidential body squarely in the equation's center began, before my astonished eyes, to take on dangerous overtones indeed. I interpreted some of that danger—or at least difficulty—as the U.S. popular imagination's continued ambivalence between actual *enjoyment* of "smut"[3] (as in a document like *The Starr Report,* but also vis-à-vis the widespread oral-sex jokes about Lewinsky and Clinton, as well as general pornography and all the possibilities, via the internet, of "secret"/hidden voyeurism, etc.) and the myth of "good" citizens' propriety. That ambivalence, when (inter)racially inflected, must immediately contend with the additional complexities of the United States' enduring historical and racialized realities. The ambivalence becomes even more complex with the addition of homophobia, the literal *fear* of—feeling of repulsion for—homosexuality,[4] and all that the sexualizing word "homo*sexual*" conjures in the squeamish, heterosexist imagination that continues to struggle with a trenchant Puritan-Calvinist legacy: repulsion over, yet fascination with, anal (male-male) penetration, oral sex, oral-anal contact, and, as associated with "diseased," "perverted" queer bodies (and especially with black queer bodies), the bane of AIDS and other sexually communicated diseases.[5]

True enough, all of the above. But what about the flabbergasted reaction of the people to whom I initially broached the question? Undergraduate students, mostly white, but numbering among them a few African American, Asian American, and Latino. We were on a State University of New York campus, where I was teaching that fall (2001) a course on contemporary (1985–present) African American "queer" writing, encompassing poetry, fiction, political essays, memoir, and film.[6] The question came to me after our reading an essay by Reginald Shepherd, "On Not Being White,"[7] in which Shepherd analyzes—not always entirely convincingly, but, I thought, always earnestly—racialized and sexualized intersections of power, privilege, fetishization, and desire between black and white men. The essay's harsh honesty regarding the author's self-professed frequent sexual desire for white men both startled and fascinated me, as did his linking of that desire to the social "cachet" of sexually "possessing"/being "possessed" by a white man. I was also struck by his pondering whether or not his being viewed by white men as sexually desirable in any way validated him, so to speak, as a black male and black homosexual who in many ways found blackness and all that he associated with it, as he defined it, *un*desirable. Simultaneously, I had for some time found myself surprised by *The Starr Report*'s grim dogged-ness in its aim to expose Lewinsky's and Clinton's sexual adven-tures—what struck me at the time as a clearly puritanical public pillorying of the two "transgressors," and of the then-president in particular: a pillorying obviously motivated, in part, by insidious pro-Republican, anti-Democrat political expediency, rendered all the more shaming for its highly public and revealing docu-mentation of sexual "badness" enacted against the "innocence" of Lewinsky's youth and inexperience, against the sanctity of Clinton's marriage and nuclear family, and against the national myth, albeit history-disproved, of the U.S. president as Honorable, Never-Philandering Supreme Being in Charge. (Thomas Jefferson and John F. Kennedy, to name only two, long ago undermined the mythic notion of president as Supreme American Family Value Sexual Saint. Jefferson's "transgressions" might be viewed by many today—and might have been seen in his time—as particularly risqué and unacknowledgeable, given that, as much evidence now indicates, he had sexual relations with numerous black women, among them the more studied Sally Hemings, who may have borne him children. Jefferson, of course, as white, male, a member of the privileged class and also a slave owner, occupied a completely dominant position over Sally Hemings as a black female chattel slave.) Rereading Shepherd impelled me to consider once more the (historical and other) connections between sexuality, race, gender, and power, but also pushed me toward the apparently unthinkable question of the white heterosexual president, himself consistently heterosexual*ized* by the media, entertaining a secret dalliance with a black man: how *would* the U.S. public feel about the possibility of a black penis entering President Clinton's (or president George W. Bush's, or any president's) white, presumably exclusively heterosexual anus? How would the nation feel about its elected Chief wrapping his lips in full-fledged desire, in secret or otherwise, about a tumescent black penis?

Would the nation be shocked into silence, then into jittery laughter, and then into more visceral reactions, judging from my students' reactions? "But why?" I wanted to know. "Why are we laughing?"

"It's crazy," one (white, male) student finally said, continuing to laugh, though blushing enough to turn the classroom itself a scarlet only Kandinsky could have imagined. "That is like, *so* not possible. I mean, the very i*dea* . . ." He trailed off into a silence of complete amazement at the fact that—as he later confided—such a discussion could even take place in a *classroom,* of all places. Weren't we studying African American queer literature, after all? What could these preposterous imaginings possibly have to do with our curriculum, and how the hell could we actually be speaking about such unheard-of things? Suddenly, a return to poring over text- and time-distanced explorations of sexuality, desire, and race had never, I suspected, so appealed to everyone. He fidgeted haplessly in his seat as I urged him to continue.

"I mean . . . it would just, like, *never* happen," he said. "I mean, come *on*—the *pres*ident of the United States having an af*fair* with . . ." His sentence trailed off once more, but I wondered what he found more unimaginable, objectionable: the president's having sex with a man, or with a black man? Or both? Or merely the president's having sex? His conviction, like those of some other students who began to speak, appeared more the result of a strong, if undefined, but for him somehow correct, feeling—an opinion informed by intuition informed by insights into his nation's history and attitudes he might not consciously have known he possessed—as opposed to the end result of a definitive, locatable knowledge.

"Even if it did happen," a black female student commented with grave certainty, "it would never be reported. Somebody would be killed before they'd let that get out." Several other students murmured agreement, many still registering incredulity that they were even being asked to consider the obviously impossible idea. Throughout the ensuing discussion, I noted that no one ever questioned who the "they" would be who would so assuredly prevent news of the president's interracial same-gender liaison from reaching the public.

It would never happen. Somebody would be killed. Serious, definite words from serious, if dumbfounded, faces. But why so profoundly unbelievable? So unimaginable?

It was after leaving the class and walking slowly home that I felt myself more consciously resisting the *Absolutely not, No way* tenor of the discussion. In the class, we had all agreed that, in the U.S. present-day popular imagination, the president—the actual presidential physical body—is perceived and conceived, for better or worse, as a reflection of what the nation wishes to see in such a position of power ("commander in chief," for example): a white, heterosexual, Christian, ostensibly virile male. A male perhaps not too overly aggressive, except perhaps in times of war, when he will use his, and by extension *our,* missiles wisely and well, with expert aim. A male somewhat conventionally good looking, à la Kennedy, Clinton, and the 2000 Democratic candidate Al Gore. Depending on his looks, he might or might not have been permitted "ascension" from the poor or working class; that is, he would be an acceptable contender for the Oval Office if he'd *once* been poor (as a child, for example), provided that he didn't seem in any way physically "tainted" or permanently touched by poverty (visible problems with his teeth, unhealthy-looking skin) during his candidacy. We agreed in the discussion that, in this present historical moment, the nation would most likely not countenance a Jewish president. (I also believed that more obvious anti-Semitism, including overtly anti-Semitic language—words such as "kike" or blunt references to "money" in reference to Jews—while privately felt by many citizens, would surely be strongly censured, if not outrightly punished, in the public realm.) If a Jewish candidate did manage somehow to succeed to the presidency, he or she would doubtless be compelled not to "appear" or "sound" "too" Jewish. (None of the students, Jewish or otherwise, could imagine a president with a stereotypically sounding Jewish surname such as Schwartz or Levine. All the students laughed outright at the idea of a President Jacobowitz, which, according to another student, herself Jewish, "wouldn't happen," as with our imagining of Clinton's interracial queer affair.) No one, including the Asian American students, could (or would) imagine an Asian American president—President Chang, or Yee, or Yamamoto? *No way,* virtually everyone said, even when Peruvian former president Alberto Fujimori's name, for one, was raised. The idea of a Latino president, even given the current statistic of Latinos as the largest group of people of color in the United States, was also unimaginable: President Salgado, or Gutierrez? No, everyone said. At least not yet. And the suggestion of an openly gay or lesbian president, squiring his "First Man" or her "First Lady" partner about the White House and displaying same-gender affection at official state functions in the media's omnipresent glare? That idea was so unthinkable to the students as to draw from them—even, or especially, those possibly queer—unrestrained hoots of laughter. (At that time, the fall of 2001, the *New York Times,* as one example, had not yet begun including on its Sunday wedding announcements page lesbian and gay civil union notices. The newspaper's featuring of queer civil unions on its formerly invincibly hetero-only page, begun in September 2002, might have struck those students, at that time, as another "could never happen" ideal, utterly unthinkable.) Privately, I reflected—not completely sardonically—that if the president were black, he would of course have to be a "good" black—light skinned, surely, thus skirting associations with darkness of evil, ugliness, and licentiousness; serious appearing (as opposed to feckless); not too young appearing, young black men equaling in the skewed popular imagination danger, frenzied sexual appetites, general depravity, and so on. The black president would greatly benefit from the "legitimization" of a (preferably) elite education: if he managed to get through Yale or Princeton without murdering or raping anyone or stealing any cars, the conventional wisdom might assume, he would probably be a safe bet on Capitol Hill—a *fairly* safe one, though still far from guaranteed. He would also have to be remorselessly capable of spelling his own name and that of his cabinet members: a combination, say, of Colin Powell, Andrew Young, and Julian Bond, but subtly deracialized out of the dangerousness of blackness and inducted, in a perhaps different way than occurred with Clarence Thomas and Condoleezza Rice, into the approved and nonthreatening realm of tacitly "honorary" whiteness. ("Honorary" whiteness, of course, ever subject to revocation by its bestowers at the slightest sign of niggerishness, the ever-lurking beast within—such beast in the black head of state hopefully permanently neutralized.) For finally, we decided, the U.S. president—definitely, in the present day, male—is and must be the corporeal and symbolic opposite of what the Old Testament has bequeathed us: not man created by God in His image, but sacred godhead (and, by extension, guardian of the nation, the national body, and the kingdom/empire) created by people—those who hold the most power and privilege—in *their* desired image: whiteness, maleness, heterosexuality, masculinity, Christianity, perceived virility, relative good looks according to culturally sanctioned standards of beauty, et cetera. An official created/elected by votes, but also by media constructions, representations, and manipulations of *who* and *what* the president should be as occupant of—at this juncture in world history—the most powerful position on earth, "checks and balances" notwithstanding.

Yet the persistent *why?* regarding the general confoundedness I'd encountered over the original question continued to nag: why was the very idea of President Clinton (for example) enjoying extended sexual intimacy and pleasure with a black male, and a subsequently glaringly revealing *Starr Report* of that liaison's intimate particulars, so utterly unimaginable, to the point of undiscussability?

I soon understood exactly where my pondering and analysis had fallen short. For while I had acknowledged to myself an understanding of general journalistic homophobia—more specifically, an understanding of journalistic squeamishness over the ostensible unseemliness of publicly discussing the intimacies of male-male sex—I also immediately understood that I hadn't yet gazed as deeply as I might have done at the presidential body: the actual physical entity as representative, to the world, of the nation, or imagined ("pure" white, heterosexual) Nation. Thus we might reasonably and realistically view the presidential body as the nation's/Nation's supreme body, in every sense, and also as icon/symbol of the hegemonic power and force of white heterosexual maleness "unpolluted" by either blackness (or any other color darker than whiteness) or homosexuality/queerness. Given the historical configuring in the U.S. national imagination of blackness as dangerous and foul, and considering historical and contemporary taboos against black-white interracial intimacy that have positioned blackness as the ever-lurking potential defiler of the "purity" of whiteness—"pure" whiteness envisioned as master race and thus one of the linchpins, if not the foundational tenet, of white supremacist ideology[8]—it would then stand to reason that the entry of an historically abhorrent, yet frequently desired, black penis into the sacred white presidential body would wreak havoc on the sacredness, and hence racial and "intact" heterosexual purity and power, of that whiteness and heterosexuality as shaped and buttressed by the U.S. historical imagination; purities, though obviously spurious, symbolically/metaphorically housed in the national iconic godhead of the presidential body, the *representative and ideal* of how a nation wishes to see itself and be seen by the world: white, Christian, heterosexual, and patriarchally controlled. Thus constructed, racially and sexually "intact" and fiercely protected from racial and homosexual *im*purifying, the symbolic white, hetero, Christian all-powerful god may stand—literally preside—as the national and nationally guarded embodiment of unassailable whiteness, patriarchal maleness ("commander in chief"), and unsullied heterosexuality; depending on what the nation desires at any given time (war, imperialist show-'em fervor, tough-guy testosterone, poor-boy-made-good myths), the god/president as *idealized* being will stand firmly at the center of national ideology as symbolic godhead.[9] Given these realities, interracial (especially black) homosexual (especially penetrative) contact with the president—Bill Clinton or any other, provided that he is white and heterosexual—would indeed be unthinkable, and is. For such contact would not only fatally endanger the mythic-symbolic ideology surrounding the sacred presidential body's white/racial and heterosexual purity but also seriously undermine, to say the least, the "real man" masculine power and force that only a homosexually *un*penetrated male body can possess and claim. (A similar argument regarding the dangers of racial and homosexual defilement vis-à-vis these ideologies might be made were we to imagine Bill Clinton, or any other president, inserting his white penis into a black anus, but for the fact that the president as penetrator would retain his dominant-male power as insertive "top" man—*el bugarrón,* as some Latino cultures name this role—and his racial power as a white man penetrating—topping—a black male, although his white penis would be *racially* "defiled" by its entry into, and sustained engagement with, a black anus. The entry of a white penis into a black body, of course, evokes enormously powerful historical images when one recalls the powerlessness, sexual and otherwise, of black male and female slave bodies subject to white slave owners' capricious sexual whims.)

A president's engagement in interracial homosexual liaisons

becomes even more unthinkable to a national imagination dead set against interracial intimacy and queerness when one imagines the sacred white presidential body *willingly* accepting a black penis into its most sacred inner sanctum, the primal preserve of male anal "virginity," which, to preserve its body's heterosexuality and the fully patriarchal power granted completely inviolable heterosexuality, must remain absolutely intact, its top-secret rosebud—the anal entry—unplucked.[10] Shielded from the impermissible intrusions of racial (i.e., blackness) and queer infection,[11] the presidential body can remain both heterosexual*ized* (via, e.g., the hetero-izing figures of the president's wife and family and the media's constant photographing and mention of them) and *actually,* actively heterosexual. In this regard, while a black male sex partner's anal rape of the white presidential body would doubtless be considered horrifying for a number of reasons, it might, per a presently anti-interracial, heterosexist and homophobic popular imagination, be preferable to the president's *consensual* interracial homosexual activity, pleasure, and entry into the ultimate infamies of racial and homo/sexual transgression.

In considering the foregoing, we should also remember that, in a homophobic and heterosexist society, the idea/ideal of male anal "virginity" is constantly threatened by the *perceived* lurking danger of anal-obsessed homosexual rapaciousness: recall, for example, pervasive fears about child molesters (envisioned frequently as older, or old, men with an unappeasable appetite for the velveteen buttocks of young boys), as well as more recent concerns about Boy Scout leaders, and enduring Don't-bend-over-in-the-shower-to-retrieve-the-soap jokes and lore. Male anal "virginity" itself, of course, remains for many, even in some progressive "queer" circles, largely a still unspeakable, if not incomprehensible, topic. Some of this unspeakability obviously has much to do with feelings of shame regarding anal penetration, with general societal ambivalence about—disgust for, and simultaneous fascination with—the anal area and anal (sexual) pleasure. It is also clearly connected to the anxiety-producing power dynamics manifested in voiced or silent questions about who, in sex, will penetrate whom, who will top whom, and, ergo, who will become—be viewed as—more of a "man" than whom, and who more of a "woman"—the latter, in a sexist culture invested in male dominance across races and white male domination over everyone, being the worst possible fate for any male, with its attendant loss of "true" (i.e., anally *un*penetrated) male status. (Much of this shame contributes to a globally still-prevailing enormous silence about, and under-reporting of, male rape of other males.) In all likelihood, few heterosexually identified males in the West—Western males who actively, consciously define themselves as heterosexual—ever, if they even regard themselves as virgins in their preadult sex lives, imagine themselves as *anal* virgins, with the idea that their anuses will one day be sites for welcome deflowering by another male.[12] The very unspeakability of male anal virginity in contemporary U.S. culture (and in many cultures), however, intones volumes to its unspeakability in the context of the presidential body: if (nongay) male citizens of the president's patriarchal nation under-stand, however tacitly, the dangers and degradation of being anally topped, which topping will ineluctably lead to a fall from patriarchal heterosexual grace, how much more critical must pro-tection of the president's anus be from such a "fall," given how much is at stake? In the president's case, not only male status and heterosexual status and privilege would be lost with such a fall, but also national and global power and prestige, and, without doubt, full human credibility. Additionally—and perhaps most unsettling to the white presidential godhead—if Bill Clinton, for example, had received sexual favors not from Lewinsky but from a black male—the hypothetical "Mr. Jacobs"—and had permitted that black male to anally penetrate him, how, if at all, would the white iconic presidential body have survived the ensuing utter depravity of racial pollution?

Kenneth Starr's report, with its circus of intimate revelations and details, obviously did little, in the end, to malign either sexu-

ally or racially Bill Clinton's presidential body, which, throughout
his romps with Lewinsky, remained (obviously) white, male dominant, and energetically heterosexual. The report certainly didn't
irreparably besmirch the presidential body as actual intimacy with
a black male sex partner would have done, although, returning to
my initial question, it remains extremely doubtful—at least to
me—that *The Starr Report* as a published text would, in all its unrelenting inquisitiveness and documentation, have glimpsed the
light of day in the first place had Bill Clinton opted not for the
oral attentions of the white Monica Lewinsky but for the penetrative probes of the black "Mr. Jacobs" (or another, actual male of
visibly African descent). "Someone would have been killed before
that got out," a student had remarked; in the puritanical, race-
and sex-obsessed United States, taking into account once more the
supreme importance of presidential power foregrounded by anxieties over national/presidential security and perceived threats to
the National/national executive body, she may have been closer to
the truth—to a highly probable truth, given allegations and realities of past U.S. clandestine intelligence activities—than anyone
could have imagined or been willing to consider. Looking back at
Clinton's priapic heterosexuality as documented in the Starr text,
however, the sexuality itself was essentially nonthreatening and, to
a heterocentric popular imagination, acceptable: man on top, orally
penetrative, and woman on bottom, receptive. *The Starr Report*
succeeded most in providing the nation with typical, if pruriently
presented, fare: less threatening *intra*-racial heterosex, transgressive
in its "naughtiness" mainly owing to the great difference between
Clinton's and Lewinsky's professional positions and the significant
difference in their ages, because of the extreme explicitness of the
Report's sexual details, and—in a society which still, by and large,
professes its belief in heterosexual marriage—because of Clinton's
marriage and parenthood. As something of a "boy next door" who
ultimately made good from modest means (and withstood and
finally overcame the possibilities of a forced resignation), Clinton

also starred—literally—in two combined popular narratives: the American dream success story (The Hardworking, High-Achieving-Yet-Humble-Hero's Tale) and the tale of the poor (white) boy who grew up to marry well, become president, get "bad" with a pretty young thing of whatever race, and, in the end, get away with it.

It remains possible that, in another time in the United States, another century, two men, one black and one white, one an elected president and the other a regular citizen, will come together to join their bodies in sexual congress and pleasure. Perhaps, by that (unthinkable?) time, whose racialized penis enters whose racialized body, who kneels before whom, and whose race-marked flesh tops or is topped by another's will pass as matters of scant importance. Perhaps. But given the United States' tenaciously racialized and race-ist history, that history's largely intransigent silences (or explosive violence) about sex, sexuality, and gender especially within *inter*racial contexts, and the contemporary nation's steadfast refusal to gaze for even one coherent moment at the sources and consequences of such a severe inheritance, the image of a future president (or any powerful white, publicly heterosexual male) enjoying uninhibited sexual intimacy with another male, and/or a male of color, especially a black male—particularly if the body of the white male in question is a public, "official" one, representative of "pure" racially "untainted" whiteness, unqueered (untainted) heterosexuality, and intact patriarchal power—appears remote indeed.

2001–2004

On the Importance of Returning from Abroad to the United States in a Time of Imperialism and War (A Meditation on Dissent)

YET THE UNCOMFORTABLE TRUTH WAS AND REMAINS THAT on that morning in April 2003 he was someone I neither fully liked nor trusted—in fact someone whom, though unbeknownst to him, I could often barely stand, luminous and interesting and even entertaining though he frequently was. Perhaps seeking to avoid unnecessary conflict, or because I was ambivalent, dishonest about my own feelings, just a regular old coward, or some combination of all three, I remained hypocritically polite in his presence but never told him. Never told him how much his socially overbearing manner and frequent self-absorption wore on my nerves. A prisoner of my own ambivalence, and even (though it's painful to say) disingenuousness, I never told him either that, along with my final distrust of him, I had also initially found him nearly fascinating —I had been almost completely enthralled by his strikingly imperious command of small social gatherings, his mellifluous voice (which later came to sound somewhat affected, as did his not-quite-British, not-quite-Jamaican accent), his effortless crossing and recrossing of his legs, his apparent utter conviction that what he had to say really did merit others' infinite listening (occasionally it did), and his somewhat flirtatious, "knowing" smirk.

I did not tell him, as he rambled on and on in his monologueish way (on the telephone; in Jamaica—Kingston, as usual—where

I had spent and would, fortuitously, spend most of that year) how very differently I felt from him, but how very much I also understood the difficult feelings he was just then expressing. He was a visiting researcher that year at the University of the West Indies. We both were residents, citizens, and offspring of two locales—Jamaica and the United States. That morning, he was agitated with concern, reluctance, anxiety, about having to return shortly to the United States, as his research time was nearly completed. I, too, knew that I would have to depart Jamaica late in the summer for the United States, in order to begin teaching again in the fall—a prospect to which, deeply immersed in the particular freedoms and joys Jamaica always offered me,[1] I would scarcely look forward as August edged its bronzed shoulders in over 2003's steadily narrowing days. There was no comparable freedom to basking in the blackness of one's own black-majority sovereign nation, far enough from the perpetually race-befuddled United States, colorism and color tensions in Jamaica notwithstanding. Few joys could compare with finding oneself again among the family and friends so beloved, who returned that love. Little pleasure could equal finding so much pleasure in sustained intimacy with the men whom, over the years, I had consistently desired, pursued, dreamed of, and sometimes loved, and who had desired and often undone me: joys backed by the always gorgeous Blue Mountains to the north and the shimmering, eternity-skinned sea to the south—all those pleasures and more, although Jamaica's murder rate, already terrifying for many years, was steadily rising, constantly cautioning one, in Kingston expecially, to be careful—*very* careful; to take care staying out late and walking the streets after dark, as I had done for years and sometimes foolishly continued to do.

But then departing Jamaica for the United States as I had invariably been compelled to do, after spending time as a child and teenager in Kingston, had always been an occasion for the most wracking of tears, the most clenched of misery-clenched hearts. Misery, revolt, wretchedness, for I was again leaving all of *them* behind—those voices, that music, that music in those voices, those cousins, those uncles and aunts, those mango trees (hairy, East Indian, Julie, Bombay); those ginneps tied in bunches in the sun-dappled kitchen, those cups of steaming tea at four o'clock in the afternoon, those lizards creeping up the walls while extending, alarmingly, their pink or red or yellow throats—and those hummingbirds: busy, furiously busy at the hibiscus each morning, no time to stop and chat with anyone; and those canes, those breaths of the sea, those purple crimson evenings, and yes, I have not forgotten, *those* every-couple-of-days trips to the Constant Spring open-air market (so like so many markets on the African continent, of course, which I would only apprehend years later)—leaving all of it behind, Jamaica, Jamaicans, people, mountains, sea, for what suddenly loomed as the grayness and colorlessness and coldness and *wizenedness* of New York.

And so I did understand his not wishing to return to the United States—the wish of this fellow whom I had met some months earlier at a dinner party in "stush" (upscale) Stony Hill. He had been on the island for nearly a year and, as happens to many who visit it, and perhaps especially to those who are linked to it and often yearn for it in spite of its many, many social problems, he had been seduced by it; swayed by the parts of it that, without question, still wrapped themselves about him with the softest caress fully imaginable only by the willing victim. He had been seduced by the fact that here, people more often than not still actually looked you in the eye when they spoke with you; he had been swayed by the fact that, for better or worse, often worse but quite often better too, people really did, once they knew you (and often even if they didn't), care about you: how you were, how you were feeling, how your mother was doing with her injured foot and whether or not your father had managed with his arthritic knees to play any cricket this year. Here, where (although the gunshots each week are increasing, the racketeering and deadly extortions are increasing), somehow, one actually *can* find time for friends: to see them, talk with them, lyme with them, and laugh. His reluctance to return to the United States and all its rush-rush-rush-money-is-all and foolish bigotry-inclined people with their frightened O-my-God-is-he-going-to-*rob* stares . . . of course I understood.

Yet, that April morning, we were speaking of very different things. Not so much of the joy of friendships and healthy family life and general love and care between human beings but of war, mayhem. Cruelty. For just that month, George W. Bush's bellicose administration, a.k.a. the New American Empire, was in the process of launching "preemptive" strikes against Iraq and, as the daily Jamaican and U.S. papers and local and cable TV channels steadfastly showed us, was, in its fierce quest for alleged "weapons of mass destruction" and the living or dead body of Saddam Hussein, bombing the hell out of Baghdad and surrounding areas. ("Bombing dem bloodclaat," as some Jamaicans gravely put it.) The cataclysmic U.S. aggression revealed in the news—that which media executives, deciding what exactly constituted "truth" or "acceptable truth," permitted ordinary citizens to see—had been, and continued to be, sickening. The constant display of George W. Bush's triumphant face, and those of his henchpeople vice president Dick Cheney, attorney general John Ashcroft, defense secretary Donald Rumsfeld, and national security adviser Condoleezza Rice, particularly when juxtaposed against the faces of tormented Iraqis (and, in some cases, against their bloody, burned, bombed bodies), was more than we—and, one would like to believe, most people in the world, including many U.S. residents—could bear. The Department of "Homeland Security" had certainly, by the spring of 2003, already begun to do its surveilling worst. Unknown numbers of foreign nationals, and others, were being held in "detainment" by U.S. security officials and agencies; applicants for political asylum, depending on where they came from and how they appeared, were being subjected to more heightened forms of scrutiny; people believed to have suspect "Middle Eastern" connections were being harassed, interrogated, and generally policed by both "the authorities" and civilians, as had already begun shortly after September 11, 2001. Apolitical, ahistorical Americans—a number impossible to estimate—blithely expressed confidence, at least publicly, in the increasingly repressive administration of a "president" the majority of the nation had *not* elected. Few public personages in the States, it seemed, with very few exceptions (Noam Chomsky, Howard Zinn, Ramsey Clark, and a few others associated with the conscientious radical left) were questioning Bush's and vice president Dick Cheney's connections with the Halliburton Corporation, which Cheney had headed for five years, and which had (among other suspicious activities) delivered gas to Iraqi citizens under at least one highly priced contract. *Extremely* lucrative contracts, the rebuilding of Iraq's fallen oil industry, deals with the KGB- and mob-connected Russian Tyumen company for Halliburton involvement in the production of Russian gas and oil, and profits for all concerned on the U.S. side—and elsewhere—were only part of Halliburton's hidden core. Meanwhile, hundreds of thousands of people in the United States, if not more, continued to storm the streets in protest against the strikes. Their hundreds of thousands were not enough—not then, anyway—to thwart Bush's contemptuous eye toward them.[2] The brave documentary filmmaker Michael Moore, upon winning an Academy Award for his latest film, *Bowling for Columbine,* denounced the "fictitious president" at the awards ceremony, on live television, to a chorus of boos but also to many cheers. (This well before the formidable success of Moore's 2004 documentary *Fahrenheit 9/11* and its considerable impact on public/lay discourse critical of Bush, so sorely needed.) In the case of the 2003 invasion of Iraq, racism and lies, the bedrocks of U.S. history, pushed their brutish way forward. All hell was breaking loose in both the United States and Iraq, assisted in no small way by the United Kingdom's venal prime minister Tony Blair and his apparently limitless and uncritical support for Bush's aggression. Blair by that time had already become known by many in Europe, appropriately, as "Bush's poodle"—the poodle also no doubt keenly aware of the future profits that would arise from the ashes of a devastated and reshaped, neo-(corporate-)colonized Iraq. Viewing all these events askance, my colleague on the telephone told me that he was returning to the United States only because he had "no choice."

"No choice"? But I knew what he meant. As choices move in human affairs, he certainly had a "choice," but also a job to return to: one to which he was connected financially and emotionally. One in which he had formed warm associations with some of his colleagues and to which he had dedicated enormous amounts of his considerable intellectual energy. He also had relatives and friends in the States to return to. In spite of my own (admittedly partly mean-spirited) dislike for him, I found myself deeply affected by his words—for I also had a job to which I felt compelled to return, if only because (although it was a job I'd actually sometimes very much liked) it would also be my main source of income in the year or so to come. Through that job, I had also come to know people about whom I deeply cared and wished to see again. And I, too, had relatives and friends in the States whom I loved and whom I couldn't imagine not seeing again anytime soon. But the idea of remaining in Jamaica throughout the tumult of the United States' ugliness in Iraq was a wild temptation: tempting, to remain in a place in which one could easily enough loudly deplore, with the rest of the decrying world, the United States' human rights abuses; in which one could easily enough dissociate oneself from *that place*—from that bullying government so fond of invasions, murder, and conquest. It would be so humanly satisfying to feel oneself at last not stuck between blind-eyed "patriots" in favor of the bombing of Iraqis, but rather in synch with a populace dead set *against* mindlessly waving the stars and stripes, and *not* supportive of Bush's (or Ashcroft's, or Rice's) doublespeak or even triplespeak rhetoric, to say nothing of their outright viciousness against the latest victim of dire U.S. foreign policy.

Yes: to remain in Jamaica amid one's own truest people—in the place of my ancestors, some of whose graves I'd already visited in Manchester and Clarendon—rather than return to the States and, with other U.S. people, be compelled to pay taxes, *again,* that would finance the artillery that brought incendiary devastation upon too many nations: U.S. artillery sometimes held by Israeli hands and directed against Palestinians; in another time, held by U.S. soldiers aiming for Vietnamese faces. Many months out of the United States had provided me with a distance extremely helpful in repressive times: I knew, as I had known for some time (certainly since Bush's theft of the 2000 presidential election, if not before), that I simply couldn't—could *not*—abide the idea of benefiting, as a U.S. citizen, from the ferocities constantly visited on others. In the midst of multiple schisms, one scathing truth looms: if one is a taxpaying U.S. citizen, bombs killing people in Baghdad most definitely *do* bear one's name on them as a member of the (presently) most powerful country in the world. And what had I, as a beneficiary of that country's wealth, done up to that point to stop it?

Unless one is actively engaged in political activism, and, by extension, connected to a vibrant political/progressive community, the question can make one feel helpless—angry. Its content of *Well, but what* are *you doing to help others?* makes one feel collusive; it can induce (as it did in me) a feeling of powerlessness, overwhelmedness: "they" in Washington are making all these dire decisions, and what can "we" do, civically, to stop them?

But one *can* do things, I thought, at least beginning with the word. The word, which can express dissent.

On that spring morning in Kingston, however, I was feeling enraged, helpless, and momentarily distanced from the word—thinking as I listened to that rambling voice on the phone that he was right: no one in their correct mind would wish to leave the Jamaica we loved, impoverished, troubled, and violent though it often was and is, to return to a country that, with Tony Blair's assistance, had made the horror Saddam Hussein ultimately became possible in the first place—only to remove Hussein, murdering innocent Iraqis in the process, when he became both inconvenient and an obstacle to capitalist gain. The notion of returning or post-poning return to the States while the devastation surged on in Iraq became, as we continued to speak about it, increasingly painful, and—as I suspect occurred for the caller—a consideration of deep moral import. For staying away would not help incinerated or suf-fering Iraqis, would it? It would only help oneself. It would enable us to feel less guilty, less part of the problem "Empire" nation; less connected to the source of so much hatred: I'm not *there* in the "first world," I'm *here* in the forgotten, cast-off "third"—and, by the way, I'm black, I in no way hail from a wealthy background, I have no connections to the Halliburton Corporation or the U.S. ruling class, I'm not part of the Ivy League to-the-manor-born elite, and, why, I'm not even heterosexual. In short, I'm in no way part of *them.* So murmured the self-deluding, comforting words, so desperately clutched.

In honest and ultimately useful discussion of such political matters and moral realities—moral truths—nothing is, of course, nor can realistically be, ever so cleanly sliced. For as one engages the analyzing intellect in a more dispassionate gaze (even, or es-pecially, for the gazes that provoke moral outrage) at the contem-porary and historical underpinnings and ideologies that inform a society and shape it to loom exactly as it does, one is compelled also to engage the emotions, if only because they exist, irrefutably are *there*: taut electrical wires that will not, though here and there flanked by reason's and analysis' coolness, depart. It was painful for me to discover in the spring of 2003 that, as a U.S. citizen during a period of such intense (post–September 11) patriotism and uncritically pro-president fervor, I was a member of a society so jarringly not my own. (I'd been processing this knowledge for years, of course—probably all my life, as a black/racially marked child of immigrants from a developing-world, largely black coun-try. The States had never quite been "my own," of course, nor my parents', but that is a long, terribly painful story for another day, that begins in another, earlier century.) Those people in the United States who supported Bush and company's "preemptive" strikes against Iraq were not, in any way, "my" people—that is, other human beings with whom, in the most profound ways, I could truly share some fellow feeling. Had they ever been? But who were they? For while I know for a fact that, had I seen them jumping from the flaming World Trade Center towers on the morning of September 11, I would have screamed, covered my eyes, and felt sick to my stomach like so many others, as I also knew that I would most certainly have helped any person I could have on that day or any other day, had I glimpsed them in distress—glimpsed them running in terror as so many did on that morning, or stumbling blindly through all that dust and debris in the great ash cloud that lower Manhattan became—while I know all that without question, like the unsettling taste of my own blood, how—*how?*—to trust and feel comfortable around people who would so unthinkingly wave the stars and stripes; who would so cheeringly champion Bush's cowboy-minded fury; who were determined to believe that, in spite of no evidence whatsoever of Iraq's harboring "weapons of mass destruction," that nation was without question a global center of "terrorism"? How—what—to feel, as one felt so very displaced among them and, at times, unsafe?[3]

And how to feel about the United States' terrorism against most of the rest of the world? (And here the act of actual *feeling* becomes extremely daunting—for in regard to the United States' crimes against others, there will always be *too much* remembering, too much grief, so much history.) How to live with the reality of all that violence out there, not so far beyond one's windows, globally speaking—just there, across the sea in Haiti or Cuba, or south of the contiguous border? How to live with all those unbearable memories on a daily basis while trying to grapple with one's own life and exist as a morally conscientious person? To exist with the aim of doing good in the world: resolutely possessed of the hope, if not the unerring belief, that many human beings, most of the time, will try to do the "right thing," will try to be "good." But then, faced with the obvious requirement of acting humanely in respect to other human beings, to *humanity* (we all, of course, being "humanity"—we who are obliged to make *it*—ourselves—"humane"), how to countenance, in a time of so much xenophobia and careless bandying about of the word "terrorism," so many Americans' willful *dis*remembering of—for example—the Ku Klux Klan's terrorism? A terrorism often tacitly sanctioned by the state? Much disremembering of torched homes and publicly burned bodies, although one certainly could understand why many of the Klan's victims would wish to forget. Such self-saving forgetting, or dimming, is born of impossible knowledge—the sort of knowledge that should not, in a humane world, ever be possible for anyone—and is in no way, in the case of the victim/survivor, morally reprehensible. The self-saving forgetting is a different creature from the determined, unconscionable amnesia that erases memory of the terrorism of U.S. right-wing militia groups—the like of those who bombed (and still target) abortion clinics and murdered or maimed abortion doctors, nurses, clinic staff. How to feel, after September 11, when so many of those believed to be Middle Eastern, Muslim, Arab, were targeted, harassed, and, in more than one case, killed? The country in which I was born of Caribbean immigrant parents had long been the nation of lynch ropes, Jim Crow, internment camps for the Japanese, internment camps for Haitians, and, not that long ago, "Whole towns wiped clean of Negroes; eighty-seven lynchings in one year alone in Kentucky; four colored schools burned to the ground; grown men whipped like children; children whipped like adults; black women raped by the crew; property taken, necks broken. . . . Skin, skin and hot blood. The skin . . . one thing, but human blood cooked in a lynch fire . . . a whole other thing."[4] Terrorism, yes. And so how to feel about *that* country? The one that had been capable of doing all those things to black and other people, and now was doing them to Iraqis? That country, in which my own Jamaican parents, seeking economic opportunities, eventually found them? They found enhanced possibilities for their children even as the "Land of Opportunity" to which they'd emigrated continued to deliver so much misery to so many others in the world, including their Jamaican own. The United States, so hated now by so many. Hated at times also by Jamaicans,[5] whose government it had tried to thwart and topple in the 1970s, when prime minister Michael Manley's increasingly close relations with Cuban president Fidel Castro, during the era of Manley's experimental "democratic socialism," engendered much anxiety in Americas-policing Washington.

A wide range of feelings notwithstanding, in wartime—aka decimate-for-corporate-gain time—however much I publicly and privately deplored U.S. foreign policy and military aggression, I remained—uneasily—a U.S. citizen, owner of the passport that grants one the privilege—the vaulting, supreme privilege—of nearly an entire visa-less world. Such is the privilege of the so-called first world: one known (and often taken for granted) by many of its citizens. No amount of remaining in Jamaica, removed (I thought, I yearned to believe) from the reactionary people I despised "up there" would change that. Yet—and it was partly because I didn't care for the person speaking to me on the phone that morning that I didn't disclose to him this reflection, but also because my thoughts in this direction wouldn't fully assemble coherently until much later—such citizenship obviously does carry privileges and even, to be sure, responsibilities. That truth became ever clearer to me that spring as, in antiwar protests organized by the new group Jamaicans Against the War, with many others, I voiced dissent outside the U.S. embassy on Oxford Road and the British High Commission on Trafalgar against Bush's and Blair's incursions ("Bush and Blair, no war for oil!" "U.S. and U.K. get out of Iraq!").[6]

It was while engaged in active dissent with the protesters, and feeling greatly empowered by it (especially when a Jordanian man visiting Jamaica came by and thanked us, as a Middle Easterner, for speaking out), that I began to understand that, comforting though life cushioned among the middle class in Jamaica might be, comforting though the illusion might be that there, in the black-majority developing-world nation that was one's own, one had nothing to do with Washington, the fact remained that, as a U.S. citizen, even a black one, one had everything to do with all of it. (Citizens' taxes paid to be used by the government for defense spending . . .) One really *did* need to return there, sooner or later, in order to make one's voice heard in the widening corridors of dissent—heard in some way even if one never attended a protest. For, above all, it was most important that dissent against the war—and against all U.S. imperialist violence—be registered most loudly *within* the United States. A protest trip to Washington would be ideal in order to confront the fictitious president with a citizen's displeasure, wherever he made one of his heavily scripted speeches or otherwise unfortunate appearances. For such a trip, it would be necessary to bring every single part of the integrated self—black, Caribbean, gay, Jamaican, educated, artistic, and more—to all moments of dissent. At all times, it would be critical to challenge the word "patriot," lately used as a sledgehammer to crush, or render highly suspect, dissent—for in a true democracy, doesn't everyone have the constant and absolute right to critique, even vociferously, the U.S. president, without having to submit to patriotism tests? For the president isn't—ought *not* to be, or be perceived as—a king. (And even if he were a king, he would still be subject to critique.) Particularly in the time of the insidious USA PATRIOT Act,[7] one needs to bring home to a conservative, censorious citizenry *and* government the unequivocal truth: that each dissenting voice, even in what is so casually and uncritically referred to as a "democracy," remains *its own*. Its own—assured, as the First Amendment guarantees, of the complete right to express itself; a voice of dissent that owns the right to challenge brazen falsehoods of how America always wants to "help" the world and "protect" its own people. ("Protect" them from Communists, blacks, homosexuals, "terrorists"—but not from AIDS, poverty, cancer, racism, sexual and gender violence, homophobia, and the increasingly high costs of medical insurance, health care, and education.) For in truth, the greatest dangers to people in the United States are not foreign enemies but the general ignorance and apathy that reign so supreme among so many, most harmfully rendered in an indifference both to the U.S. government's manipulations and to the existence of the rest of the world beyond U.S. borders—*that* world out there, filled with real, living, complicated and very interesting people. Here, now, dissent, in spite of the skulking PATRIOT Act, can shape itself as moral outrage over the chicanery of a person who was not, in the 2000 election, correctly voted into presidential office, but—with the largely Republican Supreme Court's help—seized it. Dissent can shout *No*—as in *No more, enough*: shout it in protest over the agony that U.S. corporate-driven greed has brought and continues to bring to innocent people around the world.

Dissent, I didn't tell the person on the other end of the phone, that can, and will, fire the blood. The sort that will bring me to my feet shortly after Arundhati Roy concludes her May 13, 2003, speech at Riverside Church in New York by saying, "I hate to disagree with your president. Yours is by no means a great nation. But you could be a great people. History is giving you the chance."[8] For yes, I thought just then: at last. At last someone actually dared to say those words right in the United States; someone to whom people would listen. *Yours is by no means a great nation.* Words I and so many others had long believed—known—but in the hyperpatriotic post-September 11 climate hadn't felt comfortable or even safe saying publicly: that the United States had never been in any way a "great nation"—just ask those of us whose people had been burned, lynched, driven off their land, and received (among other tragedies) smallpox-infected blankets. The United States, since its early days, had become more of an ideology than a nation; the ideology of "America" and "Americanism" now, post–Cold War, meaning so many things to so many, among them imperialism and the indefatigable, ever regenerative racism, ethnocentrism, and xenophobia that are fundamental aspects of any empire. Roy's words just then provided a more articulate form for both my dissent and my rage over the war in Iraq. But they also provided hope. Hope that, in spite of George W. Bush's and Tony Blair's determined ignoring of all the massive global antiwar protests, active, vigorous dissent could still make a difference. For, as Roy said, and as I believed and still believe, those of us who enjoy the privilege of citizenship, who need not worry about being deported, "have the power of proximity . . . [and] access to the Imperial Palace and the Emperor's chambers."⁹ For "Empire's conquests are being carried out in [our] name," she said, "and [we] have the right to refuse. You could refuse to fight. Refuse to move those missiles from the warehouse to the dock. Refuse to wave that flag. Refuse the victory parade . . . in the ultra-patriotic climate that prevails in the United States, that [dissent is] as brave as any Iraqi or Afghan or Palestinian fighting for his or her homeland."¹⁰

Today and on all future days, I choose—though not without some fear, though fear itself is hardly new—that resistance to, and over, silence. I consciously say, Not in my name, the murder of Iraqi people and the seizure of their land for oil-based future enterprises and profits. I say No to it all, to the PATRIOT Act, to U.S. bullying and violence everywhere, and to the human rights infractions the government permits—and has always permitted—among its own citizens: the devastations of racism, poverty, vigilantism, and the horrendous living and work conditions—and harassment, official and unofficial—endured by the poorest of immigrants.

I say No to it all today, but that morning on the phone in Kingston, I hadn't yet formulated these clearer thoughts, and so I didn't tell him—the man whom, as I've said, been saying, but as I wouldn't like now so much to believe, I so disliked. Perhaps if he were here now I would tell him. Say to him (though without judgment—with, perhaps, even a bit of laughter) that it really *is* important—yes, of course!—for those of us who possess the privilege of U.S. citizenship to go back. To return, in the time of a fictitious, brutally corrupt administration, and raise hell. To ensure that the fictitious president knows that he will in no way be president-for-life, and that his corruption—and that of his vice president, and defense secretary, and national security adviser, and the British prime minister, and all the rest of them—will *not* triumph, will *not* kill any more Iraqis (or anyone) for corporate gain, at least not without hearing our rage about it. For he and his administration are despised by many in the United States and around the globe. For an enormous number of people in the United States are *not* the stupid, passive, apolitical, uninformed people Bush and company presume and hope them to be. It's important to fight this corruption, I would tell him on the phone—important to shout our dissent, so that, if only for this, the rage doesn't kill us—the rage that, properly used, might do us and many others much good. Enormous good. *The most enduring good,* I would tell him. *Yes,* I would say, *of course. Because you—*

2003–4

Autumn's Relentlessness:
Crimes against Humanity

FOR YES—IT IS RELENTLESS. THIS SEASON, ONE OF FLAME that, more than ever, now does not end. The season itself as perennial as human stupidity, but generally more pleasing to the eye. As unceasing as hatred itself, the sire of viciousness that "gazes keenly at the future," one voice succinctly told us, "as only it can."[1] But autumn occasionally also reconstituted as love: as reliable as sunset, as gorgeous as the spreading, open, illimitable sea. This autumn, 2001, providing many noteworthy things: weather (some stunningly sunny, clear days), human behavior (a capacity for both generosity and cruelty, survival and self-destruction, large-spiritedness and venality—but none of that at all new), and, in recent days, though not for the first time by far, more insufferable words from a U.S. president despicably indifferent, in keeping with his predecessors, to the sanctity of human life—this season to the sanctity of Afghani life in particular.

The weather this autumn has, many would agree, exceeded all dreams and expectations. In the New York City area it has certainly done so. September, for the most part, at least until later in the month, hardly faltered in its cerulean gaze; its mostly golden light, there and here edged by hints of early autumn weariness brought into greater relief by deepening shadows, eased in each afternoon and evening, bronzing rivers and window glass out of the complacency of merely reflecting. A few birds packed up and left, early on the flyway; various trees sneezed, shuddered, and shook off late-summer somnolence for the approaching time of snow shrouds; ponds continued their twilight complaints, insects harmonized before imminent death and regret, butterflies foundered, and people (yes, and dogs, cats, other mammals, reptiles, and all manner of creatures in the sea) slept, awakened, and slept again, as the fury of leaves commenced and the season proceeded, assuredly, through itself.

The morning of September 11 dawned particularly cerulean: hard, clear. One awakened to, and prepared for, the day beneath the most cloudless sky imaginable. Neither the day nor sky wavered when one of two commercial airline jets crashed into the first World Trade Center tower; nor did day or sky register any change when the second jet slammed into the south tower and people once again immediately died, continued to die; would go on dying and being killed amid descending clouds of ash, brick, soot, pulverized concrete, steel, office furniture, paper, and more unimaginable sunderings. The sky, steadily indifferent, performed no miracles throughout those moments that stretched into hours, days, weeks, months—what quickly, strangely, became what some now call, cautiously, Life After, as opposed to Before. Still, the sky sent forth no tears of rain, nor brimstone to avenge the living or the dead. It simply *was*—there, so very far above screams, carnage, blood, human beings jumping hundreds of feet to their deaths, and voracious, jet-fuel-scented flame; there, expansive beyond televised narratives of "America under Attack" and flashes of "Islamic terrorists."

In the later hours of that day, and in the weeks that somehow, impossibly, followed (followed while much mist and daze lingered about the eyes, about the head), it felt critical to discover how the season, at last confronted with so many crueler images of its own fire, could actually continue to advance with such equanimity. How could squirrels continue their huntings-and-finds as if nothing at all had occurred as, on urban streets and in forests, trees, their limbs thick with jays' territorial disputes, continued to wither? How could steadily cooling breezes go on registering their presences along living flesh, as photographs clutched by trembling hands rose into view about the city, everywhere? Photos of the missing and the "Have You Seen . . . ?" plastered on pizza shop windows and on those of supermarkets, pharmacies; pasted on the metal sides of public telephones, in subway stations, in railroad and bus terminals, on the sides of newsstands. Pictures of the smiling and the sober and the mostly, after some time, presumed dead, eventually to be confirmed as dead or (though *extremely* unlikely, too many learned) alive. Photographs of the "disappeared"—vanished not by another repressive regime's death squads or right-wing paramilitary units dispatched to obliterate all murmurs of the most recent rising populist front or revolutionary surge in response to systematic human rights infractions and crushing poverty, but by the cataclysmic force of a modern architectural monolith's infernal shudder and collapse. On the evening that eased its way into the retreating flesh of that day, an insistent moon rose, pulling reluctant seas after it in the cyclical rounds of cosmological come-and-go. A few days later, rain descended over a city benumbed by the leavings of soot, pulverized concrete, ash. The larger physical world, intent on its own steps, did not, somehow, astonishingly, come to an end.

That grief—like the grief of all human beings—was inexorable. Palpable and, like much grief, mostly unbearable. Yet as the days began to pass and pass on, in spite of blinding grief, fear, and sorrow for those wandering the streets of New York like a newer form of the dead, holding up before them those tattered photographs—in spite of all that, one did begin to feel, as a grave matter of conscience, the powerful urge to ask questions about (for example) Iraq. Questions that, though surely difficult, might not only help one to begin to make more sense out of one's own grief and connect it to the grief of so many others in this mess often called the human condition, but would also position one more critically in relation to long-standing realities that the U.S. "mainstream" media had long chosen to ignore and render altogether invisible—purposefully, largely successfully—to U.S. audiences.[2] Questions like: How gorgeous were the days over Iraq when, with scarcely a care for human life, life as real and fleshly as our own, the United States bombed, and bombed, and bombed, and bombed, and bombed the nation? Bombed during the years of president Bill Clinton, during the tenure of president George (the elder) H. W. Bush? How lovely were the flowers there when the United States, now wracked over its own violently dead, enforced economic sanctions against Iraq that produced slow, torturous death by way of starvation and increased poverty for hundreds of thousands of people—an untold (precisely: *un*told) number of them children? Children who, though ferociously compromised by poverty's relentlessness, did, and do still, all the things that children in all countries do: laugh, play, sing, chant, misbehave, bed-wet, and—certainly in the case of people largely impoverished—work. Work much. Work, far too often, unto death. In the midst of grief and horror that are as real as their grief and horror and continued deaths, it becomes impossible not to ask: Did one Iraqi woman (or Sudanese woman, or Afghani woman, or—), or two, or two hundred thousand, veiled against the sun and sandaled in the dust of eviscerated landscapes littered with body parts that were and remain as real as those scattered about or decaying beneath the World Trade Center towers' rubble—did one of those many women cast her gaze up to the sun one morning and wonder (while in search of water and food for her children, while not knowing if her mother, father, brother, sister, husband, grandparents had survived the last bombing, the last sure-shot slinging of missiles) at the sheer golden gloriousness of the day, before the U.S.-fired missile hit, incinerating her into someone else's tortured memory and leaving her children motherless, her husband wifeless and her parents in possession of only ashes? Before that day's missile hit, did she marvel at the sky's unflinching brow over An Najaf or Baghdad? Its steady gaze over the Gulf's waters? She or someone else did, no doubt. In the aftermath of U.S. atrocities against their humanity—atrocities that far too many people in the United States remain unwilling to acknowledge, committed to ignorance, denial, self-absorption, and apathy, all buttressed and encouraged by a rampantly consumerist culture (Why Be Informed? Go Shopping Instead) and a conservative, corporate-directed media—those Iraqi names and faces will remain evermore unknown to us, as their lives, trivialized in the truncating media, will be rendered irrelevant, dismissible, and thus erased. For many of us—and by "us" I mean not only people in the United States but also those in the larger West—"they" will always be "they": the people "over there" who are "Middle Easterners"—a term as broad and muddying as "Africans" or "Asians." Meanwhile, content enough in our ignorance, content enough not to challenge the purposeful "mainstream" media misinformation designed to fuel nationalistic ire ("America under Attack"); content not to critique jingoistic comments about "patriotism"—"patriotism" that, in its most rabid form, never cowers before its cousins, racism, xenophobia, and ethnocentrism ("America Fights Back"); content to sit by, far too many of us, and subscribe to these bigotries and the intellectual laziness that the United States, in particular, has made (in)famous, we remain relentless: subscribers by and large to solipsism, passive acceptance of the U.S. government's pernicious foreign policies, and ignorance about those whom we term "other"—including those within the U.S.—which makes accelerated global hatred of the United States not only inevitable but increasingly likely.[3]

Yet, determined and desperate in our traumatized, emotional, and still largely unself-critical post–September 11 days, we hoist U.S. flags anxiously, occasionally hysterically: a flag means so many things to so many, of course, particularly in times of fear and confusion. (Would we ever, however, especially now, ask Native American nations exactly what the U.S. flag means to *them*? Would we dare ask them now, given that it was in fact really their land, their soil, which was attacked? Their land and soil wrested from them, as we know—should know: an old story few wish to hear or remember today. But no one right now seems to be asking Native American peoples anything about anything anyway. Given the way they have been treated ever since they greeted the travelers who landed here, that treatment comes as no surprise.) Suddenly, beneath the U.S. flag that has managed to find its way even to the moon—some of us would have thought, or at least liked to believe, that space, hopefully, would remain a more flagless realm—we are all "unified" in a peculiarly "national" identity as "Americans" that our savage internal conflicts have always belied. In the heat of this particular crisis—the one that has many people horrified at what "they" (whoever "they" are) have managed to do to "us"—we're all, suddenly—conveniently?— "Americans." "Americans" even with our (suspect) brown, black, or yellow skin; the same skin that had always meant we weren't *really* "Americans"—that is, full human citizens deserving of human rights, life, liberty. And so we are "Americans" now unless we happen to *look* as though we come from "the Middle East" or *look* as though we "are Muslims"; God knows, then, these days, what happens to us.[4] We will be "Americans" now even with our Asian-slanted eyes or with our "Jewish" or "black" or "Latin" features—that nose, that hair, those lips known so well by the very American Ku Klux Klan, by the profoundly American anti-Asian vigilante mobs and anti-Semitic gangs. And so, following public dictates, so swiftly united as "Americans," we all taste—or should appear to taste—outrage's bile over what "they" dared to do to "us." ("Why do 'they' hate 'us'?"—a question heard constantly in recent weeks, expressed with genuine alarm.) It is, of course, precisely the U.S. government's arrogance and contempt for human beings around the globe that, in part, has engendered so much rage toward it and its people—its people, the "ordinary," everyday citizens, who will, without doubt, in their fairly unshielded lives, ultimately bear the brunt of that rage—the rage that rarely reaches those most responsible for it, the high-level politicians who made and continue to make the life-harming decisions that ultimately made September 11's fire possible in the first place.

That same contempt and disregard for other human life around the globe—the contempt and disregard that presently fuel the desire of so many in this country to annihilate "them" with no questions asked; to retaliate against "them," Afghanis, Iraqis, whoever "those people" "over there" are perceived to be—never leads us back to perhaps the most difficult question, resolutely unanswered over the years and invariably avoided in public colloquy and elsewhere: who, in this historical moment, are "we," exactly? Faced with onslaughts of obfuscating, ahistorical news reports, demagoguery and blitzes of mind-directing media narratives ("America Rising"), shouldn't we know by now that all the co-opting languages around us must not only be analyzed but also rigorously critiqued? Critiqued and—for the shaping of a far more humane world—actually discarded? (Discarded, not recycled.) Shouldn't we know by now that we need pay serious attention, as thinking citizens, to what Elias Canetti once termed the conscience of words?[5] Shouldn't we be aware of the power of national and nationalist (and, often, xenophobic, racist) rhetoric? Who, now, are "we" in this latest "crusade"?[6] ("Crusade" was an appalling choice of words by George W. Bush in the days following September 11, but, considering the source, not altogether surprising. It was perhaps equaled only by his statement, around the same time, that the United States would shortly embark on "the first war of the twenty-first century." The *first* war? Implying that many others, without doubt, would follow?) Are "we," setting forth in the "war on terrorism" to make "the world safe for democracy," the same "we" who, as recently as the last century—the twentieth, that is—were burned, lynched, and Jim Crow–segregated? Denied our futures and, all too often because they were murdered, our children? Denied our lives by those other, still-present terrorists cloaked in white sheets and the madness of nights illumined by flame-sheathed crosses?

Are "we" those who, during and after World War II, were hustled with nary a by-your-leave into internment camps? Are "we" those who continue to suffer beneath the demonizing code-language assaults of "welfare reform" or "unwed mothers" or "the inner city"—among other phrases?

Are "we" those who have not forgotten forty-one bullets (and all the uncountable others) blasted into the flesh?[7] Are "we" Haitian immigrants remanded on Coast Guard cutters back to death beneath U.S.-financed genocidal repression?—for yes, make no mistake: that repression was, and remains, genocidal. As genocidal as the United States' bombing of Iraq, and as its supporting—enabling—General Augosto Pinochet's September 11, 1973, fiery coup against the Socialist government of democratically elected Chilean president Salvador Allende; as genocidal as so many other U.S. government crimes against humanity—but we will get to them. In any event, make sure sometime to ask all those dead Haitians how they feel about it all, then ask those who managed to survive them—for it is the living, finally, who possess a memory that can actually speak; the living who, in a different way than the dead, just might prove invincible.

Let us wonder if "we" are those of the ghettos, slums, and poor communities—including, to be sure, those of us with prison records, felony records—whose votes were summarily discounted in the 2000 presidential "election," and whose lives, like those of people in "the Middle East" and elsewhere, are consistently, systematically erased, written out, trammeled by the United States' determination to dominate at any cost. At the same time, we should wonder if "we" are the First Nation peoples now consigned to the dust-shame of reservations—the peoples who have long borne humiliating references to "Indians," when they are mentioned at all: the same ones who can tell us how it feels to observe the blood-soaked U.S. flag flying over their bones and memories, their cultural fragments, and, most of all, *their* land.

"We" should wonder how severely the outrage over what "they" did to "us" would have sounded had the jets veered into and destroyed a community of poor Vietnamese fishing people in East Texas, or a First Nation territory, or East Los Angeles, East New York, East Palo Alto, Watts, Detroit, Newark, Gary, Indiana (add to the list, name your ghetto). Would the deaths of many black people, people of color, have occasioned such outcry, such national compassion, such moral outrage?

The answer, of course, is no. Not in a nation in which people of color, and blacks especially, number the highest among the imprisoned and those on death row. Not in the nation in which all people of color, and, again, especially blacks, are relentlessly targeted for police violence,[8] systematically denied safe and healthy housing and proper medical care, and shortchanged educationally—as in California's and Texas's withdrawal of affirmative action programs, as in reprehensible conditions prevailing in underserved schools populated by the poor and working class. And so, recalling that particular relentlessness, it will be important to remember (and *never* to forget) that in the United States the lives deemed most important are those that are white, male, wealthy, primarily (but not exclusively) Christian, and, in most cases, heterosexual.

White, male, wealthy, mostly Christian: most certainly not the people who just might glance up at the sky (if the heavy load on the head permits it, if the hunger from having shared one piece of bread with five other people for a week permits it, if the weariness from having walked seven miles that day in search of water beneath a relentless sun permits it) and wonder when the so-needed rain will come; when the next bombing invasion (making the world "safe" for "democracy") will come; when the embargo that killed more than five hundred thousand people will end (ask Iraq, ask Cuba). The people who will wonder, again, when the food will come, if ever—and when it comes, will it arrive by way of air drops (in between bombs) televised for U.S. consumption?—a ludicrous, cynical public relations ploy, food drops bearing U.S. flags and the bitter charity of failed intelligence. Arrogance. When the food comes, will death finally come too? Death, the final release from relentlessness and also rage, but death itself as relentless as rage? As relentless as the United States' crimes against humanity, against the rest of "them"?

Courtesy of U.S. military forces in search of a symbol ("Bin Laden: Wanted Dead or Alive,"[9] trumpeted headlines recently, quoting George W. Bush's bellicose choice of words), autumn won't fare well in Afghanistan this year—if, after a history too brutal for human beings even to imagine, including British imperialism, a 1980s Soviet invasion, and the prolonged civil war that followed, it ever did. On certain mountain stretches, in the long arms of curving valleys, and in Kabul's strife-shattered remains, the still-active land mines that have already claimed who knows how many Afghani limbs—how many, exactly?—will claim more. Dead things—people, animals—will litter the plains and hillsides once more. It will not be as glorious a season in Afghanistan (or in Pakistan, or God knows where else) as it might have been in the United States in the last century and the century before that one and the one still before, when, throughout the American South, so many trees witnessed the incineration of human figures dangling between their leaves and, in some cases, buckled with the weight. Bodies ripped shy of their genitals, blood-soaked testicles cupped in a hand and held aloft to cheers; pregnant bellies sliced for the rowdy stamping into dust of the hated fetus. Frenzy, relentlessness, ash. Trees flaring over Native bodies decimated by smallpox-infested blankets traded to them by settlers for *land*. Those indigenous peoples evicted from their ancestral lands fortunate to survive, occasionally, until another autumn. Extinction steadfast, but so it has always been for "them." It's certain that slave masters didn't rape, slaughter, or torture only in autumn, but it is true that the season's red most accurately reflected the outcome of their deeds. And so in those earlier times, as now, autumns reddened into winters; coldness advanced, and whiteness blanketed the fields soon to suffer the onslaughts of a civil war from which, in the twenty-first century, the nation has still not recovered.

Not recovered, no, as incursions—the venal jaw of ever-widening U.S. imperialism—were made throughout every season into Panama, Honduras, Cuba; into El Salvador, Haiti, Guatemala, Nicaragua. Into nations disemboweled by militiamen and death squads trained in murder and torture techniques at the U.S.-based, though secret, School of the Americas (also known now as the Western Hemisphere Institute for Security Cooperation). Dictatorships, coups, atrocities covertly financed by Washington. Mexico, over innumerable autumns, has not ceased mourning the annexation, by the United States, of its land. Similar feelings, if not worse ones, abide throughout the rudely termed "banana republics"—the lives of millions of "them" twisted into further misery for the profits of the United Fruit Company. Relentlessness, maintaining its penchant for destruction via the eagle's farther-reaching claws, reshaped itself into growing isolationism and even greater indifference.

Did Haitians remanded from the U.S. in the 1990s to their dictatorship-riven country—sent back from these shores to poverty and violence abetted by U.S. economic and military aggression begun long before the Cold War—remark on the Caribbean's mesmerizing light? How fierce was that light throughout the nineteen or so autumns, and springs, and summers, of the U.S. Marines' occupation of the Dominican Republic? Over the years, what wreaked more havoc on the psyche and the flesh?—the U.S.-backed Dominican dictator Rafael Trujillo, one of the most vicious dictators ever known to Latin America, or the guarding presence of armed foreigners?

Soon, someone will have to ask the Vietnamese—those who survived more than a decade of war, one of the United States' most infamous mistakes—how brilliant their autumns loomed after those devastations. Did napalm, for instance, impair their ability to take pleasure in the weather? Did it in any way impede their observation of nature's, and their own, surrender to death?

Someone must soon ask the Somalians, and black South Africans, and Grenadians, and Angolans, and Indians (before and after the Bhopal disaster, courtesy of Union Carbide—thousands, *many* thousands, killed in 1984), and Cambodians, and Koreans how their autumns have progressed through eras of starvation, ethnic (and secret) U.S.-engendered wars, invasions, annihilations, and nations sundered into the weirdness of North, South. Autumns during which the United States, in its continued disregard for "them," plowed through seas of living faces and amassed skeletons that, for our TV screens, became—when they were shown at all—by way of media trivializations and our own ignorance, the nameless and unimportant dead.

Someone, sometime soon, will ask Chileans how they remember Tuesday, September 11, 1973, in the Chilean spring, the northern autumn. What do they remember of that day when General Augosto Pinochet's CIA-supported military regime bombed to death Socialist president Salvador Allende right in his own presidential palace, then proceeded, over seventeen or so autumns, to murder, "disappear," terrorize, and torture thousands of Chileans? How many mass graves throughout the country were eventually uncovered, and as the electric shocks of torture found the skin's softest parts, what exactly did each new day's gleam over all those military truncheons and bayonets reveal?

It is not—should not be—an impossible feat for any of us to understand that one of the greatest acts of humanity we can achieve, if not the greatest, is to imagine the lives of other people, no matter how outwardly distinct from ours, as fully equal to our own. If we do so—if we are brave and do not succumb to nationalist myopia, religious or other brands of fanaticism, or any other ideological or cultish dogma—we will surely understand that, as people in the United States and elsewhere mourned and wept over the September 11 dead, Iraqi women and men, on scorched and scorching plains, mourned and wept over theirs. If we expansively imagine, we will comprehend that, as some in the United States tossed and toss still in febrile nightmares choked with body parts, Afghanis have done the same, have done it much, and will do so again, and again. And again. If we bravely inhabit imagination's most radical terrain—that of compassion—we will quickly apprehend that as, horrified, we watched people burning, driven by the fury of burning jet fuel to leap to their deaths from the World Trade Center's high windows and disappear into crushes of steel and concrete, so too Lebanese people, bombed and otherwise assaulted by Israeli forces supplied with U.S. artillery, counted their torched murdered as they scratched through ravaged soil for remains. The dismembered hands uncovered in lower Manhattan might match perfectly in size those recently unearthed along the Gaza Strip, in a corpse-thickened river in Rwanda, or in yet another secret mass burial ground newly excavated in East Timor. "Their" lives *are* ultimately, somewhere, at some point, our lives, no matter how concerted our insistence otherwise. This late in the human calendar, John Donne's words have not receded. They resound ever more clearly.

Before today—October 7, 2001, the day these words are completed—this essay might have ended on a more hopeful note. It would have pleaded, as it does anyway, for stupidity and downright viciousness where human (and all) life is concerned *not* to triumph; for cruelty *not* to hulk its missile-laden shoulders and snarl; for atrocities against humanity *not* to be committed yet again; and for the wisdom and blessedness of peace, on all "sides," on whichever "side," to step forth, intelligently, humanely—*fast*—so that, for once, the truest, noblest, most vulnerable and necessary engagement might commence. But today, October 7, 2001, the first day of U.S. retaliatory strikes against Afghanistan began. Scores of already shattered people will be killed. Much flesh, too much of it, will burn. Will melt, yes, and blacken to the crispness of ash. The autumn for people in that country, and possibly in others, will be far from fine. (Pakistan, though also aggressive, holds its breath, as do others.) These words might have concluded with hope, but in the face of what we too often know to be murderous and savage intent, hope all at once, without warning, becomes elusive. As star-spangled flags sail and flutter and jingoism gambols while skeletons mount, the season, aware of human stupidity but strangely mute before it, continues. So today the United States marches forward, ferocity in its teeth. It is certain that now, some residents of this large nation, this "Empire," will congratulate themselves—for at last, once more and always, relentlessness strikes back. America Strikes Back, from the air and on the ground. America again today, as in the past, an ignoble purveyor of horror—evil—for others and itself. Horror and evil in a season of fire that will yet bear within its glow American, and more, faces and names—faces and names that, like the glow and the radically charred flesh, begin where the annihilation that is truest hatred begins, and do not end.

2001

Re-membering Steen Fenrich:
Not a Candidate
for Matthew Shepardhood

∞

IT IS IMPORTANT TO REMEMBER STEEN FENRICH. I WISH very much to re-member Steen Fenrich. I want—yes, through memory, though I never knew him, and through writing—to put him back together. To bring him once again before my gaze, a gaze I did not have the opportunity, during his life, to turn upon him.

While I do desire to re-member Steen Fenrich, I in no way wish to suggest, by my choice of words, any sort of gruesome or sick joke, or "irony." What happened to Steen Keith Fenrich in the last (nineteenth) year of his life, discovered by an unfortunate passerby in March 2000 and revealed shortly afterward to police, turned out to be far more than ironic, far more grisly than any gruesomeness; far more sick than any sickness except the dis-ease and utter depravity of the worst sort of "insanity."

Sometime during the fall of 1999 (most likely, from the medical and other evidence, in September), Steen Fenrich was dismembered by his stepfather, John Fenrich. Steen's mother, Wanda, married to John Fenrich, was, like her son, black—from all the news accounts I have been able to find, it appears African American. John Fenrich was white. The Fenriches had, at the time of the discovery of Steen's murder, a fifteen-year-old son, Steen's half brother.

I wish to re-member Steen Fenrich for many reasons, among

Steen Fenrich, 1981–2000

them the fact that to some degree he has become since his murder, like many victims of violence in the world, invisible—if, indeed, he was ever that much known. He has become a statistic in a region generally avoided: the region of horror, regret, hatred, fear. Yet it is precisely fear and horror, and some familiarity—a face of African descent in Steen Fenrich's face—that will not allow me to walk away from him; that will not permit me to watch him become over the years a Steen *who?* as opposed to Steen Keith Fenrich remembered, his story—as best as I can render it—made more known.

The exact circumstances of his death remain unclear, at least from extant news reports, although the facts of the discovery of his remains loom as sickening today as they did in 2000. On March 21 of that year, several items were found by a passerby walking through Alley Pond Park in the Bayside neighborhood of Queens. All the items were enclosed in a plastic container (a Tupperware container, according to the *New York Post*).[1] Among them police found Steen's skull, doused with bleach and completely "clean" of flesh; one of his feet with decaying flesh still clinging to it; teeth; pulverized bone fragments; an article of clothing; and a New York City subway Metrocard.

Steen's Social Security number was written ("scrawled," claimed one report) on his fleshless, bleached skull. Also written, or scrawled, on his skull was what several reports only described as a "racial epithet" and "derogatory term" for "homosexuals." The words written (or scrawled) actually were "Gay nigger number one."

The office of the New York City Medical Examiner would later ascertain that, for whatever reason, Steen's foot had been kept for a period in a freezer. The office would also determine that Steen's skull had been doused with either bleach *or* acid.

It is so very important to remember Steen Fenrich. It is so very important that he not disappear. For he was real. He *is* real.

A black man. A gay man. A black gay man.

(Gay nigger number one.)

A black gay man murdered by his white stepfather. The stepfather later confessing to the police, in an hour of pistols, rifles, and rooftop agony, that he had killed Steen because his stepson was gay.

Murdered him, yes. But how?

Words written (scrawled) on the body. On its skullbone.

A black gay man, nineteen years old, whose remains turned up in the most ignominious (to say the least) state.

Some people say it, and I have always believed it, and believe it again: there is no desecration like desecration of the dead, unless it is desecration of the living.

Unless it is rape, perhaps worse than death. (Ask those who have been raped, who have survived it.)

Unless it is torture—worse than death? But I cannot say. Ask the thousands, the millions, the many millions out there who have been tortured, who have survived torture, who have seen (or heard) their loved ones, their grandchildren, their children, their parents tortured. (And also perhaps raped. We cannot always know.) Ignominious words written (scrawled) on dead bodies. On bone, and on flesh.

Killed him because he was gay. So the stepfather John Fenrich screamed down to the police from the roof of his home in Dix Hills, Suffolk County, Long Island, New York—a beautiful neighborhood, a lovely town by all accounts, though, never having been there, I cannot say with any certainty.

Killed Steen because he was gay, John Fenrich screamed down from his roof to police. The stepfather who, in an hours-long confrontation with police on Wednesday, March 22, 2000, that would end in his suicide that afternoon, screamed at them, *Shoot me, shoot me. What are you waiting for? I'm a failure as a father.* John Fenrich, who, before pulling a trigger on himself, walked back and forth on his roof, armed with a handgun and a high-powered rifle. Walked back and forth on the roof, drinking beer. Was seen by some witnesses vomiting at least once into the chimney. Wednesday, March 22: one day after the police revealed to Fenrich and Steen's mother Wanda—and, perhaps, to Steen's surviving fifteen-year-old half brother—the facts about the Alley Pond Park discovery.

But then envision here, if only for a moment, simply Steen. Steen, who, as seen in his photograph and as confirmed by the facts, was young. Handsome. Who had, as people like to say, his "whole life in front of him." Who, according to some, had run on the track team in high school. (Half Hollow Hills East High, Dix Hills.) Who had been "friendly,"[2] one person had said. Who had—yes, it had been confirmed, attested to—played basketball, years ago, with his stepfather and a female friend. Steen, who later, in 1997, at the age of seventeen, joined the army. Was assigned shortly thereafter to Fort Jackson, South Carolina, as a worker in food service—a position from which, in April 1998, he would be dismissed for "unspecified reasons."[3]

Steen, who was involved, at the time of his death, with a "lover" or "boyfriend," in either Douglaston, Queens, or Flushing. (Which neighborhood? And which term best used? Which term would Steen himself have used? "Lover," or "boyfriend," or both, or neither?)

Killed Steen because he was gay. The actual murder having occurred in September 1999, John Fenrich told police, after Steen and he had argued. The stepson had apparently wanted to move back into the Dix Hills house after a disagreement (or worse) of some kind with his partner. John Fenrich apparently refused him reentry. Why? But no one—at least no one who has reported on the events for the press—seems to know. Because Steen was gay?—something of which John Fenrich disapproved, as he himself told the police? But no one seems to know: not all these years after Steen Keith Fenrich's death (dismemberment); after his epithet-scrawled remains turned up in a Bayside park in a plastic container, his story—the little we know of it, all the complications of a life and the life's abrupt interruption—has faded into media archives. Into the years of not knowing also tumble Steen's younger half brother and his mother (who, like her husband, had had troubles with the law).[4] And all the voices that, for all anyone knows (I do not know), just might have spent time—hours, weeks, months—uttering his name. Calling out, through darkness and through light, his name.

A more difficult part begins here. The part I wish so much not to have to confront even as I regard, in my mind and on various archival pages on the web, Steen Fenrich's smiling, handsome, young face; even as I know, looking at that face, that, though I never knew him, I will not ever forget him; as I also know that, in some measure, my attempt at re-membering him and the little I knew and know of his life has—at least for me—succeeded.

This more difficult (really painful) part involves acknowledging the fact that, from all appearances, to an untold number of people both in the United States and certainly outside the country, Steen Fenrich's death and life meant—mean—little or nothing. Steen Fenrich, like so many other victims of horrendous violence, never to be a candidate for Matthew Shepardhood.[5] Why? Perhaps in part because Steen, unlike Matthew, was black as well as gay; perhaps because, unlike Matthew, he was not particularly socially privileged. (John Fenrich, in addition to his criminal activities, had worked as a self-employed carpenter, and Steen, as mentioned earlier, had served time briefly in the army, generally not a province for the privileged.) The lives, loves, hopes, dreams, sorrows, secrets, and much else of black people are often considered unimportant, uninteresting, unworthy of remark (and, in a crass, capitalist, sales-driven market, *unsalesworthy,* unless they are sensational and involve sex and scandal of a certain sort, preferably heterosexual)—considered unworthy and uninteresting too frequently even by ourselves, even when we think we are showing interest. Similarly, the lives and deaths of people not heterosexual are often dismissed, ignored, "written out" of social history. What do these realities then mean for the lives of black queer people?

While acknowledging the horror of Matthew Shepard's torturous death (and, even more unimaginably, the grief of those who loved him and survived him), I note with both grief and rage that, in a world of unequal human lives, not everyone will be remembered, cared about—grieved over—as Matthew Shepard has been. In such a world—the same world that correctly views the deaths of three thousand people in New York City on September 11, 2001, as a tragedy but myopically regards the decimation of hundreds of thousands of Iraqi people (or Rwandans, or Vietnamese, or . . .) over decades as an unfortunate statistic—not all victims of hate crimes will, like Matthew Shepard, be remembered by thousands, if not millions, and wept over, eulogized, and recalled at vigils every year on college campuses, in cities, in smaller towns. Not everyone who is brutally murdered because of his or her queerness, or race, or gender, or because of two or all three of those, or for some other reasons, will be recalled during Sexual Violence Awareness Month or on National Coming Out Day, as has frequently happened with the memory of Matthew Shepard. Certainly not everyone will be remembered in passionate, beautifully crafted essays or books.[6] Not everyone's name, like Matthew Shepard's, will become a virtual referent for some sort of antiqueer violence.

Not everyone who is killed by hate violence will have a foundation set up in his or her name and memory.[7]

Yet here is a more difficult part still—perhaps the hardest. For while I too still feel, and felt when it occurred, horror and revulsion, and plain old deep *pain,* over what happened to Matthew (and felt it all in an even stranger way after a visit a few years ago to Laramie, Wyoming, the town where Matthew was murdered, and a visit to the University of Wyoming, where he was a student and where I met and spoke with some of his friends and associates), I feel absolute rage—and outrage—that what happened to Steen Fenrich *could* have happened to him, and could easily happen again, anytime, anyplace, to another black male, to a black gay male, to a black lesbian or to any black woman. *Gay nigger number one. Not-gay nigger number one. Nigger-bitch-bulldagger-dyke number one.* Could happen with scant subsequent protest, civic action, and morally fired ire appropriate in a society that considers itself "humane"—a society in which all human life is supposedly valued equally both in the eyes and practice of the law and in the concepts, protections, and advancements of true human rights. I feel rage and outrage that Steen Fenrich is (as one example) so ignored, forgotten, his death and memory rendered virtually invisible—invisible, certainly, in comparison with Matthew Shepard's. But again, why? For was not Steen, like Matthew, murdered because he was a homosexual? Unlike Matthew, was his body not also racially assaulted? *(Gay nigger number one.)*

In my outrage and unabated grief and horror over what happened to Steen Fenrich and what continues to happen to so many more unknown, dis(re)membered others—an outrage that I recognize occurs partly as a result of feelings of helplessness and overwhelmedness in the face of so much (surely prevent-able?) human tragedy—I know that I too make the same error, the deeply painful error, made by so many other black lesbians and gay men, black "queers," black transgendered people, and progressive supporters and allies. Like many of them, I believe, continue to believe (and this truly must be the hardest part), that our supposed "brethren" and "sistren" in the nonblack queer populations and our supposed "sistren" and "brethren" in the black nonqueer populations, including those among my ostensi-bly "own" Jamaican people, would indeed care enough (as they supposedly care about us) and be horrified enough by the details of Steen's death and dismemberment to present their own moral outrage over such a violation of human rights, with or without "prompting" from those of us who happen to share the victim's sexuality and race.

I say that we make a mistake because we ought to have learned by now, ought we not? Learned, after having lived in the United States that never loved us; after having lived in Jamaica (for example), which unabashedly hates us; after having lived in England, which seems never to know what to do with us, and in those parts of African America that have often wished that we would just shut up with our "nastiness," go away and keep our filthy business to our-selves—we ought to have learned that we simply cannot trust those people who we seem so often to wish would care for us: our col-leagues in black life across sexualities and diaspora, our colleagues in queer life across races, nationalities, ethnicities, and more. (The wish that others might care for one, as one might care for others, is, of course, a valid, even given desire in the human social contract of inevitable mutality.) Yet, these hurting realities acknowledged, one does continue—must continue—doing one's best to believe somehow in the inherent soaring possibilities of other people, our fellow humans, those whom we either care for or not but in any event without whom we cannot live on this planet, because that is how we all must live, somehow, isn't it? With the hope that keeps at bay the jarring death of the soul? With the faith that prevents the self-protecting corrosive of cynicism?—all the while doing our best to believe in people's greatest possibilities in spite of dictatorships; in spite of mass rapes and genocides and concentration camps; in spite of the decimation of human lives for oil or land (or simply the joy of killing the despised), or the ripping apart of children's most tender parts by grown-up hands and penises. In spite of all that—and it is all obviously horrible, horrifying, and that particular "in spite of" enormously daunting—I cannot imagine living without hope, without some sort of faith, in other people, no matter what color they are, no matter whom they love or desire. Such faith requires that one live slightly precariously here and there, with vulnerability; it requires that one constantly risk being terribly hurt by others' indifference to, and contempt for, one's own personhood and the personhood of those for whom one cares. Hurt, and, as happened with Steen Fenrich and Matthew Shepard and so many others and so many yet to come, perhaps even torture. Dismemberment.

In speaking of social contracts and trust, however, and my rage over the unequal remembering of victims of violence, I must also consider myself: for, in all honesty, was I always there for someone else when another person—a female, a male, of any color—had been raped, or killed? Did I speak out, say anything—even offer someone who needed it a consoling word, even when I myself was utterly exhausted, dispirited? There, when my voice as a supportive man was needed? A man doing what men so infrequently do—supporting women confronting sexual assault and violence? A man standing with women against the consistent degradation of women's lives, bodies, and all the sex workers found disemboweled on a back road last month, all the girls raped and sterilized in the newest sex-trafficking ring, in another narcotics ring . . . was I there? Were we? Men? There, shouting *No more*—shouting fury?

Although I have used the term "social contract," human support is not—and should certainly not be—offered contractually, tit for tat. Yet I must continue to ask myself: as much as I wanted to see Steen Fenrich's cruel death acknowledged by thousands, millions, as was done and continues to occur for Matthew Shepard, have I consistently done as much to help "others" (i.e., not "my own" people) as I have to help "my own"? As, in considering my response to the question, I wonder: is one of our realities as human beings that, when we do care about others we tend to care more about our "own," whomever we consider them to be? Is it because of such tendencies that we construct such divisions as "nation," as "tribe," as "race"? Is it because of such tendencies that, in the event of some disaster (an earthquake, a plane's fiery plunge to earth, or the crashing into the ground, after the seething of jet fuel within them, of twin skyscrapers), we scan the lists of victims for those names we believe to be from "our" group, sighing and giving thanks if few of "our own" numbered among the destroyed, or slumping into despair (or worse) should we discover the exact opposite? *I hope no gay people died in the crash. Were any black people killed? Were any Jews on the plane? Any Latinos? Any Jamaicans? Any Korean Americans?*

"Matthew Shepard died, and they did everything for him," a black gay man in New York said to several other people in a communication shortly after the revelation of Steen Fenrich's murder, "but what have they done for this man?" In that expectation that I also briefly felt—"what have 'they' done?"—and in the feeling of betrayal, deepened by that question, which I also felt, arose another error: the feeling, expectation, that "they" ought to have done "something." For, first of all, just who are/were "they"? Whoever "they" are, they have clearly rarely, if ever, cared about us, so why would we expect "them" to care about the murder of someone like Steen Fenrich or anyone similar to him? (Yet one does want "them," those people out there, to care—I know I do. Like the majority of human beings, one wishes—*I wish*—to believe that all sorts of human connections are possible; that one is—that I am—cared for, loved; and that, should one die, die violently or in whichever way, the death will mean something: it will be *noted,* and one, you, me, *we,* will be sorely missed. In fact, one feels about death the way one often feels about desire, being desired: I want to have made an impact; I want to have been wanted, loved, needed, *felt*.) For, finally, Steen Fenrich bears little resemblance to Matthew Shepard, the victim of antigay violence who, for whatever reasons, seems to have attracted the most grief, the most caring, the most consistent moral outrage. Steen Fenrich is not, at least as a black male, no matter what his sexuality, a candidate for Matthew Shepardhood. In the context of a race-ist United States, no black person ever can be.

Who exactly "they" are and whose lives they value or dismiss is one discussion, but another, more urgent one is this: while re-marking how little "they" did regarding Steen Fenrich and others like him, what did *we* do? We to whom Steen was obviously important? We who read the news about him and felt ourselves literally sickened by it; we who looked at him and thought, Brother. Ourselves. Many, and many thousands. We who might have desired him, who might have cared for him, who could have seen ourselves so easily in his place. What did we do?

Did we cohere in groups of mourning and remembrance? Hold our own vigils, readings, remembrances?

Did we fashion posters bearing Steen's name and photo-graph, beneath which words like "Remember Him" and "Never Again This Violence" and "We Will Always Remember You, Steen" were written—indeed, scrawled? Did we register his loss among us and within us, in that deepest place where breath and life—yes, and desire, and longing, and the longing for love—both begin and end? Where grief begins, begins to sear, gnaws at the sinews, and need not end?

Did we—perhaps for the first time, for some of us—truly feel ourselves among each other? Our force that *is,* in fact, our force? Along varied streets and in bereft parks, did we walk, march, shout, and also stand in silence, all the while bearing aloft those posters, aware of the gift—the very profound gift—of our selves among our living selves?

Did we strategize on the political (race-ist and antigay) realities of Steen's murder? And comfort each other even as we sat at tables or on floors, trying to think of more far-reaching ways to fight for our lives, loves, and the lives and loves of those to come?

Did we—black men of all sexualities—convene with each other with the intention of working through our grief over a fallen brother, and also with the aim of bravely, coherently, analyzing our differences and similarities, strengths and weaknesses? If we met, did we try our best, our differences and fears and suspicions of each other notwithstanding (accompanied by our occasional deep regard for each other in spite of, but not necessarily because of, those differences), to work *with* one another in our respective and bisecting communities and outside them? Work toward ensuring that the viciousness visited on Steen Fenrich's living and deceased person would never, so long as we could help it, be wreaked on anyone again?

While committing ourselves to that vital work, did we resolve to work with black women and other women as conscientious men devoted to the global human rights of women? Did we embark on that difficult work as men fully conscious of the fact, the incontrovertible fact, that it remained *and remains* our responsibility to stop, partly through our own behavior and self-reflection, all male-engendered sexual violence against women and the related violence against the gender "outlawry" of transgendered people?

If we felt repulsion in the presence of transgendered people, or at least unease, did we resolve to wrestle with the feelings and listen, *listen* to them and to the women—listen carefully, compassionately, respectfully—in order to learn from their experiences as people daily and nightly confronted with the possibilities—the *realities*—of sexual violence (including domestic violence) and the violence, in the cases of people of color, of racism?

Did we work to understand their analyses of the similarities and differences between racism, the hatred of women, lesbians, gay men, and transgendered people, and the global exploitation of poor people, most of whom happen to be women of color?

Finally, but at the point of another beginning altogether, did we apprehend that truth so necessary for our most productive, possible futures? The truth that makes clear that there isn't, rarely has been, and will not ever likely be any "they"—only we. Ourselves.

Ourselves, who must, in every way possible, re-member—knowing in our deepest hearts, though it is terribly painful, that "they" will not, because "they" so rarely—*very* rarely—have.

For there are—yes, we know there are—so many more to re-member. Sakia.[8] Brian.[9] Amanda.[10] Arthur.[11] And so many, many others, going back several centuries. Each one bearing his or her own name, and a face lately, or long ago, gone silent.

And so the years pass; the days widen and thin; and memories, like joy and passion in the shadows of the days, return and recede. By now, several years later, it is possible that Steen's bleached (or acid-doused) skull, hopefully cleansed of the scrawled *Gay nigger number one,* has been placed somewhere beyond the possibility of further desecrations. Someplace inviolable, even venerated, which is the right of the dead. For the respect and dignity due the memory of this brother—a brother whom I did not know—that is, once more and now always, my prayer.

2004

Abu Ghraib:
Fragments against Forgetting

Already, the scandal is fading fast from our collective memory.[1] (August 6, 2004)

But it must not. Must not ever fade. Cannot. In the fading lies the danger of repetition: the ever-recurring danger. The danger of brutality. More of it. More cruelty. Stupidity. Evil. We never did this or that, some might think, will want to think, unschooled in history. Yet *that,* that terrible thing, that awful sequence of horrendous things, is precisely what we *do* do, again and again, and again. What we do while ignorant of history, or unmindful of it. While indifferent to it. Uncaring. As arrogant as ever.

The human degradation that occurred in that prison in Iraq: much, much more than a "scandal." But yes. Without question. Crimes against humanity: a more fitting term. War crimes, sanctioned by various arms of the U.S. government. Sanctioned because, after all, who cares about those people? Are they not all pigs, all "terrorists," all anti-American sons of bitches? (Or, if they are women, just bitches?)

The wise, sad man with those eyes that had seen too much—much too much—said:

The real danger, the real evil, the major issue of our
times, is indifference. . . . The opposite of love is not hate
but indifference. The opposite of art is not ugliness but
indifference. The opposite of faith is not heresy but indifference. And, after all, the opposite of life isn't death, it's
indifference.[2]

(Yes, to be sure—he warned. Warned as others have warned, continue to warn. But when, and where, does our listening begin?)

In the case of that prison in Iraq and what was done to human
beings there by U.S. soldiers and officers (and what was done to
human beings in Afghanistan by U.S. soldiers, and what was
done, is still being done, by U.S. soldiers to human beings in
Guantánamo Bay), where does indifference begin?

Abu Ghraib. And so the photographs of male and female U.S.
soldiers torturing and humiliating Iraqi prisoners were published.
This year, 2004. Made public in newspapers, electronically, in
magazines, and on TV. All over the world. Violations revealed:
Iraqi women and men, civilians held as prisoners for indefinite
periods (and what exactly were the charges?). Iraqi people held
naked, bound, hooded. In that nakedness degraded by U.S. soldiers. Vulnerable in that nakedness to who knew what sort of
further humiliation and torture at the hands of gleeful American
soldiers. Iraqi men forced by laughing U.S. soldiers to simulate sex
acts with each other. (Yes: a profound violation of Islam.)

So much glee on those laughing American faces. Some of the
soldiers sporting the "thumbs up" sign as they humiliated the
Iraqi prisoners. (Or as they crouched over the dead ones.)

The United States began to create offshore, off-limits
prisons such as Guantánamo Bay, Cuba, maintained
other detainees in "undisclosed locations," and sent ter-

rorism suspects without legal process to countries where information was beaten out of them. . . . Concern for the basic rights of persons taken into custody in Afghanistan and Iraq did not factor into the Bush administration's agenda. The administration largely dismissed expressions of concern for their treatment, from both within the government and without.[3]

But then remember this above all else, except the torture itself: that not one of us—not the U.S. public, nor the rest of the world, and certainly not the people of Iraq—were ever supposed to know about any of it. We were not meant to know about the torture, the violations—about all that malevolence visited upon Iraqi bodies by—

Yes. By American hands.

A secret. To be kept as secret, surely, as U.S./CIA aid to mujahideen in Afghanistan fighting the Soviet Union's invasion, 1979–88. The United States having begun supplying aid to the mujahideen six months *before* the Soviets invaded.

As secret as the United States' training of the Iranian secret police under the Shah in the 1970s.

> What is clear is that the U.S. military personnel at Abu Ghraib felt empowered to abuse the detainees. The brazenness with which the soldiers at the center of the scandal [but so much more than a "scandal"] conducted themselves, snapping photographs and flashing the "thumbs-up" sign as they abused prisoners, suggests they felt they had nothing to hide from their superiors.[4]

Who, then, were their "superiors"? More importantly, their ultimate "superiors"?

The head of the CIA?
>   The secretary of defense?
>   The joint chiefs of staff?
>   The president of the United States?

Already we are beginning to forget.

The United States did sign the Geneva Conventions. It did sign the International Covenant on Civil and Political Rights. It did sign—yes, without question—the United Nations Convention against Torture. Global treaties, all. Each treaty expressly enjoining, *enjoining* the use of torture in any situation, for any reason. For *any* reason. Ever.

> *The [Geneva] Conventions . . . provide explicit protections*
> *for all persons held in an international armed conflict, even*
> *if they are not entitled to P.O.W. status. Such protections*
> *include the right to be free from coercive interrogation, to*
> *receive a fair trial if charged with a criminal offense, and,*
> *in the case of detained civilians, to be able to appeal periodi-*
> *cally the security rationale for continued detention.*[5]

"Torture should be added to the list of evils that the Bush administration is defending, in accordance with a foreign policy based on unilateral American domination of the globe."[6]

But then remember this too: that it all began long ago. Began not with a prison in a country invaded by the United States for nefarious reasons (can any invasion ever occur for a "good" reason?) but on American soil, in Atlantic waters. Centuries ago. Those bodies, raped and humiliated, torn and burned, castrated and flayed and yes, O yes, now remember: so much more. Forced to work the land, forced to breed. Forced to swallow and forced to—. . . . Those bodies that, while chained, could not speak for themselves against the torture, though many did escape. Many fled. (Fled, including by way of suicide: death, the most guaranteed route of flight.) Those bodies so long ago and not so long ago: hanged, burned. Raped, and ripped. The ones that, if they did not wind up in smoke-shrouded trees, if they were not whipped to death, knew, like the hooded, bound bodies in Abu Ghraib, the power of the commanding state. The power of the gag.

So long ago—

And yes, it is true: that torture, like slavery, like the torture of slavery, like the various forms of enslavement with which forms of torture are invariably connected and without which they cannot succeed, requires a certain secrecy. (The world would know nothing, the U.S. public would know nothing, the citizens of Iraq would certainly know nothing.) Yet, as in the case of Abu Ghraib and other sites like it, an audience for the torture—an audience that participates in the torture by doing nothing to stop it—almost always exists. An audience, in the case of Abu Ghraib, that snapped photographs, and also jeered ("thumbs up"). Laughed.

> In fact, the only exceptional aspect of the abuse at Abu Ghraib may have been that it was photographed.[7]

Yes, they did. Back then, in that time (but not so long ago). All the time. They photographed them. Photographed the people in the trees, swaying from the trees if they were not already ash, with broken necks, with stretched necks. With fire-scorched bodies. Blackened hands. (Soot, ash.) Photographed the people dangling. Dangling from those limbs. (The leaves—how beautiful, how green, despite the smoke. . . . Oak? Ash? Beech? Sycamore? But never, as far as anyone has seen, any sort of pine, conifer.) They photographed themselves looking at the dangling people. And themselves sometimes laughing. A party. A party for all, provided that they were white. Provided that they were not Iraqi. Provided that (in the case of the unfortunates massacred at My Lai by American soldiers) they were not Vietnamese.

"We—and the rest of the world—are . . . bothered by the fact that the U.S. soldiers in the [Abu Ghraib] pictures (and presumably those taking the pictures) clearly got a kick out of what they were doing. In this respect, these photos resemble the postcards circulating in the United States in the early 20th century showing white people smiling and cheering at the lynchings of black men (and sometimes women)—the photos that showed us that racial animus can amount to a kind of giddy arousal."[8]

> The commanding general in Iraq [at Abu Ghraib] issued orders to "manipulate an internee's emotions and weaknesses.". . . Abusive treatment used against terrorism suspects after September 11 came to be considered permissible by the United States in an armed conflict to suppress resistance to a military occupation.[9]

Sickened: the exact word. One is sickened, and shocked, by the brutality—by the sheer cruelty possible at American hands, revealed in the photographs taken at Abu Ghraib. (Although, yet again, if one can manage to live with an unflinching view of American history—of world history—one is not surprised. If one is black and living in the United States, one should certainly not be surprised.) As a member of U.S. society, as a human being, one might even be ashamed. Yet one learns—I learn—that shame, in the face of inhumane behavior, is not enough. Anger even is not enough, although it can fuel the correct sort of civic moves toward clarity and, in a case such as the Abu Ghraib abuses, justice. Already, here and there, various media in the United States and elsewhere are featuring stories about which individual in the president's administration should or should not have kept closer watch over the prison, over the armed forces and the soldiers and officers assigned to the prison, and over the innumerable varying conditions—political, social, some glaringly evident, others less obvious—that may have contributed to the violence (in addition to war) inflicted on Iraqi bodies. Yet few gazes seem truly interested in the fact that not only did the U.S. soldiers' behavior at Abu Ghraib betray a profound disrespect for, and even hatred of, Iraqi people and their culture, religion, and history (not surprisingly, of course—rare is the plunderer who would behave respectfully). The contempt and general inhumanity the American torturers displayed for their prisoners also clearly must in some way have been approved—encouraged—by some among their superiors, who, in one way or another, felt such contempt themselves. That contempt, known in some quarters as xenophobia or racism or both—a dire combination in men and women carrying guns, as often shown by U.S. police forces, especially when present in poorer neighborhoods and areas.

> Anti-torture laws [an August 2002 memo written by assistant U.S. attorney general Jay Bybee states] *simply do not apply* to "detentions and interrogations of enemy combatants pursuant to [George W. Bush's] Commander-in-Chief authority." All the documents [since] released by the White House reflect this same obsession with presidential war powers.[10]

> "[George W. Bush] has known for more than two years that his Administration has been pursuing policies that could qualify as war crimes under federal and international law."[11]

And so, in the wake of a memo written by the assistant attorney general and supported by the White House's Office of Legal Counsel (of course), the current president of the United States—a president not legally elected for his first term—believes that he and those who would follow him (and there are many) *can* disregard the Geneva Conventions, the International Covenant on Civil and Political Rights, and the UN Convention against Torture. And so the U.S. government in this present historical moment will not only flout human rights at Abu Ghraib. It will also do so, as it has already done, at Guantánamo Bay, Cuba, where who knows how many suspects of anti–U.S. government actions are being held. (Do their families know? Do they have legal counsel? Does anyone know where they are?) It will do so, as it did before, in Afghanistan. As it did at (among so many other places) My Lai.

My Lai   1968   Vietnamese village   more than four hundred civilians murdered there by U.S. soldiers   most of the murdered having been women   children   elderly

> Guantánamo . . . where the U.S. is holding hundreds
> of detainees in top secrecy and without access to courts,
> legal counsel or family visits. Add that to the roughly
> 1,000 civilians the U.S. imprisons in Afghanistan, the
> 10,000 civilians thought to be detained in Iraq and who
> knows how many others across the globe, and it looks
> as if incarceration is the nation's best export.[12]

Afghanistan

> [In western Afghanistan:] The Americans blindfolded
> us and, worst of all, they made us completely naked
> and made us to sit in a cold room and we were shivering
> and trembling because of the cold air. . . . [Describing
> transport to Kandahar:] I was naked and I had no clothes
> at all when I was moved. . . . [Upon arrival at airbase in
> western Afghanistan:] I was pulled out of the car and
> moved towards an airplane. At the airport, someone
> who was pretty strong held my neck under his arm and
> pressed it hard and meanwhile kept punching me hard

on my face and one punch hit hard on my mouth and two front teeth of my upper jaw fell out, which you can see now [interviewee is missing both teeth].

[In Kandahar:] They behaved very rude with me after the plane landed in Kandahar. It was cold and they threw us on the desert for more than an hour. Then some army men came and took us inside. Getting us inside the room there were some guards ready, and they were beating us mercilessly, without any reason. They were kicking and punching us. Mostly they were beating us on our backs. Later [they] gave me clothes to put on. They shaved our hair and our beards and mustaches. After that they took me for an interrogation and before asking any questions they started beating me. One person picked me up high over his head and threw me onto a desk and made me lie there. And then two or three other persons hit me with their knees on my back and shoulders. . . . The next day I was taken for interrogation.[13]

Unfortunately, unlike Los Angeles in 1992, no one happened to be nearby with a video camera.

How many voices yet to be heard

Abu Ghraib

Guantánamo

Kandahar

Kabul

Baghdad

And more

Yes, much more—
(But so important: to remember)

(Yes, critical:
to remember)

(Utterly crucial:
to remember)

to not forget

many would rather
that we forget

war   murder   death   torture

A few of the abuses the American soldiers perpetrated on their
prisoners:

Breaking chemical lights and pouring the phosphoric
liquid on detainees; pouring cold water on naked detainees; beating detainees with a broom handle and a chair;
threatening male detainees with rape; allowing a military
police guard to stitch the wound of a detainee who was
injured after being slammed against the wall in his cell;
sodomizing a detainee with a chemical light and perhaps
a broom stick, and using military working dogs to frighten
and intimidate detainees with threats of attack, and in
one instance actually biting a detainee.[14]

Abu Ghraib   now they are in a pile   bodies in a pile   they made them get naked for the   pile   why is that woman walking the man on a dog leash   why do they have those people wearing hoods   *Abu Ghraib*   so this is the prison   *Guantánamo*   but no one knows they are there   no one knows the   bodies   are there   why are the American soldiers here   the soldiers care nothing for Islam   outside Iraq is still burning   one of the oldest countries the oldest civilizations in the world is   burning   so many bombs and limbs and torn people and bones and   is it true that some of the women were raped in Abu Ghraib   is it true that they are holding children there   the soldiers   the soldiers saluting the American flag   the soldiers enjoying watching the male prisoners forced to simulate sex acts   *prison*

> In George [W.] Bush's America, denial about inmate mistreatment runs . . . rampant. As Texas governor, Bush oversaw the executions of 152 prisoners and thus became the most-killing governor in the history of the United States. Ethnic minorities, many of whom did not have access to proper legal representation, comprised a large percentage of those Bush put to death.[15]

. . . the random jailing of
     more than 15,000
        Iraqis
           reminds us that more
             black men
               in the U.S. are
                  incarcerated
              than have
            graduated
            from
            college.

Torture
was practiced in
U.S. prisons
long before
Abu
Ghraib.[16]

But who cares? (A voice, one of many: out there. Heard, sensed,
witnessed in the past. Recurring. Always there.) For after all,
They are only
Iraqi people.
They are only
black
yellow
brown
people.
They are only
those people who continually
threaten our
security,
security,
who harbor
Weapons of Mass
Destruction,
who
will never
never
never
shut up
about
slavery

The reasons for the U.S. soldiers' taking those photographs of the
Iraqi prisoners experiencing abuse? Photographs of men forced to
simulate sex acts, including oral and anal sex, with each other;
photos of a bound man cringing before a threatening guard dog;

photographs of naked men wearing hoods (but so many photos like that), and of a man pulled along at the end of a dog leash, by a female soldier—

"It was just for fun," that female soldier remarked.[17]

And doctors—

Doctors, yes. Doctors who, as disclosed in recent reports, also colluded with the torture of Iraqi bodies by doing nothing about it.[18] *Doctors seem to have colluded in covering up . . . deaths of detainees in Iraq. . . . [A] well-known case was described . . . in which an Iraqi general suffocated after his interrogators pushed him upside down in a sleeping bag and sat on his chest. An on-site surgeon, whose report was initially posted on a Pentagon Web site, said the general had died of natural causes. One of the medics . . . was called to treat a prisoner who had been punched so hard that he could not breathe. While there, the medic saw detainees stacked naked in a pile—a now well-known photograph. He failed to report the incidents. . . . Army regulations, the Geneva Convention and the federal War Crimes Act require all military personnel, not just medics, to report evidence of abuse or torture.*[19]

The United States as a Decimating Force.
The Good Citizen, Language, and Memory

In such a configuring alone—that of the U. S. as decimating force—the nation carries too much history. As if the Atlantic slave trade were not enough: the creation of (in that case) utterly unbearable history. (Yet it is astonishing—is it not?—how much human beings discover, over centuries or through nights and days, they actually can bear.) The erasing of millions of histories, including those of the peoples whose feet, millennia before, first roamed through all the ranges of the Americas. And no, we must not stop talking about it slavery

genocide

for all of it, like so many other perpetrations, has not yet been fully remembered. In future times, we might become brave enough and honest enough to term all of it, correctly, what it was: an American Holocaust. In future times, we will perhaps be brave enough (honest enough) not to shrink before the word "Holocaust."

The United States still, today, evermore, as decimating force. As if its undermining and toppling of democratically elected governments all over the world were not enough. (And what was at stake in the particular toppling? Oil? Land? Private-sector investment in, contracts with, U.S. corporate interests? The "threat" of Communism?) As if the constant denial of its own culpability in so much world misery were not enough. And so in the context of the corporate-driven empire, the antihuman empire, does memory become the Enemy of the Good Citizen? Does the Good Citizen, at his government's behest, worship amnesia? Worship amnesia's scent (foul or divine) and its substance? (The shape of its bulges . . .) Does the Good Citizen permit himself to swoon before amnesia's caresses? If he does so, does it not follow that language itself then becomes a cloaking device?—a restrained and restraining device, the adversary of actual (as opposed to ideological, regime-shaped) truth? Language as prisoner of the censoring, monitoring state. Language: the most powerful resource of both dissidents and despots. Corralled language: restrained by—cloaked within—the state and statist regulated official untruths ("Iraq harbors weapons of mass destruction"). The language of official untruths in the grip of obscurantists and ideologues, including those of totalitarian regimes. Language that, in their grip, becomes not only the foundation of the Good Citizen's amnesia ("Was the Vietnam War really that big a deal?" "Did the Holocaust *really* happen?" "Why do we have to keep talking about slavery?") but also its most depraved counterpart as the enemy of testifying memory—the memory, state, faculty, that is most crucial to human dignity and possibility. The memory that refuses to forget—*cannot* forget, *must not* forget—that *something happened here*: Torture. Murder. Rape. Genocide. Invasion.

The memory that refuses to bow before indifference. Indifference, the comrade-in-arms of amnesia and of corrupted, state-enslaved, ideological language.

We must not forget

Abu Ghraib

Guantánamo

And more

More—

What the U.S. government is perennially capable of

What human beings are always capable of—

2004

Again, the Sea

The sea would forever be larger than me.

—DIONNE BRAND, *A MAP TO THE DOOR OF NO RETURN*

AND LARGER AND LARGER AND EVER LARGER THAN ME, O sea: water: waves and foam: this girlpoet this womantongue does speak the truth, says I: does speak the truth, she womantongue, from she selfsame mouth. Poet, poetry. Make she come back to she island and sing to me and we. Make she come back and read she words to we. Make she tell we what we does already know: how the sea would take I and wrap I deep in it. How it would drown I, mash I up, wash I into bits. The girlpoet with she womantongue and she words would tell I so. And so I does say now that I know the sea this same sea like I does know the back of me hand, says I: these currents,
these waves,
these foams,
says I,
like I does know the smell and form of my own shape that the Lord God did once pon He holy time giveth to me. What the Lord God did giveth to me the sea shall not take away, I does pray. Let this sea not take I, but let it talk to I. Let it sing. The sea, the sea. Yes, water. Waves. Wetness, poundsurf, that I does love.

. . . while the sea soft,
and leaves of brown islands stick to the rim
of this Caribbean . . .[1]

(This Caribbean)

(But then do not hanker after it, said those whom you the traveler had long known to be [yes, without question] wise, and whom you loved: do not hanker after that sea which you have always loved and far from which you cannot live happily for long: neither cling to it nor summon it, but *Let it go,* they urged, and do your best to exist "in the moment," they said—referring to that place in which, so very far from that sea you so adore, you now are. In another place which is always somewhere north. Somewhere cold. Somewhere where the sea you so love cannot know how much you dream of it, long for it, caress it in thy sleep. Somewhere *where you now are,* which once again [soon again], you know, will become that town, that upstate mountain-surrounded town where—at least for now, until you can escape—you work, yes, every day, and which you hate.)

(Far from the sea, and I am yearning. Far from les antilles, las antillas, and I am sad.)

But do not hanker, they warned. No. *Leave it behind,* they said.

Surrender it, they warned. Yes. *Jettison it,* they advised.

All of them speaking of,
(speaking of)
    all of them speaking of
    that sea.

        That sea,
        but not just any sea. Not

the Ionian, no, nor
the Aegean, no—
nor the South China,
nor the Tyrrhenian, nor the great,
old,
formid-
able
Red.
They

were speaking of
(but of course!)
the Caribbean.
El mar caribe.
La mer antillais.
Once upon a time
the Spanish Main.

But leave it behind, some said. (Still say.) Migrate northward. Eastward. Northeastward. Return to the empire. (But you were always part of someone's empire.) Return to "civilization," where people, *people,* know the meaning of a good pot of tea. *Leave it all behind.* History. Memory. Poverty. Backwardness. Thirdworldness. Ignorance. Fear. Anxiety. *Behind, behind.* As if some would—but many had no choice, had to: children needed things, life had to go on. But some could not: the ones simply too poor to leave, forced to stay where they were in poverty. Forced to "endure," that was the word, exactly: or die. *Leave it all behind.* Can you leave it behind? Life, or death? But children are in need, in need of things. People are so in need. In need of their own lives.

Returned: here a traveler originally of that sea finds himself returned to an upstate town in the north of a coldish country; an upstate town he deeply hates. A town from which permanent departure will, for him, he knows, without question someday occur.

Someday, yes. (But he must remain there for the while; remain there until the opportunity to depart forever looms.) In that backwoods eyesore of a town and hating it so, how could he not dream, devouringly, of el caribe? Of la mer antillais? The Caribbean. His sea. The sea of poets, womanpoets and men. The sea of time.

Dream, *dream of returning to it*—

Dreams, yes. The region in which, so many believe, that elusive thing known as "true freedom" (or "truest freedom") begins. The region in which all can live unassailed, unencumbered, when so little *out there* promises (life becomes more bleak, more lonely, without the sea) and the sky simply, mutely returns stares *(how it stares!)* and you, I, we are *so far, so very farfar from the sea not only of deepest dreams, but also of desires.*

> . . . we could look back
> with widening memory
> on the hot, corrugated-iron sea
> whose horrors we all
>
> shared.[2]

Once upon a time, in fact not that long ago, on an afternoon of scalding sun, the sea was—yes, exactly, it is true—made of corrugated iron. Hard. Deep. And the horrors that lurked beneath it? But I came to know them, of course. I myself had only recently emerged from the sun, from the blazing, glaring sun, and sought, with the naïveté of youth, a cooling surface for my more recently singed limbs, my arms, the delicate feathers at the nape of my neck. (My strongest wings, those that would later emerge from my shoulders, had not yet begun to form.)

And so how could I not plunge headlong into the sea so far below— plunge, with a great cry, through its hot corrugated iron and right

through to the deeper depths, down, down, to the darker green depths,
down, to the blue, aquamarine,

    (All beginning in water, all ending in water. Turquoise,
aquamarine, deep green, deep blue, ink blue, navy, blue-
black cerulean water)[3]

to the beginning and ending that were there in that water, down in
the deepest deepest part where, as I plunged and plunged more still, I
began to see the horror: the faces, of course. The hands, still reaching.
The bones, still whitening. The mouths, still grinning. Some of the
hands clutching others (those of their children, perhaps, or those with
whom they had decided to jump overboard hand in hand: this is the
end of it all for us, they thought, we shall jump together, we shall
never see this new place, we shall reawaken back over there from
whence we came, in a field. Beneath trees. Reawaken far from these
stenches we have endured, these screams we have endured, this death
through which we have suffered and witnessed—children, old people,
women with child, it did not matter: death, death, all was death,
down there, shackled. Give us the sea, they thought, and so jumped,
sometimes holding hands). Some of the hands . . . but we all shared
those horrors. Yes, even I, though recently emerged from the sun.
For the sun, like a few of the stars, knows all the secrets of the sea:
knows its sorrows, its gravities, its complaints, its dirges. It knows,
and so, though not yet fully winged, though glowing and blushing in
the naive bloom of utter youth, do I know. These horrors. Plunging,
still downward, I weep. Yes, and cry out. My sorrow is the sorrow
of the sea and of stolen time. My tears are the salt of the sea of their
wounds of their tears of the sea so unmerciful so broad so beckoning
so terrifying so endless eternal when they

jumped

or when, in darkness, in the suffocating heat of what it all was down
there, shackled,

they died.

I share it. I weep. When shall I return to the above and to the light to which, though I am not yet fully possessed of my most powerful wings, I am compelled to return? But a little more time down here to plunge, I beg you. For they still all are reaching. Still so many of them are staring (though many fish swim through their sockets, through their hollow eyes). Still so many of their bones, even here in this cooler darkness, whiten. I must be near them. I must, though I come from the sun. And yes, I do hear their voices. For am I not too one of them? Have I always, even in the sun's hottest core, not been one of them? This, then, only part of my widening memory. I plunge, though the light above will soon pull me upward unto its breast. Through the corrugated iron. That hardness. Through the waves that today are all iron. But for now, here, I feel the bones. They are holding hands. They jumped, many of them. Others, once confirmed to be deader than dead, were tossed over the side. I hold them. Feel them. They are me. Reach out to me, I to them. They are, will be, my wings to come. (And I theirs . . . ?) I plunge, awaiting the light that has always known my name. L-i-g-h-t, as in "gleam," as in "day." It will come. It is coming. Down, up. Darkness. So much of it. But then light—

But they do not understand. They who warn and advise against hankering ("Stop hankering for the blasted sea!") simply *do not understand* what it, el mar caribe, means to one when one is pulled away from it.

And regard (I):
Here are the words (alongside them, between them, imagine, once more, the sound of waves):

It's difficult to live near the sea.
It overwhelms. . . . It owns. Your
small life is nothing to it. The sea
uses everything. Small things like
bits of black bottles and rusty
bottle tops, smoothed transpar-
ent fish, fish bone, cockles against

small rocks. . . . The sea can make
a tree into spongy bits, it can wear
away a button to a shell. It can wash
away blood and heal wounds.[4]

And regard (II):
*Letter from the Sea, Scrawled by Its Most Eminent Hand, to Three
Corpses—Each Felled in a Different Century, Two by Its Ravaging
Waters* (O Sometimes Cruel Sea!)
Dearest Ones,

To each of you—but what can I say? For you each know,
each of you trapped still within me, so deep within me, that
her words, written above in her very own womanpoettongue,
are true: it is difficult, at times, to live near me. It is difficult, at
times, to not feel owned by me. (I own: she states it, it is true.) It
is difficult, at times, not to resent how I use everything—every
utter last little striking thing. "Small things," she writes, "like
bits of black bottles"—yes, or your corpse's eyes, or your whitening bones, or the shoelaces you were unable to untie before you
wound up, choking, sputtering, clinging still to life so desperately, within me.

But in this you were not, of course, alone—for how many others, millions of others over as many years, wound up within me?
Alongside me, beneath me? Too many to count, dearest ones, and
far too many to remember, though I personally have forgotten
none of them. They are there, deep within me, where buttons
wear away to shells, where trees become bits of sponge. Where
all sadness is at last caressed, all outrage smoothed over. Has it
not been said by at least one that I and I alone possess the power
to wash away blood, to heal wounds? One of you came to me in
the jaws of a shark, and I washed away your blood myself, spread
it throughout my farthest selves. One of you bobbed upon me
with the strokes of a cruel whip upon your naked back, the scars
of manacles on your wrists, and did I not slowly pull you into

the nothingness that is utter calmness, the complete tranquility of nonbeing?

One of you came to me in the night—a victim of some sort of rebellion, or regime, or some other terrible thing involving sharp blades, explosions, bright flames, and guns. You came—or were tossed by those bearing the long, sharp blades—like the many others they tossed in on later nights: with your head missing, your hands slashed through and dangling at the wrist, and your insides completely gone—ripped out and fed, I know, to the dogs that followed the swift feet of those who, in that place, along those shores, ran each night from village to village doing to others with their blades exactly what they did to you. And I washed you, and erased you—you, whose face I would never get to know, for they never returned that part of you with the rest. That part is still out there—seeing nothing, and speaking (perhaps) of death.

One more of you came, of course—she who was the one who truly loved, loved without fear or shame; the last of you. She came of her own choice, intending to throw herself into these waves—yes, these same waves now recounting to you. But she was refused—by me, by them. Refused because it was not yet her time. Not her time yet to choke, to splutter, to thrash and then, so still, not yet stiffened, descend into nothingness and nonbeing, down, farther down. She was—yes, it is known by all who saw her and heard her, it is known as fact by all who were there, birds, stones, trees, particles of sand, and every last fish, so help them all—she was screaming and crying, prostrate, for her lost love. And undone, completely, because of what (she screamed) they had done to him. She stamped, beat herself, tore apart her clothes and wept, and was prepared, on that very shore, to give herself, her body, to the sea. To me. But she could not. For as I have already told you, it was not her time. She—yes, none other than *she*—was not yet ready.

Here: The Dreamer
And so the Dreamer tells you, here, now, that he is the Dreamer. His

*face, once more, is blue—partly blue, the color of the sea today out
of which, blue- and green-dreadlocked, he rises: dripping, yes, and
veiled, amidst his sopping sea-locks, in sea-things—weeds, myriad
leavings, all manner of clutter wrenched, by the sea, by its manifold
undulating creatures, from the dead: gleaming buttons wrested from
the tattered blouses of drowned women; sea snails pulled rudely out
of twilight copulations; crabs' moltings; and all the fingers, fingers
not yet whitened to, to*

    Yes. To bones.

    *And ah, Dreamer, he thinks, smiling his sea-smile. Smiling and
knowing as he does that you can, with no trouble at all, without any
struggle, read all his thoughts. He blushes, but revels too in your gaze.
Ah, me, he thinks: the special one. The one so beloved by the sea, by
this sea. The one who exists only in dreams, especially in dreams of the
sea, especially in the dreams this sea itself has—teal and aquamarine
beloved, waters warm but so often vengeful, and always indifferent:
Sea Magnificent, those upon the shore do frequently call it. Sea of
coconuts, of tamarinds, of guavas, star-apples: sea forevermore upon
which I, the Dreamer, in bliss, walk; through which, in joy, I who
is he swim.*

    *By nightfall, he thinks, knowing that you hear the thought, I will
be gone.*

    *And so it happens today, a day like any other (the sun blazing
overhead, the fishermen in the distance on their boats farther out calling out to each other news of the day; the sky ever so far beyond gazing
impassively yet ever watchfully upon the sea): it happens that the sea of
this region, las Antillas/les Antilles, possesses the Dreamer—indeed,
possesses all dreamers. Possesses not only them, but also all wanderers
(regard those upon the shore, suddenly dazed, stopped dead in the act
of scrounging about for shells), vacationers (they might not ever return
home), children (stopped dazed by the sea, they have already forgotten
their proper names), and all the others—all the one-day wayfarers,
the wedding celebrants and praise singers (they will soon dance and
sing praises to all undulating things far beneath the blazing sun, deep
in the sea), sailors, long-armed fishers, divers, and lifesavers (large*

*chests); and coastal monitors, and beach-strolling whores: the sea has
done to them today, Sea Magnificent, what it long ago did to the
Dreamer. To the Dreamer—*

He is a magician, of sorts—
     He floats upon the sea, upon his back, and does not fear it,
His head thrown back as he floats,
     Thrown back to the sun,
          Regard the sun above him, so stern, so powerful,
               So it is—is it not?—in a region of dreams,
               Of teal-colored sea,
                    He dreams of dying near the sea,
               Within it,
                    O upon it,
                         Let it lick and caress his carcass,
                    Let it move through,
                    between,
                       all his parts,
                    his dreams.

*The sea curls itself about his throat; it plunders him; it washes its foam
over his mouth, across his lips;*

*It enters him; swirls through him; caresses his most private parts in
that way, like that—holding him, holding. Rocking him back and
forth upon itself.*

*Rocking him that way (as if he were a twig, a bit of ruined boat,
nothing more), the sea expels him. Explodes him. He shoots up out of
the water upon which he had been floating, with one great shudder.
With a convulsion.*

*Exhausted, he awakens. Thinks that he ought to—yes, perhaps he
really ought to—head back to shore.*

And so he does. He does make it back. Of course—for the sea, this sea, would never kill him. Not this way, by drowning. Not yet. It is entirely possible that, on his exhausted way back,

[stroke,
stroking,]

a dolphin, curious about his parts, or about his blue and green dread-locks, or merely about the evidently plundered state of his form, bumped him—nudged him, yes—back to the shore. A dolphin, that (regard its grave eyes, the smooth turn of its snout), in more secrecy, away from the watchful sky, might have indulged in a little something-or-other with him. A dolphin that, had it not bumped him so determinedly to shore, might have done who knows what with him, for how long, leaving behind a watertrail of blood, foam. Leaving it behind.

The dolphin did do things to him. It did interfere with him. He knows: for later, after he has crawled, with great effort, out of the sea and up onto the shore, he becomes aware of the slicing pain in some of his parts—it is there, it is all knives. He becomes aware of the foam still dripping along some of his parts. The dolphin had done those things to him, and Sea Magnificent made it all possible, but the waters did not kill him. No, he knows. Of course not. Not that day. Not yet.

That night, all about the place where lives the Dreamer (that place of frangipani, coconut trees, hibiscus, bougainvillea; night-blooming jasmine, otaheite apple, and always lizards, lizards, scarlet throated) blows on the ceaseless breeze the message that he is now *carrying a child,* it says: *yes, deep within his belly. A dolphin's child, or the sea's.* He was *fertile,* it breathes, *soon will be heavy.*

(The Witness)

"And it is true," the witness says (young, youngish; also blue-and green-dreadlocked; now bobbing above the waves far out at

sea; now and then greedy for the taste of guava, of soursop, of
sun-fermented pineapple), "the sea put a child into him. Or the
dolphin did. But in any event they are the same, out of the same.
And so it came to be that in some months' time he did indeed give
birth, far beneath the waves, to not one, not two, not three, not
four, but *five* perfectly formed young ones, young things, already
dreadlocked (yes, green, with blue among the females—although
it was invariably difficult to tell which was male, which female).
He gave birth, straining with great cries and pleas for mercy, *Sea,
Sea, what hast thou done to me*—so he screamed down there, but
Sea Magnificent paid him no attention; it swirled about him, it
sent its dolphin minions to attend to him; it commanded them to
provide their milk to his young ones, seeing as he had not enough
milk, or the determination to provide it, for the five reaching
mouths. I do not think that he ever saw again, after it happened,
the face or form of that dolphin that interfered with him—that
left all that sea foam all over him, and nudged him back to shore
leaving behind a trail of foam and blood. A thousand years may
pass, and still he will be about here, the young ones gone from his
side, on their own . . . I have no idea what has become of them.
But he—he with his dreadlocks in blue and green so beloved by
those randy dolphins—he so beloved by so many creatures, by the
sea itself—he, the Dreamer—he will not fade, think I. He will
always be here. He will always return here. He will always be of
here. Yes, say I, the Witness. Only one of many," says he, before
disappearing beneath the waves, perhaps forever—"one of many
who, in these waters, at these times, with just this feeling between
the legs, *this* one—ought to know."

The sea would forever be larger than me, wrote that womanpoet,
but it is exactly for that largeness that I will return to you and
return again to you and again and again and once more O yes
without question to be sure to be certain yes again, my sea: return
to you at the end of this year, return in my blue-tinted dreams:
return in those dreams in which I will see and know, I am certain,

the beautiful Dreamer of your most prolonged caresses. I will
return to you, and wherever it may be,
Jamaica, Martinique
Trinidad, Cuba
(and let me not forget, how could one ever forget you, Sainte Lucie)
I will carry within me their memory, too, for certain, yes, and their
bones: even now they are holding hands in your deepest depths.
*They are me. Even now, down there some of them jumped, provided
the chance   they would not feel the whip one more time provided
the chance   they knew once they jumped they would awaken back
there, over there again from whence they had been taken/the sea
provided them the chance   jump   jump   come let us live
forever   better to jump now and go down down   down   than
to live forever in chains   I do not know what is down there   I
am terribly afraid   come take my hand and   we jump   the
waves swirling waves greet us   we will awaken once more over there
back there   we will not live forever in chains   I will carry their
memory I will   we will not live forever in their   The sea,* she
wrote, *would forever be larger than me*

And at last: twilight. The quick, brusque twilight common
throughout these parts. Twilight that blues, then purples, all the
little villages nestled on the cliffs so high, *high* above the sea.
Twilight that folds beneath its belly all the little towns, lights,
fires, people, animals upon the cliffs so high, very high, above the
sea. *The sea,* a young wise girl with twilight eyes once said, *is the last
thing you see when you leave the island. Yes, this island. It is the first
thing you see upon approaching.* Each night, unbeknownst to her
parents, that same young girl becomes a dolphin. She cavorts out
there, in the great deep darkness, with all of *them.* She snorts and
spouts as they do; she leaps and twists herself as they do, without
care, upon and beneath the deep, dark sea during the hours when
no one, no fisher, no lone swimmer, no unfortunate child on the
beach can see. I do not know what will happen to her. Already, for
more years than even I can possibly remember, she has called me

with her twilight eyes and called me, called me again: *come back, return,* she calls, in absolute silence, as if I did not intend to. As if I were not already there, feeling that dolphin—her, perhaps, or one of the males, or another of the younger ones—interfering with me again. Doing those things to me even though I have returned. Poking me, nudging me—pushing me back to shore, yes, leaving behind us on the water's surface skin a trail of blood and foam. I am the Dreamer. I want so much to be the Dreamer, my belly heavy after the sea and the dolphin have been within me. I do not know what will happen to her. Night after night cavorting with all of *them. But how difficult it can be to live near the sea,* her eyes so often say, *how it uses everything for itself. In this dream which is in fact no dream, I am at last a dolphin. I am cavorting. I am at last free. Leave it all behind. But I will never forget any of them, down there, still reaching. They jumped. Yes, I am prepared to jump. Let us awaken back there. O sea magnificent, blow your breath upon me. Now hold me in your grasp. Now help me to remember. I want so much to remember. You are memory. You are—yes, magnificent water, CaribbeanAtlantic, caribe, holder of those so far down within you still, so far down within you after the centuries, so far down within you the ones who jumped some still all bones all bones O yes children old people and everyone all of them down there, down there so dark and silent, now still holding hands . . .*

2004

Acknowledgments

WITH ALL-OF-IT-AND-MORE, BUT MORE STILL, PLUS African violets this time—plus much, much love—to Anne Higginbottom. (And so indeed, as Ms. Brand wrote long ago, "to be awake is lovelier than in dreams.")

With special thanks and love to the Prescods of Roselle Avenue; to Shelley Ruth Glaze, recalling (at least) Port Royal, and so much more—sardonic words, earnestness, and still more laughter by the sea; and, out in Clarendon, to one Ms. Gennie Prendergast Harrison. The Jamaica I remember in your company, abiding national troubles not withstanding, remains the one I love most, and the one I will continue to hope for and believe in.

With profound gratitude for the generosity and support of Joyce M. Glave, Roderick Ferguson, Rinaldo Walcott, Michelle Cliff, Maryse Condé, Sonia Sanchez, Jonathan Ned Katz, Paule Marshall, Heather Burns, Patricia McFadden, Mary Poggione, Laura Westlund, Daniel Leary, Stacy Zellmann, Norman Riley, Linda Duggins, Lisa Li Shen Yun, Ricardo René Laremont, Carole Boyce Davies, Elizabeth Alexander, Robert Olen Butler, Darryl C. Thomas, Ali Mazrui, Rebecca Schleifer, Leo Wilton (brother, colleague!), Beverly Facey, Don Weise, Mary Helen Washington, Gene Jarrett, B. G. Firmani, Michael Thelwell, Charles Henry Rowell, Masani Alexis DeVeaux, Robin Coste Lewis (always, and more), Toby Thompkins, David Lenson, Carole Maso, Daylanne K. English, Aishah Shahidah Simmons, Lisa C. Moore, Susan Strehle, Juanita Díaz-Cotto (estimada colega y compañera), Maureen T. Reddy, Donald Lindo, Thalia Field, and Hugh "Barty" Cresser.

Most special appreciation to Richard Morrison and Doug Armato, who, along with their belief in this work, both extended warm hands. Broad hands. To you two and to all, I would like to say once more, always, Thank you.

Notes

Baychester: A Memory

Since the 1993 writing of this essay, matters have changed considerably regarding documentation and attention to human rights violations against lesbians and gay men. Both Amnesty International and Human Rights Watch, two of the largest, most visible human rights organizations, now frequently track and report homophobic hate crimes in many parts of the world. Lesbian and gay organizations such as the 1978–founded International Lesbian and Gay Association (ILGA), among others, were, of course, the leaders in this arena.

1. Assotto Saint (Yves Lubin) died of AIDS-related illness on June 29, 1994. For his long struggle against death, for his unequaled heralding and support of so many black gay writers, and—most of all, never to be forgotten—for his nurturing and guidance of my work and vision, and for the love and privilege of his friendship, this essay is dedicated to his memory. My teacher. My brother.

2. Looking at this essay in 2005, I note with chagrin my own unfortunate ethnocentrism of earlier years, vis-à-vis notions such as "coming out." "Coming out" is still, as this book appears in print, neither a commonly accepted nor widely practiced phenomenon in Jamaica; nor, for now, is it generally, across social classes, conceptualized in such language in Jamaican culture. In 2005 I know this, but as a younger, more naive person in 1993—a person to whom Jamaica had always meant an enormous amount, as it does today—I didn't.

3. At the time of this essay's writing—the early 1990s—I had not yet encountered the work of three Jamaican writers whose work centrally featured homoerotic themes: Patricia Powell, Makeda Silvera, and Andrew Salkey. Powell's gay (male)-themed novel set in Jamaica, *A Small Gathering of Bones,* was first published in Heinemann's Caribbean

Writers series in 1994. I had no way of knowing then that I would be asked by Powell nine years later to write the introduction for Beacon Press's 2003 reissue of the novel, which Heinemann had let go out of print. Some years earlier, I had also discovered Powell's better-known novel *The Pagoda,* which, set in nineteenth-century Jamaica, focuses on the life of a transgendered Chinese Jamaican living as a male with a female lover. After Powell's work, I would also find Silvera's story collection *Her Head a Village* and her wonderful essay "Man Royals and Sodomites: Some Thoughts on the Invisibility of Afro-Caribbean Lesbians," as well as Salkey's novel *Escape to an Autumn Pavement,* set in London and concerned with a Jamaican man's homoerotic yearnings.

Toward a Nobility of the Imagination

1. This writing comes on the heels of the formation of the Jamaica Forum for Lesbians, All-Sexuals, and Gays (J-FLAG), of which I am a founding member. It is my hope that this essay, first published in the local Jamaican press, will assist in amplifying and enhancing an incipient activist-humanist dialogue that, like several of its proponents, continues to struggle for equal voice in a Jamaican climate of prevailing virulent homophobia, sexism, and ongoing psychological, social, and physical violence aimed at lesbian, gay, bisexual, and transgendered people. The views conveyed in this essay are expressly my own as an individual and do not necessarily represent those of J-FLAG.

2. "Out of many, one people," Jamaica's national motto.

3. Cf. the ragingly homophobic lyrics of the Jamaican singer Buju Banton's 1992–93 infamous dancehall hit "Boom Bye-Bye": "Boom bye-bye in a battybwoy [homosexual's] head / . . . nah promote de nasty man, dem haffi dead" (Don't "promote" homosexuals/homosexuality, they should be killed). From its release, this song was greeted with widespread approbation in Jamaica—due clearly in part to Banton's notable vocal and musical gifts, but also to its theme in keeping with many Jamaican antigay cultural beliefs. After the song's content was translated from Jamaican creole by Caribbean-affiliated, U.S.-based black gay activists, Banton's outright bigotry and calls for violence against homosexuals were protested by numerous lesbian and gay activists throughout the United States and Europe.

4. "Smaddi": somebody, person, in Jamaican creole.

5. "Battyman," "man royal": derogatory terms for gay man and lesbian, respectively.

6. ICI, informal commercial importer. Term applied, occasionally sardonically or cynically, to the enterprising street vendors who purchase goods abroad, largely in the United States and Curaçao, and return to sell them at varying profit levels in Jamaica. While a number of these vendors, an overwhelming majority of them female, sometimes manage to earn what would appear to some in Jamaica to be a fair to substantial income, relatively speaking, the majority of them remain among the country's severely socially disadvantaged and uneducated ever-burgeoning urban underclass.

7. Michael Norman Manley (1924–96), former Jamaican prime minister.

(Re-)Recalling Essex Hemphill

1. Essex Hemphill, "Heavy Breathing," in *Ceremonies: Prose and Poetry* (New York: Plume/Penguin Books, 1992), 4–5.

2. I refer specifically here to the continuing rise in the United States of white nationalist, white supremacist hate groups, including neo-Nazi and "skinhead" organizations and so-called patriot groups, all of which demand another essay's comprehensive analysis and discussion. More information on the proliferation of hate groups can be accessed from the Southern Poverty Law Center based in Birmingham, Alabama, an excellent resource; and from the Institute for Research and Education on Human Rights, in Kansas City, Missouri.

3. See Robert Reid-Pharr, "Memory and Man: Essex Hemphill," *Gay Community News* 24:3–4.

4. Recalling the Abner Louima case of New York City. Louima, a Haitian-born immigrant to the United States, was physically tortured in a bathroom of the 70th police precinct, Brooklyn, by Officer Justin Volpe on August 9, 1997. The principal and, to many, most horrifying cruelty inflicted on Louima by his assailant was Volpe's sodomizing him with a toilet plunger's handle, causing Louima severe injuries to his rectum and bladder, after which Volpe brandished the stick in Louima's face. Louima was also threatened by Volpe with death if he told anyone

about the incident. After almost two years of in-court wrangling, bureaucratic and other tensions, and outrage displayed by citizens activist and nonactivist alike, Justin Volpe pled guilty on May 25, 1999, to federal charges, including conspiracy to obstruct justice and conspiracy to deprive civil rights.

5. Remembering the literally torturous death of James Byrd Jr.: a forty-nine-year-old black man who on June 7, 1998, was picked up not far from Jasper, Texas, by John William King and Shawn Berry, both twenty-one, and Lawrence Brewer, thirty-one. All three men were white. Byrd was driven by the men in their pickup truck to a deserted area, where they chained him to the back of the truck and dragged him along the road for three miles, toward Jasper. Byrd was soon decapitated by a concrete drainage culvert; his torso wound up in a ditch, approximately a mile from where the rest of his body was discovered by a passing driver and later by police. When found, Byrd's face was spray-painted black. King's very body entered the case as evidence for the prosecution, marked as it was with racist and neo-Nazi tattoos, the words "Confederate Knights of America" and "Aryan Pride" (see note 2 above), and a tattoo of a black person being tree-lynched. King was convicted of murder on February 23, 1999, and sentenced to death—the first white sentenced to death in Texas for killing a black person since the state reinstituted capital punishment in 1976.

6. Comment attributed to either Eric Harris, age eighteen, or Dylan Klebold, seventeen, as they shot and killed black student Isaiah Shoels, eighteen, in the library of Columbine High School, Littleton, Colorado, on April 20, 1999—Adolf Hitler's birthday. Shoels was one of thirteen people killed, not including the two killers' suicides, and one of two people of color.

7. Cf. the comment made by the Columbine High School English teacher Paula Reed on an April 21, 1999, *Oprah Winfrey* TV show: "This is a school that's very safe. . . . It's in a community that cares and . . . supports its schools. You . . . think of . . . things like this happening in the *inner city,* where maybe socioeconomics are a problem, where poverty is a problem. That's not the issue here at Columbine. *We are predominantly an upper-middle-class neighborhood*" (my italics).

8. From an unpublished poem by Gwendolyn Brooks.

9. See Toni Morrison, *Beloved (New York: Alfred A. Knopf, 1987).*

10. Hemphill, "To Some Supposed Brothers," in *Ceremonies,* 132.

11. In reference to Amadou Diallo, twenty-two-year-old Guinean immigrant and street vendor living in the Bronx, who was shot and killed by four white police officers in the Bronx on February 4, 1999. Forty-one shots were fired at Diallo, of which nineteen hit him. Diallo was unarmed when shot, was not known to possess any firearms, and had no previous criminal background. According to court testimony by Sean Carroll, one of the shooting officers and a defendant during the officers' trial in Albany, New York (moved there from New York City due to defense attorneys' fear that "public clamor" over the shooting would make a "fair trial" for the officers "impossible" in the Bronx), Diallo, just before the officers opened fire, had been acting "suspiciously," "slinking" back toward the building where he lived. Carroll also testified that Diallo, to the officers' eyes, fit the "general description" of a "serial rapist" who had been active in that part of the Bronx; Carroll also stated that he suspected that Diallo might have been a "lookout for a push-in robber." On February 25, 2000, the officers were acquitted of all charges, including murder in the second degree, manslaughter in the first and second degrees, criminally negligent homicide, and reckless endangerment. (See Jane Fritsch, "4 Officers in Diallo Shooting Are Acquitted of All Charges," *New York Times,* February 26, 2000, A1; and Tara George, "4 Diallo Cops Go Free," *New York Daily News,* February 26, 2000, 2).

12. Billy Jack Gaither, age thirty-nine, a white gay resident of Sylacauga, Alabama, was picked up in Sylacauga on the evening of February 19, 1999, by Steven Eric Mullins, twenty-five, and Charles Butler Jr., twenty-one, both also white, and driven to an isolated nearby area, where he was beaten by both men, forced into the trunk of his own car, driven farther, then beaten to death with a wooden axe handle. His body was placed on two tires his killers had set afire. Mullins and Butler later confessed that they had killed Gaither principally because of his sexual orientation; Butler stated that he had been angry at Gaither because the latter had allegedly made a "pass" at him.

13. Matthew Shepard, age twenty-one, a gay white University of Wyoming student, was beaten into a coma on October 6, 1998, by Aaron McKinney and Russell Henderson, both twenty-one and also white. Shepard was found the following day, laterally tied to a fence. His skull

had been crushed by his assailants' hitting him with a pistol. He died on October 12, 1998.

14. The actions and words of the white supremacist Buford Furrow, Los Angeles, August 1999.

15. See Audre Lorde, "The Master's Tools Will Never Dismantle the Master's House," in *Sister Outsider: Essays and Speeches* (Freedom, Calif.: Crossing Press, 1984), 110–13.

16. Hemphill, "Does Your Mama Know about Me?" in *Ceremonies,* 41.

17. Hemphill, "American Wedding," in *Ceremonies,* 171.

Fire and Ink

This keynote address was delivered at "Fire and Ink: A Writers Festival for Gay, Lesbian, Bisexual, and Transgendered People of African Descent," University of Illinois–Chicago, September 21, 2002.

1. See Essex Hemphill, "American Wedding," in *Ceremonies: Prose and Poetry* (San Francisco: Cleis Press, 2000), 184.

2. See Pat Parker, "Where Will You Be?" in *Movement in Black: The Collected Poetry of Pat Parker, 1961–1978* (Ithaca, N.Y.: Firebrand Books, 1978), 74.

3. See Václav Havel, *The Art of the Impossible: Politics as Morality in Practice* (New York: Alfred A. Knopf, 1997).

4. Toni Morrison, *The Nobel Lecture in Literature, 1993* (New York: Alfred A. Knopf, 1994), 22.

5. James Baldwin, "Sonny's Blues," in *Going to Meet the Man* (New York: Dial Press, 1965), 139.

6. Joseph Beam, "Brother to Brother: Words from the Heart," in *In the Life: A Black Gay Anthology,* ed. Joseph Beam (Boston: Alyson Publications, 1986), 239, 242.

7. Audre Lorde, "A Burst of Light: Living with Cancer," in *A Burst of Light: Essays* (Ithaca, N.Y.: Firebrand Press, 1988), 80.

8. See Nadine Gordimer, *Living in Hope and History: Notes from Our Century* (New York: Farrar, Straus and Giroux, 1999).

9. Arundhati Roy, "The Ladies Have Feelings, So . . . Shall We Leave It to the Experts?" in *Power Politics* (Cambridge: South End Press, 2001), 9.

10. This quote and the two following are taken from Toni Morrison, *The Nobel Lecture,* 33.

Whose Caribbean?

This convocation address was delivered in slightly different form for Caribbean Heritage Week, Brown University, March 10, 2003.

1. See http://www.jflag.org.

2. Recalling Buju Banton's notoriously homophobic dancehall song "Boom Bye-Bye" (1992). "Battybwoy": profane Jamaican creole word for gay man or homosexual, literally "ass man" or "ass boy"; "sodomite": condemnatory word for lesbian, occasionally also used in reference to males. "Battyman fi dead": "Faggots should be killed." "Battyman fi bu'n": "Faggots should be incinerated."

3. While I use the words "gay," "lesbian," "bisexual," and "transgendered" here, I much prefer the all-encompassing term "queer," which includes all the aforementioned not only as sexual *identities* that are often, though not always, self-selected, but also as sexual behaviors, as in "gay" (male-male) sex. "Queer" also makes room for various political/ideological practices, such as lesbian and transgender feminism. It is critical to remember, however, that much of what some Western quarters term "gay," "lesbian," "bisexual," or "transgender" is not necessarily so viewed or named by those who practice the behavior. Thus "men who have sex with men," a term seen frequently in some North American and European (and increasingly Latin American and Caribbean) AIDS/HIV education contexts, accurately describes the *behavior* of individuals who participate in same-gender sexual and romantic unions but do not particularly, if at all, view themselves as "gay," "homosexual," or even "bisexual."

While the word "queer" also makes room for varying behaviors and identities that would be viewed by many as unquestionably "nonheterosexual," it also includes behaviors often viewed as "subversive" by many, such as that of "straight" men who enjoy cross-dressing in their female partner's undergarments, "straight" people's use of body piercings, hair dyes, and tattoos (some of which presentation has come to be seen as "queer," but not necessarily a definitive statement of "gay," "lesbian," or "bisexual" sexuality), various or all sadomasochistic practices, same-gender participation in sexual fetishes by people whose sexual or romantic lives are otherwise "heterosexual," and so on.

The word "queer" has also been used much in recent years as both verb and adjective by many (principally North American and European, although this too is changing) scholars, as in, for example, "queer" theory/theoretical discourse, vis-à-vis the need to "queer" or "queer*y*" a text (provide a "queer" reading of or "queer"-ed investigation of a text). With such linguistic and intellectual fluidity and expansiveness, almost anything can be "queer"-ed or "queer*y*"-ed: texts (queer theory applied to the works of Derek Walcott or C. L. R. James, for example), other cultural products, philosophies, scholarship (the "queering" of an historian's scholarly gaze), public and private spaces (the "queer-ing" of Buckingham Palace, or a "queer"-ing study of the cricket match as a homosocial, homoerotic bonding ritual), ideological, cultural, historical, and national narratives (the still largely unexplored reality of "queer"/same-gender sexual/romantic desire between slaves and/or between masters and slaves, for example), metaphors, allegories, and so on. While I believe in and support the inclusive, imaginative, and political possibilities of the word "queer," I chose not to use it in this essay principally because it is not (yet), in the Caribbean at large, a word that has either been used much or considered for its potential in applica-tion to nonheterosexual sexualities, practices, and identities. By way of amplification with regard to "queer," a similar, but somewhat differently employed, term has recently emerged in some African American lesbian and gay circles: "same-gender-loving."

4. As cited in the "Parliamentary Submission" section of J-FLAG's website (www.jflag.org), "The Offences against the Person Act prohibits 'acts of gross indecency' (generally interpreted as referring to any kind of physical intimacy) between men, in public or in private. The offence of buggery is created by [the act's article] 76, and is defined as anal in-tercourse between a man and a woman, or between two men. No force is required for the commission of the offence of buggery. Most of the prosecutions in fact, involve consenting adult men suspected of indulg-ing in anal sex." Article 76, "Unnatural Crime," states that "whosoever shall be convicted of the abominable crime of buggery [anal intercourse] committed either with mankind or with any animal, shall be liable to be imprisoned and kept to hard labour for a term not exceeding ten years." Article 77, "Attempt," states that "whosoever shall attempt to commit the said abominable crime, or shall be guilty of any assault with intent to commit the same, or of any indecent assault upon any male person, shall be guilty of a misdemeanour, and being convicted thereof shall

be liable to be imprisoned for a term not exceeding seven years, with or without hard labour."

5. See George Orwell, *Animal Farm* (New York: Harcourt, Brace, 1946), 112.

6. Interestingly—and sadly—toward the end of 2004, roughly one year and a half after this essay was written, Human Rights Watch issued a report entitled *Hated to Death: Homophobia, Violence, and Jamaica's HIV/AIDS Epidemic.* The report featured some harrowing (to say the least) documentation of antigay, antilesbian human rights violations in Jamaica. Within days, the report and its recommendations for future progressive action were brusquely dismissed by members of the Jamaican government, including the prime minister and members of Parliament. Reactions to the report in the Jamaican press and on local radio stations ranged from occasional grave consideration of the report's findings to outright contempt.

7. I use only the term "gay" here, meaning self-identified gay or homosexual men, and do not include lesbians because, to date, the significant majority of political asylum cases involving Jamaican refugees fleeing homophobic persecution have been those of men. This reality comes as no surprise, given the ways in which homophobia and homophobic violence are leveled in such radically different measures toward men, women, and transgendered people in Jamaica. (In this regard, one might rightly assume that transgendered people, unless they are able to "pass" visibly as a person of one gender or another, bear the discriminations visited on people who, in a strictly gender-demarcated society, possess the physical and visual attributes of both genders. Even if they are able to "pass" completely as women, they must still contend with the hostility and sexism regularly visited on women.) It is also important to remember that the oppression of women who are perceived to be lesbians in Jamaica (and in many, if not most, societies) occurs within and beneath the prevailing oppressions of sexism and misogyny, which, in their stern ideological insistence on adherence to rigidly imagined and constructed gender roles, impact women's lives differently from, but similarly to, the ways in which they bear on the lives of men who stray from the gender role "normative" male behavior expected of all men. Men of whichever sexuality, of course, always possess some measure of male, patriarchal privilege, which is especially, though not only, granted

to the male perceived as "masculine," within a given society's specific definitions of masculinity.

8. Wislawa Szymborska, "Children of Our Age," in *With a Grain of Sand: Selected Poems* (New York: Harcourt, Brace, 1995), 149.

The Death and Light of Brian Williamson

1. "Sketel": Jamaican creole for a "trashy," somewhat tawdry person; if used by someone in the middle or upper classes, the insult often makes clear that the "sketel" is not, though might be, of one's own social class. The insult might also be directed toward someone imagined as sexually "loose."

2. "Butu": an "ill-bred" or coarse person; someone who doesn't know how things "ought" to be.

3. "Nyam": eat.

4. Ting: Jamaican grapefruit soda.

5. "And ting": literally, "and thing(s)," meaning all the rest, everything else.

6. "Get on like batty and bench": literally, to get along as well with someone, or keep company with someone, as much as a person's backside ("batty") does with a bench.

7. "Go on bad": behave badly, rudely.

8. "Fenke-fenke": highly particular, hard to please, finicky.

9. "Tek bad tings mek laugh": to use unfortunate events for jokes; to use gallows humor.

Regarding Carolivia Herron's *Thereafter Johnnie,* So Long Swept Aside

1. Carolivia Herron, *Thereafter Johnnie* (New York: Random House, 1991), 3. All italics in the quoted sections of the novel are mine. In 2001, Carolivia Herron published a revised edition of *Thereafter Johnnie*. All notes here, along with the entire essay, refer to the original 1991 Random House edition of the novel.

2. Ibid., 3.

3. See Brenda O. Daly, "Whose Daughter Is Johnnie? Revisionary Myth-Making in Carolivia Herron's *Thereafter Johnnie,*" *Callaloo* 18, no. 2 (1995): 472.

4. Herron, *Thereafter Johnnie,* 95–96.

5. Ibid., 227.

6. Even as this essay is written in 2004, thirteen years after *Thereafter Johnnie*'s original publication, Herron is still known far more for her (in)famous, controversial children's book, *Nappy Hair,* than she is for the novel.

7. See, for example, Elizabeth Breau's article "Incest and Intertextuality in Carolivia Herron's *Thereafter Johnnie," African American Review* 31, no. 1 (Spring 1997).

8. I often feel infuriated at how much Butler and Marshall are also overlooked, along with superb fiction writers like Helen Elaine Lee, the Jamaican Michelle Cliff, and the occasionally recognized Gayl Jones—but that fury will without doubt lead to other writings, and for that I am also grateful. I should make clear here that in these paragraphs I am speaking about African American women writers, and not, principally, about those of the larger diaspora.

9. As "general" a population as one can get at any given moment in the United States. By "general" here, though, I mean a less academic audience, but also one interested in reading a wide variety of books.

10. See Breau, "Incest and Intertextuality."

11. Herron, *Thereafter Johnnie,* 21.

12. Ibid., 242.

13. Ibid., 242–43.

Between Jamaica(n) and (North) America(n)

This essay was delivered in slightly abbreviated form for the Faculty of Literatures in English/Postgraduate Seminar Series, University of the West Indies/Mona, Jamaica, March 28, 2003.

1. See Anthony Winkler, *Going Home to Teach* (Kingston, Jamaica: LMH Publishing, 1995), 76.

2. A predominantly upper-middle-class suburban neighborhood, north of Kingston proper.

3. "Helper": Jamaican term for a maid.

4. The "claat" words: Jamaican profanities, such as "rassclaat," "bumboclaat," "bumborassclaat," "pussyclaat," and "bloodclaat." "Claat" is a patois-ization/creolization of the word "cloth," originated in the days when neither processed sanitary napkins ("pussyclaat,"

"bumboclaat," or "bloodclaat"—the latter literally "bloodcloth") nor toilet tissue ("rassclaat") was available, and "cloth"/rags of one kind or another were used for dealing with bodily functions. "Bumborassclaat" is a compounded form, often used for extreme emphasis. Some years ago, the use of these words in public could bring harsh consequences to the user from the police, although, as remains true today, the working class and poor were more likely targets for police harassment and violence in this and every regard than were the privileged. The "claats" are commonly heard now among all age groups, both genders, and are considered in some quarters as much aphrodisiacs as vulgarities.

5. "Stush": upscale, fancy.

6. Jamaica Omnibus Service.

7. "Where's your woman, faggot?"

8. Much has been written elsewhere about the "policing" of sexuality, but of particular interest is an essay by Cathy J. Cohen and Tamara Jones, in which the authors delineate the specific difficulties of heterosexism, homophobia, and the "policing" of sexualities perceived to be deviant. The authors write: "In its full force, heterosexism is not satisfied with merely categorizing behaviors as deviant or normal, but works systematically to (re)produce conformity to 'normalcy.' Heterosexism thus requires that . . . communities engage in continuous policing of members by each other. It demands an environment of constant surveillance in which individual members must adhere to strict codes of conduct or risk being attacked. Specific gender roles are an inevitable consequence of a heterosexist belief system." See Cathy J. Cohen and Tamara Jones, "Fighting Homophobia vs. Challenging Heterosexism: 'The Failure to Transform' Revisited," in *Dangerous Liaisons: Blacks, Gays, and the Struggle for Equality,* ed. Eric Brandt (New York: New Press, 1999), 90.

9. "Out of many, one people," Jamaica's national motto.

10. "Faggots should be killed."

11. "Sketel": a "trashy," somewhat tawdry person, a term often used as an insult by people in the middle or upper classes to describe sexually "brash" or "rude," sometimes exhibitionistic behavior (or just general "slacknes"), especially among the working class or poor. The term "rasta sketel" is especially interesting because its very existence suggests, correctly, that if "rasta sketels" exist, there also exist *actual, orthodox* Rastafarians who are *not* "sketels"—that is, who are not in any way

interested in sex tourism or the pandering of their bodies for sex tourism or prostitution/"rastitution" purposes. Unfortunately, the complexities of orthodox Rastafarianism have in some ways been obscured by (among many other things, including much ignorance about Jamaica's cultural and historical complexities in general) the more visible, highly sexual, fetishized and fetishizable bodies of sex tourism "rastitutes."

12. Carole Maso, *Aureole* (Hopewell, N.J.: Ecco Press, 1996), 5, 6, 15.

13. Jamaica has since changed the size and color of its passport, but the "old" large blue one, presently possessed, still resides close to the heart.

Regarding a Black Male Monica Lewinsky, Anal Penetration, and Bill Clinton's Sacred White Anus

1. From "Narrative," section I, "Nature of President Clinton's Relationship with Monica Lewinsky," subsection C-2, "Sexual Contacts"/"Ms. Lewinsky's Account," in *The Starr Report: The Findings of Independent Counsel Kenneth W. Starr on President Clinton and the Lewinsky Affair* (New York: PublicAffairs, 1998), 39.

2. From "Narrative," section VI, "Early 1997: Resumption of Sexual Encounters," subsection D, "February 28 Sexual Encounter," in *The Starr Report*, 79.

3. In using the word "smut" here I quote directly from the *Washington Post* journalist Joel Achenbach who, in the "Analysis" opening section of *The Starr Report*, writes: "The Starr Report is a challenging piece of literature. It does not fit precisely into any of the familiar genres. It is certainly not a romance in the traditional sense. At moments it can be read as farce, other times as tragedy. But probably the genre into which the report fits best would be 'pornography.' . . . Quite frankly, this is *smut*, an incredibly offensive and numbingly repetitive tale of sex and its consequences. The main characters, 'The President' and 'Ms. Lewinsky,' are repulsive. But so, gradually, is the narrator himself." From Joel Achenbach, "Dreary Prose, Silly Plot. Can't Put It Down," in *The Starr Report* (my italics).

4. For an especially interesting look at homophobia and its roilings in the public/political sphere, including concerns centered on and directly resulting from U.S. national(ist) ideology and Cold War "national security" obsessions, see Robert J. Corber, *In the Name*

of National Security: Hitchcock, Homophobia, and the Political Construction of Gender in Postwar America (Durham, N.C.: Duke University Press, 1993).

5. Indeed, keeping in mind the United States' relentless puritanism, the very idea of sex—any kind of sex but especially "wrong" (i.e., "casual" or nonmonogamous), demonized, same-gender sex—might be abhorrent enough, even as the perceived "badness" of those sexual practices beguiles, sexually and homophobically speaking, to one's own certain peril. The many secular and religion-based public messages and homophobic diatribes in the United States against AIDS as punishment for sex, especially for "bad," "dirty" sex, attest to the power of these ambivalent, deeply entrenched anxieties.

6. The course was titled "Politics and Courage: Contemporary African-American 'Queer' Writings"—a course I'd begun dreaming of either taking or teaching when I was an undergraduate, and which I finally developed while a graduate student, and taught for a complete semester for the first time at the State University of New York at Binghamton. The word "queer" was used in quotes in the syllabus to call attention to its perhaps debatable place in an African American cultural/historical context: was it, for example, a word many African American "queers" or same-gender-interested people would use to describe themselves? A word nongay African Americans would use to name black "queer" people? Was it a "black" word, found in any of the diverse and highly regionalized African American vernaculars? But then could language be so placed within a racial category or "claimed" by a "race"? In this instance, what might the differences be between "race" and "culture"? Did they exist, and if so, were they, for us, valid? The word "queer" was also employed with the hope that our scrutiny of it would push us all toward more useful, comprehensive definitions and expansions of the word itself.

7. See Reginald Shepherd, "On Not Being White," in *In the Life: A Black Gay Anthology,* ed. Joseph Beam (Boston: Alyson Publications, 1986), 46–57.

8. Explorations into the notion or myth of "pure" whiteness—what "pure" whiteness as ideal, property, and "race" might and should be, and has been—have been assayed extensively elsewhere; I nonetheless raise the issue here as a reminder that U.S. ideas and constructions of "pure" whiteness often, but not always, exclude Jews, white-(self-)identified

Latinos, Latin Americans, Chicanos (if any Chicano can truly be considered "white"), and other "ethnic" (i.e., Slavic) Caucasians.

9. In this instance, the word "nation" or "Nation" itself must be scrupulously analyzed: *who* and *what,* exactly, constitute "the nation"? Who are its supreme and most representative citizens, sentimental and ultimately dishonest splutter about the U.S. "melting pot" aside? For all nations have citizens, but the citizens are rarely equals—and, saddled by white supremacist ideology, ethnocentrism, religious fundamentalisms, heterosexism, sexism, misogyny, and "othering" of the poor and elderly, the citizens (of the United States, at least) will never be. These questions regarding the *actual* identity of "the nation" loom particularly large and troubling in the wake of post–September 11 U.S. jingoism, xenophobia, and increased intolerance and suspicion directed toward Muslims and others perceived to be non-Christian, especially in an era when the word "terrorist" becomes increasingly synonymous to many with "Muslim," "Islamic," or "Middle Eastern."

10. This point, of course, is obvious: in a patriarchal society, self-identified "gay" men, and any men who have sexual or romantic relationships with men, possess male privilege and dominance over those not male. However, *non*heterosexual men—or, more specifically, men who are *known* to be nonheterosexual, as well as those perceived to be effeminate or less masculine, whatever their sexuality—are assuredly granted less patriarchal power than those men deemed to be "real," invincibly heterosexual men, whatever the slippery, even illusory, criteria for invincible heterosexuality may be. Things get complicated here, however, vis-à-vis behavior: for what happens in terms of patriarchal power with men whose heterosexuality is assured and publicly known but whose behavior is markedly effeminate, and thus suspect? Similarly, what happens with evidently same-gender-interested men who are macho? And if all this were not complex enough, where do transgendered males whose biological reality was originally either male *or* female enter the picture? (In the case of transgendered people, the amount of patriarchal power available to them will depend on how much is known in their present society about their biological male or female origins, and how male/masculine-appearing they presently are.) All considerations about patriarchal power must also be evaluated taking into account class, racial, and age differences, as well as differences in ability.

11. If one accepts racial categories and constructions at all—and in the United States and the world beyond at present, most, if not all, do—we remember that whiteness, too, need be configured as a racialized category. But as we also know, U.S. whiteness invariably stands as the dominant, "default" *un*raced category situated squarely at the racial equation's center: the category against which all other "colors" are marked as "other" and hence ascribed a "race," or become "raced," against whiteness's central "racelessness." "Raceless" whiteness as the norm positions all nonwhiteness as "other" in contrast to itself.

12. While many U.S. males wrestle, consciously or otherwise, with anxieties about their masculinity as defined, in part, by the virginal "intact"-ness of their anus, these anxieties are not necessarily common—or at least not common in the same way—in other, non-Western, societies, as illustrated in several excellent comparative anthropological texts. See, for example, Stephen O. Murray and Will Roscoe, eds., *Islamic Homosexualities: Culture, History, and Literature* (New York: New York University Press, 1997); Murray and Roscoe, eds., *Boy-Wives and Female Husbands: Studies in African Homosexualities* (New York: St. Martin's Press, 1998); Murray, ed., *Latin American Male Homosexualities* (Albuquerque: University of New Mexico Press, 1995); Devdutt Pattanaik, *The Man Who Was a Woman and Other Queer Tales From Hindu Lore* (Binghamton, N.Y.: Haworth Press, 2002); and Ruth Vanita, ed., *Queering India: Same-Sex Love and Eroticism in Indian Culture and Society* (New York: Routledge, 2001).

On the Importance of Returning from Abroad to the United States in a Time of Imperialism and War (A Meditation on Dissent)

1. "Freedoms and joys" more possible, of course, if one numbers among the more socially privileged, which, in Jamaica, by virtue of my education, family (somewhat), U.S. citizenship, and, to some degree, skin color—not necessarily in that order—I do. Jamaica, already so compellingly gorgeous in spite of its present frightening crime rate, becomes even more so, and more enjoyable, not only with the money to enjoy more of life's comforts, but also with sufficient funds to escape from time to time from the island's considerable stresses, as those with such cash are occasionally inclined to do—escape for shopping in Miami, trips to London, trips to New York, to Atlanta, to other parts

of Jamaica's extensive diaspora, and more. Without enough money or time to enjoy the country's range of activities and events, fully nurture one's loved ones in it, or protect oneself from its unpredictable violence, Jamaica today—like many other nations—can quickly become an absolute hell, and one never to be taken lightly, especially in an era of continued government and police abuse of the poor. These facts are not always admitted by the more socially privileged; nor are they readily admitted by many who have migrated to other countries and persist in viewing Jamaica—"Home"—through the distorting, revisionist lenses of nostalgia—the lenses through which daily life on the island is rendered flawless and supreme, incomparable to anything else. These distorting lenses are the expatriate's especially seductive pitfall.

2. See, for example, Joel Brinkley, "Bush Says Worldwide Protests Won't Change Approach to Iraq," *New York Times,* February 18, 2003; and Richard W. Stevenson, "Antiwar Protests Fail to Sway Bush on Plans for Iraq," *New York Times,* February 19, 2003. Although I mention two *New York Times* articles here, it's important to remember that the *Times* itself, like some other "mainstream" newspapers, did not earlier steadfastly (or even accurately) document the increasing antiwar protests or the great numbers of people who attended them. Then and later, one was compelled to go not to the *Times* for more accurate coverage but to places like the United Kingdom's *Guardian,* DemocracyNow's and *The Nation*'s websites, and, in several instances, Canadian newspapers. In an age of continued attempts to silence dissent, one thanks the skies for the web.

Bush and company may have attempted to ignore—or at least sidestep—the winter 2003 dissenters, but those who participated in the protests were surely impressed by their own magnificent numbers and their collective anger's palpable force. Not since the Vietnam era had such antiwar protests been seen in the United States.

3. This question might sound naive coming from someone born and grown in a nation that decimated Native American peoples in its early days and went steadily, brutally downhill from there. Still, I have always wanted to live with some faith in people's best, most inspiring possibilities from moment to moment (and, by extension, faith in myself), no matter how ignorant or parochial those people might appear. That faith means a great deal to me, and keeps at bay the "easy" out of cynicism. Nonetheless, the question at hand would become even more

jarring and painful—and frightening—in the aftermath of the 2004 U.S. presidential election, when George W. Bush actually was elected by the popular vote, albeit by a narrow margin. Like many people the world over, I honestly did not believe that Bush would regain the White House he had initially stolen. But in 2003, when this essay was originally written, I barely gave a thought to such an impossible-seeming future, preoccupied as I was with the United States' perpetration of widespread murder and misery in Iraq.

4. Toni Morrison, *Beloved* (New York: Alfred A. Knopf 1987), 180.

5. This hatred was brought sharply home to me by a Jamaican friend who told me, a few days after September 11, how jubilant he felt upon seeing on TV the destruction wrought on the World Trade Center and the Pentagon. A few other Jamaicans with whom I was close expressed similar sentiments, although several also expressed horror over the loss of life. The first friend did later say that he began to feel compassion, and also horror, when he viewed images of people jumping from the Trade Center towers to their deaths.

6. The protests I attended, organized by Jamaicans Against the War, were populated by—not surprisingly—mostly, though not exclusively, middle-class, upper-middle-class, and generally well-educated Jamaicans. They, unlike poorer Jamaicans, certainly had, by and large, more uninhibited leisure time to devote to such activity. They also generally had the mobility—a car, or one of several family cars—to get to the rallying sites easily. (I, for example, lived near the U.S. embassy and the British High Commission, both in central, upscale New Kingston and both within walking distance of my apartment. Joining the group on a Saturday afternoon was not, for me, a person without children and unconstricted by a taxing job, in any way a hardship, as it might have been for some of the country's poorer and poorest people.) Perhaps most significantly, it gradually became clear to several people at the protests— those who wondered and discussed among themselves why more people hadn't shown up each time—that a number of less financially secure Jamaicans might very well have been concerned about who at the U.S. embassy or British High Commission might see them and photograph them, thus, to their minds, ruining any future chances of their obtaining a visa to either of those countries. Obtaining a visa for travel from Jamaica to the United Kingdom and the United States remains generally far easier for the more socially privileged than it is for the working class

and poor—a fact far too many of Jamaica's socially privileged continue to take for granted. In this regard, I felt doubly motivated to protest: both as a privileged U.S. citizen who would never need a visa to enter the States and as a socially privileged Jamaican one: someone who could be physically present to protest, as opposed to someone who, for the reasons just outlined, felt he or she could not be.

7. The USA PATRIOT Act (Uniting and Strengthening America by Providing Appropriate Tools Required to Intercept and Obstruct Terrorism), passed only forty-five days after September 11, 2001, is without question one of the most ruthless, most bold-faced attempts of the U.S. government to increase control and uninhibited scrutiny over its citizens. The act—something George Orwell's Thought Police could have conjured—grants the government unblocked access to (among other things) one's medical records, library borrowing records, and student files. It increases the government's authority to place and keep under surveillance, at its own arbitrary discretion (after all, anyone might be a "terrorist"), *anyone*: the surveillance includes wiretapping and search-and-seizure. Those under surveillance need not be (and surely would not be) notified that they're being monitored, of course. The FBI, CIA, National Security Agency (NSA), and who knows who else all participate in this revised totalitarianism, with—as the act stands so far—virtual impunity. For more information on the USA PATRIOT Act, consult the American Civil Liberties Union's Web site, www.aclu.org.

8. See Arundhati Roy, "Instant-Mix Imperial Democracy (Buy One, Get One Free)," in *An Ordinary Person's Guide to Empire* (Cambridge: South End Press, 2004).

9. Ibid.

10. Ibid.

Autumn's Relentlessness

1. See Wislawa Szymborska, "Hatred," in *Poems New and Collected, 1957–1997* (New York: Harcourt, Brace, 1998), 230–31.

2. By "mainstream" media I obviously do not mean the more conscientious, evenhanded, left-centered entities such as *The Nation, The Progressive, Z* magazine, South End Press, CommonDreams.org, DemocracyNow.org, et cetera, but more clearly corporate-dominated

organs such as CNN and Fox News, among others, which, in the United States and across the world, have far wider reach and visibility; and the larger U.S. newspapers, the *New York Times* and the *Washington Post* among them.

3. This essay was written in 2001, eventually—though I didn't know it at the time—to be included in this volume published in 2005. Looking back at this essay and then at the 2004 U.S. presidential election which *legally* put George W. Bush back in the White House, I wonder how much global hatred for the United States has increased since the election and since the 2003-begun U.S./U.K. war waged on Iraq. It's a question I honestly fear to answer.

4. Hate crimes against people perceived to be Muslim or from the Middle East—assaults, other forms of public hostility, and even murder—increased with terrifying speed in the United States after September 11, 2001. Given the ferocity of some of the assaults and their frequency, however, one must wonder how much of that xenophobic, racist hostility was already present in the U.S. population, quietly seething beneath an ostensibly—or even grudgingly—accepting veneer. If, in U.S. history, blacks and other people of color, Jews, and Irish and Eastern European laborers could be lynched or otherwise destroyed, why would those perceived to be Muslim or from the Middle East be left behind?

5. See Elias Canetti, *The Conscience of Words* (New York: Farrar, Straus and Giroux, 1984).

6. Five days after September 11, in a globally broadcasted speech, president George W. Bush said, "This *crusade,* this war on terrorism, is going to take a while." (my italics). Bush's careless use of the word "crusade"—possibly informed by his reputed born-again Christian fervor—did not go unnoticed, to say the least, by many Muslims throughout the world, and by others.

7. Keeping in mind the dreadful fate of Amadou Diallo, a Guinean immigrant to the United States, who was murdered by four white police officers in the Bronx on February 4, 1999. He was shot by them forty-one times; nineteen of the shots penetrated his body. A little over a year later, the police officers, tried in upstate New York, were acquitted of all charges.

8. See, for example, Jill Nelson, ed., *Police Brutality: An Anthology* (New York: W. W. Norton, 2000).

9. The "Bin Laden: Wanted Dead or Alive" slogan gained popularity in a few quarters after Bush's public utterance of the words on September 17, 2001. T-shirts, posters, and other items with the slogan and bin Laden's face at the center of a target circle, among other designs, rapidly appeared. See, for example, Toby Harnden, "Bin Laden Is Wanted: Dead or Alive, Says Bush," *Telegraph* (U.K.), September 18, 2001; and "Bush: Bin Laden 'Prime Suspect,'" September 17, 2001, www.cnn.com/2001/US/09/17/bush.powell.terrorism.

Re-membering Steen Fenrich

1. See Kieron Crowley, Rocco Parascandola, and Maggie Haberman, "L.I. Dad in Suicide Over Stepson's Body," *New York Post,* March 23, 2000, 7.

2. See the remarks of Tara Brady in "Rooftop Drama—Man Shoots Himself after Confessing to Stepson's Slaying," *New York Newsday,* March 23, 2000.

3. Ibid.

4. According to several news reports and the confirmed information provided by at least one private investigator, both Wanda Fenrich and her husband had been involved in federal mail fraud and insurance fraud schemes. For several of the latter, John Fenrich had gone so far as to mutilate himself (cutting an earlobe, slashing his groin, and claiming that a finger amputated years before had been lost in a car accident) in order to deceive insurance companies. An insurance fraud investigator who interviewed the Fenriches in 1998 suggested that "anybody that appears to be mutilating themselves for insurance money does not strike me as a very stable person." In October 1999, the Fenriches pled guilty to several counts of federal mail fraud, among other fraud-related charges, and were to be sentenced on March 31, 2000. See "Rooftop Drama—Man Shoots Himself after Confessing to Stepson's Slaying."

5. As of this writing, Matthew Shepard's murder remains arguably the most discussed and represented late-twentieth-century antigay violence case in the United States, documented in plays and films such as *The Laramie Project,* in texts such as Beth Loffreda's *Losing Matt Shepard,* and in innumerable other writings, a made-for-TV film, and other artistic and civic ventures. Shepard himself, a student at the University of Wyoming at the time of his death, was beaten into a coma

on October 6, 1998, by Aaron McKinney and Russell Henderson. All three men were white. Shepard was found the following day, cross-tied to a fence. His assailants had crushed his skull by repeated blows with a pistol. He died on October 12. Since then, both McKinney and Henderson have received life sentences without parole for his murder.

6. I recall especially the essay "Matthew's Passion," an editorial in the November 9, 1998, *Nation* by Tony Kushner, a writer whose work and moral and political conscience I have long admired; and the incisive, provocative text *Losing Matt Shepard: Life and Politics in the Aftermath of Anti-gay Murder* (New York: Columbia University Press, 2000), by another writer whose work I respect, Beth Loffreda.

7. The Matthew Shepard Foundation states on its website (www .matthewshepard.org) that it "was created in December 1998 to honor Matthew in a manner that was appropriate to his dreams, beliefs, and aspirations." The foundation provides material and other support to individuals and groups working against violence aimed toward lesbian, gay, and transgendered people. The foundation is clearly doing some extremely powerful and important—necessary—work, much of it through the speaking engagements of Matthew's mother, Judy Shepard. I will admit, however—not in critique of the Matthew Shepard Foundation, but in sheer pained reaction—how psychically jarring it often feels to witness the bigotry crime of Steen Fenrich's murder, and the murders of so many other queer people, go virtually unremarked, while an entire foundation is set up in the name of one young murdered gay man, whose death, though horrifying, deeply tragic, is not—cannot be—more "important" than that of Steen Fenrich and hundreds—thousands—of others.

8. Sakia Gunn, an African American lesbian who was murdered on May 11, 2003, in Newark, New Jersey. Her murder was correctly classified as a hate crime. Regarding the difference between media coverage of Gunn's murder and Shepard's, cultural studies scholar Mark Anthony Neal notes: "Using the Lexis-Nexis database, [one professor] has uncovered that there were 659 stories in major newspapers regarding Shepard's murder, compared to only 21 stories—21—about Gunn's murder in the seven month period after their attacks. [The professor] also notes that not only were Shepard's attackers tried and convicted during that period, but that it took nearly that long for Gunn's accused murderer to even be indicted." See Mark Anthony Neal, "Critical Noir: Remembering Sakia," www.africana.com.

9. Brian Williamson, Jamaican gay activist and a personal friend, was stabbed and machete-chopped to death in Kingston, Jamaica, on June 9, 2004. See, in this volume, "The Death and Light of Brian Williamson."

10. Amanda Milan, a twenty-five-year-old black transgendered female, was stabbed to death after a bias-related altercation in New York City on June 20, 2000. Before stabbing Milan, one of her assailants was heard by witnesses to use, in reference to her, the word "faggot."

11. Arthur Carl Warren Jr., an openly gay twenty-six-year-old African American man who lived in Grant Town, West Virginia, was beaten to death there on July 4, 2000, by two seventeen-year-old males and possibly also by one sixteen-year-old male, all white. Warren's murderers later took his body to a quiet road and ran a car over it several times in order to mask the killing as a hit-and-run accident.

Abu Ghraib

1. Bradford Plumer, "Remember Abu Ghraib?" *Mother Jones,* August 6, 2004.

2. Attributed to Elie Wiesel.

3. Reed Brody, introduction to *The Road to Abu Ghraib* (New York: Human Rights Watch, June 2004), 2–3.

4. Ibid., section IV, "Iraq: Applying Counter-terrorism Tactics during a Military Occupation."

5. Ibid., section I, "A Policy to Evade International Law, Circumventing the Geneva Conventions" (my italics).

6. Patrick Martin, "U.S. Seeks to Block Enforcement of Anti-torture Treaty," World Socialist website, August 5, 2002, www.wsws.org.

7. Brody, *The Road to Abu Ghraib,* 1.

8. Susan J. Brison, "Torture, or 'Good Old American Pornography'?" *Chronicle of Higher Education* 50, no. 39 (June 2004): B10.

9. Ibid.

10. Bruce Shapiro, "Rehnquist, Cambodia and Abu Ghraib," *The Nation,* June 25, 2004 (my italics).

11. The Editors, "Orders to Torture," *The Nation,* June 7, 2004.

12. Heather Wokusch, "From Texas to Abu Ghraib: The Bush Legacy of Prisoner Abuse," www.CommonDreams.org, May 10, 2004.

13. This Afghani prisoner's testimony, recorded on February 11, 2004, describing abuses experienced in early 2002, was included in a report on

abuses of Afghani prisoners by the U.S. military and the unexplained deaths of three Afghani prisoners in the custody of the U.S. military. The report also states that, according to the recorded testimonies of Afghani detainees, "detainees who were held in Kandahar airport in early 2002 reported being stripped naked, kicked and punched, and forced to endure freezing temperatures. . . . U.S. officials have told journalists and Human Rights Watch that U.S. military and intelligence personnel in Afghanistan employ an interrogation system that includes the use of sleep deprivation, sensory deprivation, and forcing detainees to sit or stand in painful positions for extended periods of time." See "U.S.: Systemic Abuse of Afghan Prisoners, Open Files on Detainee Deaths," by Human Rights Watch (London, May 13, 2004), www.hrw.org.

14. Seymour M. Hersh, "Torture at Abu Ghraib," *New Yorker,* May 10, 2004, 43. The tortures described in this quoted passage, enacted by, among others, troops in the 372nd Military Police Company, were quoted by Seymour M. Hersh from a report written by U.S. Major General Antonio M. Taguba. The report, not originally intended for public consumption, was finished in February 2004.

15. Wokusch, "From Texas to Abu Ghraib."

16. Bob Wing, "The Color of Abu Ghraib," *War Times,* no. 18 (Summer 2004), www.war-times.org. I have taken the liberty here, in quoting Mr. Wing's text, of arranging it on the page in a nontraditional format. Mr. Wing's text appears in a traditional prose text format in his article.

17. Suzanne Goldenberg, "We Did It For Fun, Claimed Iraq Jail Accused," *Guardian,* August 4, 2004.

18. Donald G. McNeil Jr., "Reports Criticize Medics for Overlooking Abuses," *New York Times,* August 27, 2004.

19. Ibid. (italics mine).

Again, the Sea

1. Derek Walcott, "The Schooner Flight, 1: Adios, Carenage," in *Collected Poems, 1948–1984* (New York: Noonday Press, 1986), 345.

2. Derek Walcott, "Laventille," in *Collected Poems,* 86.

3. Dionne Brand, *A Map to the Door of No Return: Notes to Belonging* (Toronto: Random House of Canada, 2001), 6.

4. Ibid., 9–10.

Publication History

"Baychester: A Memory" originally appeared in *Massachusetts Review* 35, nos. 3–4 (1994).

"Toward a Nobility of the Imagination: Jamaica's Shame" originally appeared in the *Jamaica Observer,* January 9, 1999. It has been reprinted in *Gay Community News* 24, nos. 3–4 (1999); *Black Renaissance/Renaissance Noire* 2, no. 3 (2000); and *Small Axe,* no. 7 (2000).

"(Re-)Recalling Essex Hemphill: Words to Our Now" originally appeared in *Callaloo* 23, no. 1 (2000).

"Fire and Ink: Toward a Quest for Language, History, and a Moral Imagination" originally appeared in *Lambda Book Report* 11, no. 3 (October 2002). It has since been reprinted in *Black Renaissance/Renaissance Noire* 5, no. 1 (2003); and *Callaloo* 26, no. 3 (2003).

"Whose Caribbean? An Allegory, in Part" originally appeared in slightly different form in *Callaloo* 27, no. 3 (2004).

"These Blocks, Not Square" originally appeared in *Massachusetts Review* 44, no. 4 (2003).

"The Death and Light of Brian Williamson" first appeared in slightly different form as "Remembering Brian Williamson," *Jamaica Sunday Gleaner,* June 20, 2004. It also appeared in slightly different form as "The Lion in Brian," *Now Toronto* 23, no. 48 (July 29–August 4, 2004). It was reprinted in *Freedom in This Village: Black Gay Men's Writing, 1969 to the Present*, edited by E. Lynn Harris (Carroll and Graf, 2004).

"Between Jamaica(n) and (North) America(n): Convergent (Divergent) Territories" originally appeared in *Black Renaissance/ Renaissance Noire* 6, no. 1 (2004).

"On the Difficulty of Confiding, with Complete Love and Trust, in Some Heterosexual 'Friends'" originally appeared in *Massachusetts Review* 44, no. 4 (2003). It later appeared in *Lambda Book Report* 12, no. 11 (June–July 2004); and *I Do/I Don't: Queers on Marriage*, edited by Ian Philips (Suspect Thoughts Press, 2004).

THOMAS GLAVE was born in the Bronx and grew up there and in Kingston, Jamaica. He was a Fulbright scholar in Jamaica, where he studied Jamaican historiography and Jamaican/Caribbean intellectual and literary traditions; while there he also worked on issues of social justice and helped found the Jamaica Forum for Lesbians, All-Sexuals, and Gays (J-FLAG).

He now teaches in the English department at SUNY Binghamton and has received numerous honors, including an O. Henry Prize for fiction and fellowships from the National Endowment for the Arts and the Fine Arts Center in Provincetown. He is the author of *Whose Song? and Other Stories,* which was nominated by the American Library Association for a Best Gay/Lesbian Book of the Year Award and by the Quality Paperback Book Club for a Violet Quill: Best New Gay/Lesbian Fiction Award.